Accountability, Parliamentarism and Transparency in the EU

For Basia and Agnieszka

Accountability, Parliamentarism and Transparency in the EU

The Role of National Parliaments

Adam Cygan

University of Leicester, UK

Edward Elgar

Cheltenham, UK • Northampton, MA, USA

Published by
Edward Elgar Publishing Limited
The Lypiatts
15 Lansdown Road
Cheltenham
Glos GL50 2JA
UK

Edward Elgar Publishing, Inc.
William Pratt House
9 Dewey Court
Northampton
Massachusetts 01060
USA

A catalogue record for this book
is available from the British Library

Library of Congress Control Number: 2013935025

This book is available electronically in the ElgarOnline.com Law Subject Collection, E-ISBN 978 1 78254 865 2

MIX
Paper from responsible sources
FSC® C013056

ISBN 978 1 84720 131 7

Typeset by Columns Design XML Ltd, Reading
Printed and bound in Great Britain by T.J. International Ltd, Padstow

Contents

Table of cases

Numerical Order

Alphabetical Order

United Kingdom Cases

German Cases

Table of legislation

EU Legislation

National Legislation

Introduction

Since the start of this millennium the European Union (EU) has been preoccupied with securing a new constitutional settlement with the primary purpose of making the EU a more accountable, democratic and relevant organisation in the lives of its citizens. Though the project for a Constitution for Europe was abandoned, the Treaty of Lisbon 2007 maintains many of the constitutional principles and values that were contained within the Constitutional Treaty and which arose from the Laeken Declaration and the Convention on the Future of the European Union. The Laeken Declaration 2001 noted that:[1]

> The European Union derives its legitimacy from the democratic values it projects, the aims it pursues and the powers and instruments it possesses. However, the European project also derives its legitimacy from democratic, transparent and efficient institutions. The national parliaments also contribute towards the legitimacy of the European project. The declaration on the future of the Union, annexed to the Treaty of Nice, stressed the need to examine their role in European integration.

The significance of this statement is that it is recognition of not only the democratic credentials of national parliaments and that they remain constitutionally relevant institutions in the EU polity, but also that national parliaments have a definitive role to play in the future of EU integration. In the first formal recognition of the democratic credentials of national parliaments in the Treaty, Article 12 of the Treaty on European Union (TEU) provides that national parliaments will contribute 'actively to the good functioning of the Union'. In the post-Lisbon EU national parliaments are endowed with new prerogatives of subsidiarity monitoring which, under certain circumstances, may lead them to conclude that an EU legislative proposal breaches the principle of subsidiarity in Article 5 TEU and that it should be withdrawn. The challenge facing national parliaments since 1957, and which is explored in Chapters 1 and 2, is the ongoing process of Europeanisation which has witnessed a transfer of significant legislative competence to the EU. The

[1] Laeken Declaration on the Future of the European Union, at 5.

primary effect of this Europeanisation is what has been termed a 'deparliamentarisation' of the EU. In short, the EU, while pursuing closer integration has, through Treaties since the Single European Act 1986, pursued an agenda of democratisation which has seen the rise of the European Parliament within the EU polity.

However, unlike national parliaments, which are the expressions of popular democracy in each Member State, the European Parliament does not share the democratic credentials of national parliaments and within the process of EU decision-making may be viewed as part of the legitimacy problem. To this extent, increased legislative powers for the European Parliament have not reduced criticisms of a deparliamentarisation; on the contrary, and as the discussion in Chapters 3 and 4 illustrates, with the increased use of Trilogues in the ordinary legislative process, the expansion of qualified majority voting (QMV), the growth of technocratic decision-making and the greater reliance upon soft law, national parliaments continue to face numerous challenges to their legislative competences. The formal recognition of subsidiarity monitoring by national parliaments in Protocols 1 and 2 of the Treaty of Lisbon offers new opportunities for national parliaments over which they are able to exert some control over the legislative process. There is no doubt that such competence monitoring contributes positively to the legislative process and that it may help to inject some improved democratic legitimacy into EU decision-making. The defining feature of subsidiarity monitoring is that Protocol 2 envisages that this takes place as a 'collective exercise'. Thus, if national parliaments can secure the relevant thresholds contained within Protocol 2 then the Commission may be required to reconsider the legislative proposal. This is significant because it marks a change from the pre-Lisbon position in which national parliaments focussed on securing the accountability of their minister to the parliament. Yes, competence has always been an important issue, but pre-Lisbon any concerns about the exercise of EU competences would be communicated via the minister in the Council. Protocol 2 creates a new political opportunity by permitting national parliaments to make representations concerning the compatibility of a legislative proposal with the principle of subsidiarity directly to the Commission. Does this make Protocol 2 a 'game changer' for national parliaments and alter their position within the EU polity? First, do the prerogatives of Protocol 2 afford to national parliaments some 'quasi-institutional' status within the legislative process? Secondly, are national parliaments now to be considered as a coherent bloc of institutional actors who are all pursuing the same agenda when reviewing EU legislation? Both these questions are explored in Chapters 5 and 6, as well as the question of whether by engaging in subsidiarity monitoring national parliaments are providing improved output legitimacy to EU legislation. That is to say, if national parliaments conclude that a legislative proposal does not breach the principle of subsidiarity, will EU citizens be more accepting of it? The overarching issue that is therefore explored within Chapters 5 and 6 is whether subsidiarity monitoring helps to maintain the chain of legislative legitimacy to EU citizens which the Laeken Declaration identified as being absent.

The discourse surrounding improved legislative legitimacy has tended to focus on the position of national parliaments in their capacity as the legislative institutions of the Member States. However, and as the Treaty of Lisbon recognises, the EU possesses a multi-level governance structure in which regions and sub-national governance are increasingly important. It must be borne in mind that in the discussions surrounding the exercise of EU competence and the application of Article 5 TEU, the EU will often be sharing competence, not with national parliaments, but with sub-national institutions. Article 5 TEU and Protocol 2 for the first time recognise that when assessing subsidiarity, regional consequences of EU legislative action must also be considered. In conjunction with this, Protocol 2 affords opportunities for subsidiarity review to the Committee of the Regions, as the representative of regional governance within the EU polity, in circumstances where its prerogatives are affected. As Chapter 7 explains, though the Treaty of Lisbon's acknowledgement of regional competences is important, the provisions of Article 5 TEU and Protocol 2 are limited because there is no EU-wide consensus of precisely what competences regional governance should have. Regional competences are heterogeneous across the Member States and largely depend upon domestic constitutional arrangements.

These variations across the Member States remain a barrier to the improved participation by sub-national institutions in EU affairs and one which participation by the Committee of the Regions in subsidiarity monitoring does not sufficiently remedy. The constitutional consequences of EU integration on national parliaments have been considered predominantly in a negative manner. In addition to concerns of deparliamentarisation, national parliaments have been portrayed as 'victims' or 'losers' of integration when their overall participation in EU affairs and the integration process is considered. The inclusion of Article 12 TEU and Protocols 1 and 2 was intended to remedy this perception. While it may be fair to conclude that national parliaments are no longer marginalised in the EU polity, and that the Treaty of Lisbon does formally recognise that their democratic credentials and traditions do have a formal role to play in EU integration, it would be incorrect to conclude that national parliaments exist as some collective bloc that has acquired an institutional status. Under the Treaty of Lisbon national parliaments have been granted improved recognition of procedural rights to undertake competence monitoring, but this activity takes place against a background in which the EU is pursuing closer integration and harmonisation to solve the socio-economic challenges which it is facing. In particular, this entails the increased use of QMV and soft law to achieve Europeanisation, both of which, as the book explores, significantly impact upon the ability of national parliaments to influence EU decision-making. This provides a challenging political environment within which national parliaments will be operating. In writing this book I have had the benefit of many fruitful discussions with academic colleagues, parliamentarians and officials working within national parliaments and the EU institutions. Though we have not always agreed on the position of national parliaments in the EU, this discourse has helped my understanding of what is and, perhaps more accurately, what should be the constitutional status of national parliaments within the EU polity. In this respect I would like to acknowledge Professor Stephen Weatherill, Professor Miroslaw Wyrzykowski, Professor Erika Szyszczak, Dr Phillip Kiiver, Paul Hardy, Dominic Rowles, Haris Kountouros, Loreta Raulinaityte and Ilmãrs Solims. In particular, I would like to thank Dr Lorenzo Spadacini and Auke Baas for reading the manuscript and providing me with their very useful comments. I would also like to thank everyone at Edward Elgar who has supported me throughout this project and especially Ben Booth and Laura Seward. Finally, I want to say thank you to Basia and Agnieszka, who have been very patient and understanding with me while I have been writing *that* book. This book reflects the law and practice at 31 January 2013.

1. National parliaments, accountability and transparency in a European perspective

1. INTRODUCTION

Democracy is a fundamental and core value within any system of governance. Moreover, it is the accountability of decision-makers, who govern in the name of the citizens, which is an integral part of the democratic process and which ensures the legitimacy of legislative acts. In the context of the evolvement of EU integration and especially the emphasis, since the Treaty of Maastricht 1992, of the EU seeking improved democratisation and accountability, the debate has focussed on how to secure both input and output legitimacy within the EU legislative process. This debate has focussed primarily on the improvement of accountability of the institutional actors which participate in decision-making. Academic commentators, for example Scharpf, have drawn a distinction between input and output legitimacy when assessing the democratic credentials of the EU.

In particular Scharpf identifies that democratic governance requires legislators and policy-makers to make choices that reflect the priorities and preferences of the citizens. In the EU's system of governance this has witnessed a process of EU democratisation with an increase of powers for the European Parliament, which is intended to provide input legitimacy within the legislative process.[1] Weatherill and Menon have described this need to connect with citizens within the legislative process as requiring a 'chain of accountability linking those governing to those governed'.[2] Following the Treaty of Lisbon 2007 the two key links in the legitimacy chain are the directly elected European Parliament and national parliaments which through subsidiarity monitoring are expected to inject some element of output legitimacy into the legislative process.

[1] Scharpf, F. (1999) *Governing in Europe*.

[2] See Menon, A. and Weatherill, S. (2002) 'Legitimacy, Accountability and Delegation in the European Union' at 116.

The search for democratisation of the EU, through the allocation of increased powers for the European Parliament, should not be underestimated, but the European Parliament, though performing a representative function, has not displaced national parliaments as the foremost representative institutions that reflect the views of the citizens. The paradox of this process of EU democratisation is that it would appear to have distanced the EU from the very citizens who are the intended beneficiaries of the legislation.

This book explores the role that national parliaments have in EU affairs, the contribution that they can bring to improving accountability and legitimacy in the EU, and what if any role they have with helping to reconnect the EU with its citizens. The central concerns are how, and to what extent, national parliaments can use their established democratic procedures to ensure that the EU legislative process delivers outputs which are acceptable to EU citizens. Following the Treaty of Lisbon 2007 this means national parliaments monitoring the application of the subsidiarity principle. However, subsidiarity monitoring should not be viewed as a panacea which on its own can deliver more accountable decision-making. Within the EU decision-making process there have existed clear deficiencies in both input and output legitimacy which Treaty reform since Maastricht has sought to address with only limited success. For Scharpf, while the need for input legitimacy should not be underestimated, it is the requirement of output legitimacy that is crucial for connecting with EU citizens. He views Member States and their institutions as part of the equation to help secure this legitimacy. Moreover, Scharpf has argued that in some key EU policy areas policy legitimacy may be judged by virtue of the output itself and the benefits to the citizen, even if the input legitimacy is weak. Thus effective EU outcomes, which deliver tangible benefits to citizens and which the citizens accept as legitimate political goals, are an important consideration and suggest that a regulatory understanding[3] of EU governance may be sufficient to secure democratic legitimacy. However, from the perspective of national parliaments, the matter is less clear cut than has been expressed by Scharpf. As democratically elected institutions with a long tradition of pursuing accountability of decision-makers, national parliaments cannot be expected to assume a passive approach towards accountability in an EU context where the ends can be said to justify the means.

---

[3] Giandomenico Majone has described the EU as a regulatory State, which implies a technocratic approach to governance which is results driven. See Majone, G. (1996) *Regulating Europe*.

Accordingly, national parliaments have a political duty to pursue accountability. Within the EU context this means national parliaments (i) holding to account individual ministers for their actions in the Council; (ii) monitoring the EU legislative process to ensure competences are properly exercised; and (iii) benchmarking legislative proposals for their compliance with the principle of subsidiarity. The challenge of securing this accountability is that national institutions are seeking accountability of a supra-national governance process over which they have very limited influence. The overarching question explored within this book is whether after fifty years of political, economic and legal integration, which has witnessed a significant transfer of competences to the EU, national parliaments are able to remain as relevant actors in EU affairs.

2. THE SEARCH FOR IMPROVED ACCOUNTABILITY

Scharpf's core assertion that the key feature of a democratic system of governance is the presumption that the exercise of all public authority and legislative actions emanates from the consent of the citizens is undoubtedly correct. But, in terms of the legitimacy as derived from the citizen, this cannot be determined merely by a regulatory model of governance where the output, or results of the decision-making process, is used as the benchmark of legitimacy. The search for legitimacy in the EU, both in terms of the input into and output of the legislative process, requires effective institutional accountability both horizontally and vertically across all levels of the EU's multi-level governance structure. The hallmark of a democracy is that it observes the rule of law and that accountability is secured through institutions that are representative of the citizen. However, caution must also be maintained whether this form of accountability can ever be realistically achieved within the EU's complex multi-level institutional architecture.

2.1 The Democratic Principles of EU Integration

In the search for democratic accountability and legitimacy the EU is no different from its constituent Member States, where the challenges of multi-level governance regularly bring conflicts between central government and federal or devolved governments with regard to the exercise of competences and the powers of elected institutions. The challenge is to ensure that each level of governance remains constitutionally relevant. In the EU Treaties, Article 2 TEU provides a clear expression of the democratic foundations of the EU and its respect for, inter alia, democracy and the rule of law. It is assumed that this includes respect for democratically elected national institutions which form a constituent part of EU multi-level governance. Within the EU's institutional architecture it is the European Parliament which provides the institutional expression of the views of EU citizens through the process of direct parliamentary elections. Accordingly, Article 2 TEU describes democracy as being based upon the principle that 'every public authority must be directly elected or answerable to a directly elected parliament',[4] which would appear to place the European Parliament at the centre of achieving this accountability. However, the generic nature of this provision would also appear to leave room to imply that *national* parliamentary institutions, at all levels of governance, have a role to play in promoting good governance, and this is recognised within Article 12 TEU. Moreover, Article 2 TEU further suggests that democratic accountability and adherence to the rule of law are not the only considerations of legitimate governance, but that a democratic system of governance also requires a comprehensive system of checks and balances to prevent the concentration of power and the consequences of abuse of power which this can bring.

The concept that the exercise of legislative power by institutions arises from the citizen, which also participate in and/or supervise the process of decision-making is a prerequisite for all Member States prior to seeking EU membership.[5] Thus the EU consists of nation States which are all founded upon the principle of parliamentary democracy, and the EU can take action under Article 7 TEU to suspend the membership of any Member State which breaches these core values. On this analysis the EU Treaty uses the benchmark of a parliamentary democracy coupled with the potential sanction of suspension from the EU as a mechanism through which the concentration of legislative and administrative power is discouraged. Superficially, this is encouraging and suggests that the EU itself is not interested with the centralisation of legislative power, though, as the discussion in Chapters 2 and 3 suggests, this assertion can be rebutted. Though the Treaties do create a fully fledged federal structure, such as that provided for by the Constitution of the German Federal Republic, the Treaty, through the inclusion of the principle of subsidiarity in Article 5 TEU, recognises that in the multi-level EU, all levels of

---

[4] OJ C120/01. Article 17 (2) of the Declaration of Fundamental Rights and Freedoms adopted by the European Parliament on 12 April 1989.

[5] See further Verhoeven, G. (1998) 'How Democratic Need European Union Members Be?' at 217.

governance which derive a clear legitimacy have a role to play in the governance of the EU.

The question addressed in Chapters 5 and 6 is whether the monitoring of subsidiarity and the mechanisms put in place by the Treaty of Lisbon to regulate its application provide sufficient guarantees against the centralisation of legislative power at the EU level. Articles 9–12 TEU, which lay out the democratic principles upon which the EU is founded, represent a much clearer statement, by comparison with previous Treaties, of how the EU will seek to meet the standards of democracy and accountability which it places upon all its Member States.[6] While this is to be welcomed, these Treaty provisions cannot be viewed as a panacea, that their inclusion can remedy all the institutional defects, or that they provide a comprehensive set of provisions through which citizens will engage more readily in EU affairs. It is doubtful if Articles 9–12 TEU adequately answer the dual problems of accountability and disconnection which were articulated by the Laeken Declaration,[7] the Commission's White Paper on European Governance[8] and the subsequent establishment of the Convention on the Future of Europe. The Convention highlighted the accountability challenge facing the EU and stated that the EU must 'rethink its role, improve its operation and go down new avenues of progress and democracy'.[9] Though the inclusion of the Citizen's Initiative in Article 11 TEU offers a novel way for the EU to engage with its citizens, it is questionable whether this form of direct democracy significantly improves legislative legitimacy or prevents the Initiative from being considered anything other than mere 'window dressing'. Article 10 TEU identifies that the cornerstone of EU democracy is that it engages with the citizen and so its reference to the principles of representative and participatory democracy underscores the importance of consent of the citizen to EU integration. Under the Treaty of Lisbon the EU seeks to secure this consent in two specific ways. First, under Article 10 (1) TEU the Treaty states that the functioning of the Union is founded

---

6 For a comprehensive review of the constitutional landscape post-Lisbon and how the Treaty promotes democracy and participation see Wouters, P., Verhey, L. and Kiiver, P. (eds) (2009) *European Constitutionalism beyond Lisbon*.

7 Laeken Declaration on the Future of Europe, December 2001, available at http://www.europa.eu.int/futurum/documents/offtext/doc151201_en.htm (accessed 27 October 2012).

8 COM (2001) 428 *European Governance – A White Paper*.

9 See CONV 67/1/02 The Role of National Parliaments in the European Architecture at 8.

upon representative democracy and identifies that this will be provided directly by the European Parliament. Secondly, Article 10 (1) TEU implies indirect representation for EU citizens and that 'Member States are represented in the European Council by their Heads of State or Government and in the Council by their governments, themselves democratically accountable to their national parliaments or to their citizens'. It is securing this accountability of ministers to national parliaments for their participation in the decision-making process which has traditionally been the preoccupation of national parliaments through the operation of their national scrutiny mechanisms and which was recognised by the Amsterdam Protocol on national parliaments. This scrutiny of national ministers has been referred to as the individual scrutiny function. A novel aspect of Article 10 TEU is that Article 10 (4) TEU identifies the importance of political parties in decision-making, which in the European Parliament are organised on lines of political affiliation rather than on national lines. This cross-national organisation of political groupings attempts to create a strong pan-EU representative institution[10] out of the European Parliament and reinforces, albeit very weakly, the concept of a European demos which Scharpf has identified as both lacking from EU integration and essential to improving citizen participation. However, it is highly questionable whether Article 10 (4) TEU can transcend traditional national allegiances, or that EU citizens will elect MEPs solely on the basis of EU issues rather than being influenced by the domestic political agenda.

The undoubted absence of an EU demos, which is central to Scharpf's analysis, has been contested by Weiler, who sees a problem of translation in that 'the very language of modern democracy, its grammar, syntax and vocabulary, [which] revolve around the state, the nation and the people – its *demos*' is transposed to the Union, which is not a State.[11] Weiler's core assertion that it is wrong to impose the criteria of nation-State democracy on to a supra-national EU is not without merit. Instead, Weiler has argued for 'the very conceptual decoupling of nationality from citizenship' and advocates that democracy beyond the nation State becomes possible if one understands the European demos in *civic* and political rather than ethno-cultural terms.[12] Such ideas have found some favour within the

[10] See Case 138/79 *Roquette Frères* v *Council* [1980] ECR 3333 at paragraphs 33–35 where the Court highlighted the importance of political groupings and the representative function they perform.

[11] Weiler, J.H.H. (1998) *The Constitution of Europe* at 268.

[12] Ibid. at 344.

citizenship line of case law in the European Court of Justice,[13] but politically there is far less consensus for moving away from the idea of an EU of nation States. For example, judgments such as that of the German Federal Constitutional Court in the *Lisbon Treaty judgment*, illustrate that there remain real concerns about handing over further competences to a supra-national organisation that fails to have adequate constitutional safeguards.[14]

2.2 Improving Participatory Democracy in the EU

Another key feature of the post-Lisbon EU is the emphasis placed upon improved participatory democracy, though this occurs without any explicit reference to participatory democracy within the Treaty.[15] Article 11 TEU requires that the EU institutions give citizens and civil society associations the opportunity to make an input into decision-making processes and make known their views publicly in all areas of EU action. The main feature of this participation can be found in Article 11 (2) TEU whereby the EU institutions maintain an open, transparent and regular dialogue with civil society.[16] The key issue here is one of transparency, given that the EU decision-making process has been criticised for being opaque and technocratic,[17] reinforcing the sense of disengagement with

---

[13] In Case C-499/06 *Halina Nerkowska* v *Zakład Ubezpieczeń Społecnych* [2008] ECR I-3993 Advocate General Maduro argued that EU citizenship, to have its full effect, should not be determined by reference to nationality. At paragraph 23 of the Opinion, the Advocate General stated: 'Citizenship of the Union must encourage Member States to no longer conceive of the legitimate link to integration only within the narrow bounds of the national community, but also within the wider context of the society of the peoples of the Union.'

[14] Judgment of 20 June 2009, *Bundesverfassungsgericht*, BVerfG, 2 BvE 2/08. See also Steinbach, A. (2010) 'The Lisbon Judgment of the German Federal Constitutional Court' at 376; Doukas, D. (2009) 'The Verdict of the German Federal Constitutional Court on the Lisbon Treaty' at 887.

[15] This is a change from the Constitutional Treaty, which explicitly referred to participatory democracy as an additional means of representing the views of citizens. See Articles I-46 and I-47 of the Constitutional Treaty.

[16] Declaration 23 annexed to the Treaty of Maastricht formally stressed the importance of co-operation between the European Community and 'charitable associations and foundations as institutions responsible for social welfare establishments and services'. See further Kendall, J. and Anheier, H.K. (1996) 'The Third Sector and the European Union Policy Process' at 295–296.

[17] See for example Menon, A. and Weatherill, S. (2002) 'Legitimacy, Accountability and Delegation in the European Union' and Kiiver, P. (2012) *The Early Warning System for the Principle of Subsidiarity* at 118–121.

citizens who are unaware of what legislative action is being taken in their name. Transparency is an important value in EU decision-making and one without which participatory and representative democracy cannot be achieved.

In highly technocratic decision-making procedures such as the comitology procedure the challenges faced to secure accountability and legitimacy are even more acute. In circumstances where legislative acts are devised under the comitology procedure and have a significant impact upon EU citizens, there is an overwhelming need for transparency. The comitology process has been consistently criticised for its lack of transparency and democratic legitimacy, primarily because of the peripheral role of the European Parliament, but it is also important to note that national parliaments themselves rarely engage in scrutiny of comitology proposals. To address this criticism there is undoubtedly a greater need for improved transparency with the better provision of information to elected institutions, including national parliaments.[18] More generally, the exclusion of national parliaments from comitology is another factor that has helped to reinforce the criticism of a departiamentarisation within the EU and which is explored in Chapter 2. The importance of transparency as an integral value to EU integration cannot be overstated. Democratic and accountable governance not only requires representative and participatory institutions and mechanisms for citizens, but it also is based upon the key principle of the rule of law and the protection of citizens against the exercise of arbitrary power. Securing effective accountability to prevent the exercise of arbitrary power in the EU is complex, not least because this involves monitoring the activities of the physically and politically distant Commission and Council, which also includes the activities of national civil servants and permanent representatives in Brussels who are responsible for negotiating much of the legislation. One specific problem with this growth of executive power is that its exercise is not necessarily representative or readily accountable, a problem made all the more acute because of the absence of effective parliamentary scrutiny procedures of such executive action.[19] In the absence of effective political accountability it has been left to the European Court of Justice

---

[18] Improved transparency and accountability of the comitology procedure are core objectives of the Regulation (EU) No. 182/2011 of 16 February 2011 laying down the rules and general principles concerning mechanisms for control by Member States of the Commission's exercise of implementing powers, for example in Article 5 of the Regulation.

[19] See further Cygan, A. (2006) 'The EU Constitutional Treaty from the Perspective of the Parliament from the United Kingdom' and Besselink L.M.

to protect against the exercise of arbitrary power and protect against the abuse of the rule of law in circumstances where the procedure lacks transparency.[20] However, notwithstanding this judicial accountability democratic and accountable governance dictates that effective parliamentary accountability of executive action is also necessary.

In a new development Article 12 TEU explicitly recognises the democratic credentials of national parliaments and the contribution which they can make to enhance 'the good functioning of the Union'. The inclusion of Article 12 TEU is encouraging because it indicates a participatory function for national parliaments in EU affairs and constitutes the first formal Treaty acknowledgement of the contribution that national parliaments can make to improve the governance of the EU. However, the precise scope and effect of Article 12 TEU is unclear. This is primarily because, irrespective of Article 12 TEU referring to 'national parliaments' – thereby constituting some form of horizontal collective bloc of national institutions participating in EU affairs in a coherent fashion[21] – it is abundantly clear that national parliaments across the Member States are heterogeneous and, notwithstanding the developments within the Treaty of Lisbon, remain variable actors in EU affairs.[22] In the context of EU decision-making, where the EU institutions continue to dominate the agenda and the procedure, it remains challenging for national parliaments to participate and exert their influence. Given that national parliaments represent the citizens who have elected them, their marginal position in EU affairs has consistently been identified as a weakness of the EU's governance framework.[23] Addressing this aspect of the democratic deficit within the EU's legislative process has proved challenging, and in the period of constitutional debate leading up to what became the Treaty of Lisbon there was a lack of consensus as to precisely what future political role national parliaments should have.

(2006) 'National Parliaments in the EU's Composite Constitution' at 15–26 and 117–130 respectively.

[20] See for example Case C-518/07 *Commission* v *Germany* [2010] ECR I-1885.

[21] See Kiiver, P. (2006) *The National Parliaments in the European Union* at 41–42, and Cygan, A. (2011) 'The Parliamentarisation of EU Decision-Making?' at 478.

[22] See Auel, K. (2007) 'Democratic Accountability and National Parliaments' at 492–494. This issue is discussed in more detail in Chapter 2.

[23] See O'Brennan, J. and Raunio, T. (2007) 'Deparliamentarisation and European Integration' at 2–8.

3. THE LAEKEN DECLARATION, THE COMMISSION'S GOVERNANCE WHITE PAPER AND THE EUROPEAN CONVENTION: A FRAMEWORK FOR IMPROVED ACCOUNTABILITY?

The December 2000 Inter-Governmental Conference (IGC) in Nice[24] adopted a Declaration on the Future of Europe.[25] The primary objective of Declaration 23 was to stimulate a broad and inclusive debate with regard to the future direction of EU integration. In particular, Declaration 23 highlighted a number of key issues which needed to be addressed and which would seek to address what was considered to be the core problem of citizen disconnection. This included, inter alia, in paragraph 5 what should be the future role of national parliaments in the EU and the need for a clearer delineation of powers between the EU and Member States. On the question of competences and how they were to be exercised this raised questions over how the principle of subsidiarity should be applied and what institutions were best positioned to execute this task.

3.1 The Laeken Declaration

As stated in paragraph 4 of Declaration 23 the process would require the European Council to agree a framework of how the EU would take forward constitutional and Treaty reform to address the specific concerns expressed in Declaration 23. At the end of the Laeken European Council the Presidency Conclusions included the Laeken Declaration which stated that EU citizens 'feel that deals are all too often cut out of their sight and they *want better democratic scrutiny*'.[26] This was undoubtedly an acknowledgement that the EU's multi-level polity requires a clearer and more effective framework for accountability which must include participation by national parliamentary institutions. The Laeken Declaration further stated that there was a particular 'need to improve and to monitor the democratic legitimacy and transparency of the Union and its institutions, in order to bring them closer to the citizens of the Member

---

[24] The Nice IGC was criticised by many as an example of EU decision-making at its worst, with deals and agreements reached behind closed doors and without having the full support of all Member States.

[25] Treaty of Nice, Declaration 23.

[26] European Council Presidency Conclusions, December 2001, emphasis added.

States',[27] which can be interpreted, even at that formative stage within the constitutional review process, that national parliaments were being identified as undertaking the role of subsidiarity monitoring. The need for improved participation by, and representation of, EU citizens was, simultaneously, identified by the European Parliament. The Constitutional Committee of the European Parliament argued that the primary causes of disaffection with the EU arise not just from shortcomings in what the EU does, but also from a sense of 'alienation, the serious difficulties encountered in understanding and participating, and a fear of helplessness in the face of imposed decisions which cannot be influenced or controlled'.[28] It is clear from these and other statements that, at least amongst the directly elected actors comprising the European Council and its elected Heads of State and Government, and the European Parliament, there was some consensus with regard to the *nature* of the problems facing the EU and that the root of these problems was the consequence of weak institutional mechanisms through which to secure the accountability of decision-makers.

3.2 The Commission's White Paper on Governance

In 2001 the Commission published its contribution to the constitutional debate in the form of a *White Paper on European Governance*[29] which stated that it was concerned with how the EU uses the powers given by its citizens.[30] For the Commission, governance was rather narrowly defined as 'rules, processes and behaviour that affect the way in which powers are exercised *at a European level*'.[31] This indicates that the Commission viewed EU democratisation and improved accountability as being primarily based upon the reform of the EU's institutional architecture in tandem with reforms to the legislative process. This definition not only marginalises national parliaments, but would also appear to ignore the complex nature of the EU's multi-level polity and the need for accountability that this governance structure requires. The Commission's

---

27 Ibid.

28 *Report on Relations between the European Parliament and the National Parliaments in European Integration*, January 2002, A5-0023/2002, explanatory statement, at paragraph 3.

29 COM (2001) 428 *European Governance – A White Paper*.

30 Ibid. at 3.

31 Ibid. at 8, emphasis added. This definition is merely contained within a footnote in the White Paper.

definition of good governance is based on five key principles of openness, participation, accountability, effectiveness and coherence.[32] Within the parameters of these five principles, it is possible to identify two key themes that the White Paper addressed. First, was the question of input into and legitimacy of the EU policy-making process and how this procedure could become more accessible to EU citizens. Secondly, the White Paper examined the output and efficiency of EU legislation by considering how multi-level governance could become more involved with implementation. This analysis resonates with Scharpf's regulatory model of EU governance, where tangible results are considered as the primary objective of the legislative process and can be seen through programmes such as Agenda 2020, where there is a clear results-orientated methodology. The primary criticism to be levelled at the White Paper is that it failed to move much beyond a review of the Community method and how this could be reinvigorated. Implicitly this focussed on the inter-institutional dynamics of the legislative process and in particular identified how an enhanced role for the European Parliament could improve the democratisation of the EU. This analysis was at the expense of examining how accountability could be more broadly achieved by encompassing and harnessing the accountability procedures and traditions of, inter alia, national parliaments and perhaps pursuing greater parliamentarisation of the EU. Consequently, the White Paper failed to provide any significantly new solutions to the exercise of power in a system of multi-level governance. If EU citizens felt alienated, and it must be remembered that the White Paper sought to address criticisms arising from the Irish 'no' vote[33] to the Treaty of Nice,[34] then proposals for improving governance should also have included provisions for the more meaningful involvement of national institutions.

---

[32] Ibid. at 10.

[33] The Irish referendum took place on 7 June 2001 with a result of 53.9 per cent to 46.1 per cent against ratification of the Treaty. However, the turnout for the referendum was only 30 per cent. For an analysis of the Irish 'no' vote and its potential implications see House of Commons Research Paper 01/57 *The Irish Referendum on the Treaty of Nice*, available at http://www.parliament.uk/commons/lib/research/rp2001/rp01-057.pdf (accessed 14 March 2012).

[34] It is important to remember that the Irish 'no' vote in the Treaty of Nice referendum is only one of several occasions when EU citizens, having been asked directly to approve new Treaties which would lead to deeper integration, have decided against supporting the Treaty. This includes Denmark in 1992, following a referendum over the Maastricht Treaty, France and the Netherlands in 2007 which both voted 'no' to the Constitutional Treaty (though for different reasons) and the Irish 'no' vote to the Treaty of Lisbon in 2009.

The need for engaging with national institutions was not completely lost upon the Commission. In the White Paper, the Commission regularly alluded to the need for more diverse representation in the Community method, especially in the form of regional representation. The focus on regional institutions and enhancing their role in EU governance is perhaps based upon the Commission seeking to engage with institutions which were less hostile to EU integration than parliaments which represented nation States as well as an attempt to promote a distinctly regional agenda to EU integration.[35] The reforms proposed in the White Paper were ultimately very modest and the White Paper itself recognised the outer limits of what could be achieved and stated that they could not provide a 'magic cure for everything'.[36] Moreover, the five principles of good governance identified by the Commission are crucial components of *any* system of democratic government and will have a relevance to all levels of decision-making within a multi-level polity. However, though essential, these principles should not be considered as an exhaustive list for good governance. For example, one principle not expressly mentioned is that of representation and particularly how this may be provided by national parliaments. Furthermore, some principles articulated in the White Paper were not necessarily new to the debate, for example the inclusion of openness merely re-stated the already established Treaty principle of transparency.[37]

3.3 The Convention on the Future of Europe

The Convention on the Future of Europe considered in detail the question of what role national parliaments should undertake in EU decision-making[38] in two separate Working Groups. Working Group I considered the application of the subsidiarity principle in EU decision-making and Working Group IV examined the future role of national parliaments, focussing primarily on procedural questions and how practice could be improved to promote more effective scrutiny of EU legislative proposals through better horizontal co-ordination between national parliaments.

---

[35] This was a point noted by Hopkins, W.J. (2010) 'A Tale of Two Europes' at 55.

[36] COM (2001) 428 *European Governance – A White Paper* at 3.

[37] At the time this was contained in Article 235 EC.

[38] See CONV 74/02 Mandate of the Working Group on National Parliaments, which provided the mandate of Working Group IV on the role of national parliaments.

Without being radical, the Conclusion of Working Group IV[39] was generally welcomed in a positive manner and identified that national parliaments should have a key role in subsidiarity monitoring. It described them helping 'to strengthen democratic legitimacy of the Union and bring it closer to the citizens',[40] suggesting that subsidiarity monitoring by national parliaments would not only help to secure improved output legitimacy of EU legislation, but that by engaging in this task national parliaments would also improve the legitimacy of EU integration more generally.[41] What was described as 'anchoring and ownership'[42] of the EU in the Member States through the scrutiny activities of national parliaments was considered of major importance to the achievement of the goals of improved legitimacy and accountability. This recognised that domestic legislatures could have a central role to play in addressing the question of disengagement through promoting citizen participation in EU affairs, but one which national parliaments were, and still are, generally sceptical of fulfilling. Despite recommending to the Convention that the future Constitutional Treaty recognise the role of national parliaments, Working Group IV suggested that this recognition should be in line with the Amsterdam Protocol on National Parliaments which recognised procedural rights of participation rather than through some constitutional position equal to that of the EU institutions. Thus there was no proposal of an EU institution composed of national parliamentarians or that there should be a second revising chamber added to the European Parliament, composed of national MPs, which undertook subsidiarity monitoring. The Working Group regarded this 'as reflecting that provisions on the European level are aimed at facilitating the involvement of national parliaments, without interfering in constitutional arrangements on the national level'. In essence, this conclusion suggested that the role of national parliaments should be limited to the procedural issue of scrutiny, albeit scrutiny which occurred in a more co-ordinated fashion, rather than their seeking a larger role in more substantive questions of policy formulation and providing input legitimacy.[43]

---

[39] See CONV 353/02 Working Group IV The Role of National Parliaments.

[40] Ibid. at paragraph 4.

[41] See further Peters, J. (2004) 'European Democracy after the 2003 Convention' at 37.

[42] CONV 353/02 Working Group IV The Role of National Parliaments.

[43] Ibid. at paragraph 5. The Working Group recognises that national parliaments, together with a variety of other actors, can become involved in the consultation process through reacting to Green and White Papers. The Working

4. THE PERIPHERAL POSITION OF NATIONAL PARLIAMENTS

The search for accountability in the EU culminated in the Treaty of Lisbon, which has shaped a framework for accountability which seeks to draw together actors and institutions from across the EU's multi-level governance structure. As well as national parliaments the Treaty recognises a formal role for regional governance in subsidiarity monitoring and grants new privileges to the Committee of the Regions to review legislative proposals for compatibility with the principle of subsidiarity. For national parliaments their role primarily, though not exclusively, manifests itself in the form of subsidiarity monitoring as now laid out in Protocols 1 and 2 of the Treaty of Lisbon and through the execution of the role identified for national parliaments in Article 12 TEU of 'contributing to the good functioning of the Union'. Provision of this form of output legitimacy,[44] which the Treaty of Lisbon has assigned to national parliaments, is, however, only one constituent part of a broader accountability agenda which also seeks to ensure inter-institutional accountability.

4.1 The Effect of Europeanisation on National Parliaments

Europeanisation[45] has created a shared policy and legislative agenda which Member States are bound to implement. 'Hard' law, as a tool of harmonisation, is complemented by an increased reliance on 'soft' law and policy co-ordination following the adoption of the Lisbon Agenda in 2000 and, more recently, under the Agenda 2020 Programme. Europeanisation has necessitated a distinct governance framework at the centre of which is the ordinary legislative procedure which is now complemented by the use of soft law. The primary effect of Europeanisation is the transfer of legislative powers to the Council and European Parliament at

---

Group does not propose a privileged position for national parliaments in such a consultation process, merely that they receive such documents directly. See paragraph 14.

[44] See Scharpf, F.W. (2010) 'Legitimacy in the Multi-Level European Polity', at 89.

[45] See Bulmer, S. and Lequesne, C. (eds) (2005) *The Member States of the European Union*, especially Chapters 13–16 and Dimitrakopoulos, D.G. (2001) 'Incrementalism and Path Dependence' at 405.

the expense of national institutions and actors.[46] This has caused what has been described as a 'deparliamentarisation'[47] due to the absence of national parliamentary participation in decision-making and the limited domestic accountability of the executive in EU affairs.[48] Though national parliaments have engaged in domestic scrutiny and sought to review EU legislative proposals, this domestic scrutiny has by and large focussed on ministerial accountability, varied in effectiveness across the Member States, operated independently of the EU legislative process, and has not been an adequate substitute for the loss of legislative competence. In the light of the peripheral position of domestic legislatures in the EU legislative process the marginalisation of national parliaments could be more accurately described as 'de-national-parliamentarisation'. Working Group IV of the Constitutional Convention acknowledged these criticisms and the Treaty of Lisbon[49] includes several new provisions designed to address this deparliamentarisation, for example Protocol 1 on National Parliaments[50] and Article 12 TEU, which states that 'national parliaments contribute *actively* to the good functioning of the Union'.[51] This 'active contribution', through participation in subsidiarity monitoring under Protocol 2,[52] creates an expectation that, collectively, national parliaments will inject democratic legitimacy into EU legislation.

4.2 National Parliaments as Political Bystanders

In recent years national parliaments have assumed an increased political significance within the EU, arising from national constitutional requirements which have necessitated parliamentary approval for EU action in relation to the financial crisis which began in 2008. Tasked with approving financial rescue packages for indebted Member States and

---

[46] See Kassim, H. (2005) 'The Europeanisation of Member State Institutions' at 297–303.

[47] See O'Brennan, J. and Raunio, T. (2007) 'Deparliamentarisation and European Integration' at 2–8.

[48] See Kiiver, P. (2006) *The National Parliaments in the European Union* at 41–42 and Chapter 2 of this book.

[49] See Dougan, M. (2008) 'The Treaty of Lisbon 2007', especially at 657–661.

[50] Protocol 1 of the Treaty of Lisbon on the Role of National Parliaments in the European Union (hereafter 'Protocol 1').

[51] Emphasis added. Article 12 TEU is the first reference to national parliaments in the main text of the Treaty.

[52] Protocol 2 on the Application of the Principles of Subsidiarity and Proportionality (hereafter 'Protocol 2').

taking action to secure the stability of the Eurozone, national parliaments are, according to the President of the European Council, Herman van Rompuy, behaving in a manner which is similar to EU institutions.[53] Herman van Rompuy stated that 'maybe not formally speaking, but at least politically speaking, all national parliaments have become, in a way, European institutions'.[54] However, the extent to which the assertion of Herman van Rompuy may be considered accurate or shared by national parliaments themselves is open to significant debate. It is beyond question that national parliaments have become more prominent actors in EU affairs and the financial crisis has brought to the fore the overriding need for improved co-operation between EU institutions and national parliaments. But it is questionable whether they can be considered as 'EU institutions' in the strict Treaty sense of the definition, even by reference to the particular circumstances alluded to by Van Rompuy. Moreover, if Van Rompuy is suggesting some form of 'associate' institutional status it is not clear how this will formally change the existing status of national parliaments. It remains questionable whether national parliaments, answerable to a domestic electorate and which first and foremost pursue the accountability of their executives, share this interpretation of the role of national parliaments in the EU polity.

From a domestic parliamentary perspective, the view that national parliaments are 'EU institutions' would, in accountability terms, relocate national parliaments to the same level of governance as the EU institutions. From the perspective of national parliaments this would make them 'part of the institutional problem' and not offer any obvious improvement to the EU's accountability mechanisms. At a time when the EU consisted of six or even twelve Member States, and when their influence and contribution could arguably have been greater, national parliaments remained peripheral to the development of European integration and their democratic features were largely ignored. Yet in an EU of twenty-eight Member States, the Treaty has repositioned national parliaments and creates an expectation that they will contribute to improving democracy and accountability to EU decision-making largely through engaging in subsidiarity monitoring. Despite this expectation, national

[53] Herman van Rompuy further stated that 'in the old days, exaggerating just slightly, the European Community used to exist on one planet, and national politics on six, nine, twelve, fifteen other planets. This is over now. The debt crisis, difficult and painful as it is, brings home the fact that the Union is us.'

[54] See EUObserver.com, 28 February 2012, 'Van Rompuy: National Parliaments are EU Institutions', available at http://euobserver.com/institutional/115395 (accessed 1 March 2012).

parliaments, such as that of the United Kingdom, have repeatedly recognised they have a limited role in EU policy and decision-making and have tended to focus on securing ministerial accountability.[55] This is recognition that within the EU context Parliament fulfils a different political and legislative function by comparison with that when it exercises its own legislative powers.[56] The growth of Europeanisation and integration has undoubtedly presented challenges for national parliaments to remain both relevant and to continue to fulfil their primary democratic function of controlling their executives, including in the context of EU decision-making. While all Member States share certain constitutional principles such as respect for the rule of law, separation of powers and democratic and accountable government, the manner in which those concepts take shape varies within particular political and constitutional arrangements. These different constitutional and political traditions pose further challenges to securing coherent and uniform accountability mechanisms for EU policy and decision-making which are effective both at the EU level and within all Member States. Chapter 2 explores in more detail how national parliaments have, in the context of Europeanisation and the accompanying transfer of political and legislative sovereignty to the EU, sought to secure the accountability of EU law and policy while simultaneously protecting their constitutional status as representative institutions.

5. DEMOCRATIC LEGITIMACY AFTER LISBON: TWO STEPS FORWARD AND ONE STEP BACK?

Accountability is one of the defining features of good governance, but a precise definition and how it is to be achieved within the multi-level governance structure of the EU have been the source of much political and academic debate. The primary issue within the EU context is that, unlike traditional debates concerning the role of parliaments and the courts in nation States, the debate in the EU has been made more complex by the supra-national nature of EU integration. It is the absence of a traditional parliamentary system of governance and direct accountability to the electorate that has caused the Treaty-makers to search for

---

[55] See HC 152 xxxiii-I (2001–2) *Democracy and Accountability in the EU and the Role of National Parliaments*.

[56] See Cygan, A. (1998) *The United Kingdom Parliament and European Union Legislation*; Cygan, A. (2001) *National Parliaments in an Integrated Europe*; Kiiver, P. (2012) *The Early Warning System for the Principle of Subsidiarity* at 7–11.

democratic legitimacy and accountability through a hybrid system of multi-level political accountability between actors and institutions at the EU and national levels, together with the judicial control by the European Court of Justice. The search for effective political control is closely tied up with improving institutional accountability within the EU legislative process. Since the Single European Act 1986, the Treaty has sought to develop a system of checks and balances which places the European Parliament at the centre of this accountability process. While a more expansive role for the European Parliament is logical, this does not indicate the creation of a parliamentary system of governance in the EU. Furthermore, this does not herald a move towards the parliamentarisation of the EU because the exercise of political power by EU institutions is not subjected sufficiently to a form of accountability which is responsive to the views of EU citizens. Historically, this has been the result of the absence of national parliaments from the formal review of the legislative process, but with the introduction of subsidiarity monitoring there may be improved opportunities through which national parliaments, acting collectively, would be able to exert improved control over the EU institutions.[57]

5.1 Accountability to Whom?

The two main sources of democratic legitimacy in the EU are national parliaments and the directly elected European Parliament. However, for the overwhelming majority of EU citizens it remains the executive, accountable to their national parliament as the central element of democratic legitimacy. Yet this view does not correspond with the supra-national character of the EU and the practical difficulties that exist when seeking to secure effective accountability of ministers who take decisions in the Council of Ministers. Within a purely domestic context, a new legislative proposal will undergo rigorous review and debate, offer opportunities to propose amendments and require the assent of the national parliament or, in some constitutions, require a referendum. In bicameral parliaments there will also be a second revising chamber that can propose amendments. By contrast, at the EU level government ministers act in a capacity without most of the procedural safeguards that

[57] See, for example Kiiver, P. (2011) 'The Early Warning System for the Principle of Subsidiarity' at 98; Passos, R. (2008) 'Recent Developments Concerning the Role of National Parliaments in the European Union' at 35; Jancic, D. (2008) 'A New Organ of the European Union', available at http:// www. fedtrust.co.uk/uploads/Parliaments_Jointly.pdf (accessed 10 January 2010).

are the hallmark of a parliamentary democracy. Though the consent of the European Parliament is required under the ordinary legislative procedure and the absence of this consent can lead to a termination of the legislative process, the overwhelming majority of legislation is being agreed at the first reading stage or within the Trilogues, leaving limited scope for review or amendment.[58] Moreover, the Council of Ministers may still act independently when agreeing some legislative proposals adopted outside the ordinary legislative procedure. This Council autonomy is further compounded by the lack of transparency and the confidentiality which still prevails within Council proceedings. This principle of transparency, which Curtin has identified as a key value and fundamental principle of all decision-making, is an essential part of ensuring both the legitimacy and accountability of decision-makers,[59] and is particularly pertinent for national parliaments when seeking to hold to account ministers for decisions taken within the Council. While the Treaty does not formally create the collective accountability of the Council, other than to the European Parliament through the procedures of the ordinary legislative process, the individual ministers who comprise the members of the Council remain, in theory at least, individually politically accountable to their domestic legislatures. But, in practice, sufficient control over individual Council members has been difficult to achieve, given the lack of transparency and the extensive use of qualified majority voting procedures within Council which have diluted the impact of individual ministerial voting in circumstances where the veto could previously have been exercised, in favour of a majoritarian procedure where a 'collective' decision is arrived at.[60] Improved direct accountability of the Council to the European Parliament has been identified as the most appropriate way to remedy this deficit.[61] In some respects, for example through the exercise of its veto over legislation under the ordinary legislative procedure, the European Parliament has more power

---

[58] In evidence to the House of Lords EU Select Committee, Professor Damian Chalmers notes that the eight week period for review is inadequate and equates to the same period granted to private parties to make written observations to the Commission under its consultation process. See HL 62-I (Session 2007–8) *The Treaty of Lisbon* at 243, paragraph 11.42; HL 62-II (Session 2007–8) *The Treaty of Lisbon* at 333; HC 563 (Session 2007–8) *Subsidiarity, National Parliaments and the Lisbon Treaty*, at 33 paragraph 44.

[59] See Curtin, D. and Egeberg, M. (2008) 'Tradition and Innovation' at 649–650.

[60] Ibid. at 651.

[61] See Curtin, D. (2009) 'The Council of Ministers' 125; Kiiver, P. (2012) *The Early Warning System for the Principle of Subsidiarity* at 15.

than national parliaments. The ability to formally block legislation goes far beyond the scope of what national parliaments can do, even through subsidiarity monitoring. Yet despite this pivotal position, there remains little popular support for the European Parliament amongst EU citizens, raising significant questions with regard to how democratic this form of accountability really is. Turnout at European Parliament elections remains low by comparison with national parliamentary elections[62] and there is little knowledge of its political activities amongst the electorate, who tend to be motivated by national, rather than EU, issues.[63] The effect of this is that political parties and individual MEPs who participate in the ordinary legislative process are not necessarily being held fully accountable for their actions and decisions taken at the EU level.

5.2 A New Democratic Deficit

Democracy is traditionally associated with sustainable and active national parliaments which play an integral role in securing the legitimacy of the legislative process. This participation manifests itself in a variety of forms, but the overriding consideration is the need to ensure direct accountability of the ultimate decision-makers to a directly elected legislative body. While this traditional understanding of accountability is appropriate within the context of the nation State, it does not sit comfortably within the multi-levelled and supra-national integration of the EU, where there is no comparable parliamentary system to provide the necessary accountability. Moreover, the process of integration has had an impact upon the legislative functions of national parliaments and changed the domestic constitutional relationship that exists between the legislature and the executive. The primary effect of the institutionalisation and democratisation of the EU is that this has led to a progressive transfer of competence to supra-national institutions for policies that were previously within the exclusive sovereign jurisdiction of Member States. In many cases the Treaty provides that competence is shared between the EU and the Member States, leading to inevitable tensions concerning the application of these competences. For example, in the regulation of the Internal Market, in circumstances when competence is shared, the determinant of EU action at the EU or national level is

[62] The Commission described the 43 per cent turnout at the 2009 European Parliament elections as 'real failure for democracy'. See Special 320 Eurobaromoter Post Electoral Survey 2009 at 6.

[63] HC 152-xxxiii-I (Session 2001–2) *Democracy and Accountability in the EU and the Role of National Parliaments*, at 16 paragraph 15.

whether EU legislation is necessary and that the desired result can be more efficiently achieved through a single legislative measure. When the Commission makes such judgments, which should be based on quantitative and qualitative factors,[64] such a decision is then benchmarked against the principle of subsidiarity in Article 5 TEU. However, though the political judgment of national parliaments may decide against EU legislation, the Court of Justice has consistently held that once it is considered necessary to adopt common rules to regulate the Internal Market then this can only be achieved through EU action.[65] The presumption underlying the Court's reasoning has been that the legislative measure will comply with the principle of subsidiarity and, from a political accountability perspective, this would appear to imply that national parliaments have accepted the efficiency argument. However, this presumption is not without difficulty and while it may be procedurally correct to conclude that the legislative measure conforms to the principle of subsidiarity, this does not immediately confirm that the legislation can be considered legitimate. As will be seen from the discussion in Chapters 3 and 4, there are increasing concerns that the reasons given by the Commission for EU legislative action tend to lack sufficient quantitative and qualitative justifications. This undoubtedly raises questions of whether the EU is legislating excessively and to this extent legitimacy also raises important questions concerning the legislative content which highlights additional questions of proportionality as well as subsidiarity under Article 5 TEU. It is this ability of national parliaments to sufficiently enforce both subsidiarity and proportionality under Protocol 2 TEU that leaves real scope for the evolution of a newly formulated democratic deficit rising at the national level as a result of national parliaments not being able to apply the principle of subsidiarity with consistency and consensus.[66]

---

[64] This is part of the Commission's broader 'Better Regulation Agenda'. See COM (2005) 97 final *Communication from the Commission to the Council and European Parliament* and the discussion in Chapters 3 and 4.

[65] See Case C-49/01 *R* v *Secretary of State for Health ex parte British American Tobacco and Imperial Tobacco* [2002] ECR I-11453, in particular paragraphs 177 and 185.

[66] See further the discussion in Chapters 5 and 6.

6. CITIZEN PARTICIPATION AND DEMOCRATIC LEGITIMACY

Participatory democracy can roughly be defined as 'self-government by citizens rather than representative government in the name of citizens'.[67] This implies two objectives: first, maximum *participation*, as opposed to merely passive representation, and, secondly, *political equality*. The Treaty of Lisbon encompasses these principles and includes new provisions in Title II TEU which are designed to improve the democratic credentials of the EU and which identify that citizens are at the core of EU integration. These provisions, and especially the Citizen's Initiative in Article 11 TEU, seek to engage citizens more directly in decision-making and are to be broadly welcomed as part of the overall aim of improving legislative legitimacy. But the Citizen's Initiative should not be viewed as an appropriate substitute for, or alternative to, a system of parliamentary government. It is difficult to understand how the provisions of Article 11 TEU, which harness citizen participation directly in the legislative process and offer a rudimentary form of input legitimacy, correspond with the objectives of Article 12 TEU to improve institutional participation by national parliaments.

6.1 The Citizen and the Democratic Deficit

This 'constitutionalisation' of representative democracy within the Treaty and the guarantee contained within Article 10 (3) TEU that 'every citizen shall have the right to participate in the democratic life of the Union' are an attempt to forge a new form of 'contract' between the EU and its citizens by which the EU commits itself to a more representative and accountable model of governance. To some extent Article 10 (3) TEU draws upon the constitutional traditions and norms that are the constitutional backbone of all Member States and which guarantee constitutional government. But while the Treaty provisions may be new in substance they are not necessarily new in terms of their objectives and constitute a reinvigorated attempt by the EU to pursue an agenda, first identified by the Treaty of Maastricht, of bringing the EU closer to the citizen. Post-Lisbon the task of bringing the EU closer to the citizen encompasses more general EU principles such as transparency and subsidiarity. In the case of subsidiarity this political principle is intended to regulate the exercise of competence within a multi-level governance framework and is

---

67 See Barber, B. (1984) *Strong Democracy* at 151.

carried out on behalf of citizens by their national parliaments. National parliaments holding ministers to account, on behalf of their electorate, for their decision-making in Council provides an indirect form of citizen representation and seeks to harness the relationship that national parliaments have with their electorate. This form of proxy representation by national parliaments is also intended to contribute to the overall accountability framework of the EU and create an inter-dependent system of checks and balances which transcends the tiers of the EU's multi-level governance structure. Whether these developments will help to deliver the closeness and relevance in the lives of EU citizens which the Treaty-makers intended, and perhaps more crucially whether this improves the legitimacy of EU legislation, remains to be seen. Despite over twenty years and four Treaties in which the Member States have tried to democratise the institutional and governance structures and processes of the EU, there has been only limited success in convincing citizens that the EU is relevant in their daily lives. Placing the citizen at the centre of EU integration was undoubtedly a major objective of the Treaty of Lisbon and has been reinforced through Commission initiatives such as naming 2013 the 'European Year of Citizens'. While it has been recognised that EU citizens have significant rights of free movement or rights afforded by virtue of the EU citizenship provisions, it is the lack of influence and participation of EU citizens in decision-making which remain the weak link. Thus while national parliaments *may* provide output legitimacy through subsidiarity monitoring, it is the absence of direct input legitimacy by citizens which the Treaty has tried to address. The Laeken Declaration and the Constitutional Convention both acknowledged that the Community method of decision-making operated as a centralising legislative process which placed significant legislative power in the hands of the EU's political institutions and in particular the Commission, which enjoyed the monopoly of legislative initiative. While this monopoly remains, at least in the context of legislative proposals under the Community method, the Commission is, under Article 11 TEU, required to consult with civil society and EU citizens and maintain a transparent and direct dialogue with them during the policy formulation process.

6.2 Article 11 TEU: A Paradigm for Improved Citizen Participation and Legitimacy?

In order to facilitate this participation by citizens and European civil society more generally, the Treaties have established additional obligations for EU institutions to promote increased openness and transparency and the dissemination of information.[68] As a general principle this right of participation by civil society can be found in Article 10 (3) TEU, which states that every citizen has the right to participate in the democratic life of the Union, and for that purpose EU decisions must be taken openly and as closely as possible to the citizen. This latter requirement of decisions being taken 'close to the citizen' dovetails with the subsidiarity requirements of Article 5 TEU, and if these two provisions are read together they suggest some form of Treaty presumption that the legislative process must be more citizen focussed. The innovations in the Treaty of Lisbon indicate an attempt to establish a framework through which EU citizens can become a formal part of the decision-making process. For example, under Article 11 TEU the EU institutions are required to inform citizens and civil society organisations of policy proposals and they must publicly exchange their views in all areas of EU action. Furthermore, Article 11 TEU includes an explicit mandate for the European Commission to consult with parties concerned in order to ensure that the EU's actions are both coherent and transparent.

The backbone of these Treaty provisions is a principle of good and accountable governance which recognises that the EU legislates in the name of its citizens. This is reinforced through Articles 15 and 16 of the Treaty on the Functioning of the European Union (TFEU), which require the EU, its institutions, agencies and other bodies to participate in a discourse with civil society and which helps to create a climate for dialogue. But – and this is the crucial omission – there is nothing in these Treaty provisions which creates institutional representation for citizens at the EU level which replicates that provided by national parliaments in the domestic political context, and which could have significantly contributed to bringing the EU closer to its citizens. While the European Parliament provides representation, unlike national parliaments it does not sustain a government nor does it initiate legislation, and both of these are integral to participatory democracy and parliamentary government. Faced with criticisms that the EU legislative process was devoid of legitimacy, distant from the citizen and that it frequently led to over-intrusive legislation, the Treaty of Lisbon includes an innovative provision for a Citizen's Initiative in Article 11 (4) TEU. If the broader objective of Article 11 TEU is to bring the EU closer to its ordinary citizens, then the provisions for improved dialogue, together with the new right for the Citizen's Initiative, ostensibly provide a framework which offers some

---

[68] See Smismans, S. (2003) 'European Civil Society'; Saurugger, S. (2010) 'Interest Groups and Democracy in the European Union' at 164.

new opportunities by which citizens may participate in policy-making and inject some element of input legitimacy.

Notwithstanding the provisions within the Treaty of Lisbon to promote better accountability within the legislative process through subsidiarity monitoring by national parliaments, these institutions do not provide input legitimacy and remain outside the process of policy formulation.[69] In an attempt to stimulate citizen participation and directly 're-engage' with the citizen, the Treaty of Lisbon introduced the Citizen's Initiative, which operates without any reference to national parliaments. Article 11 TEU states that 'not less than one million citizens who are nationals of a significant number of Member States may take the initiative of inviting the Commission … to submit any appropriate proposal on matters where citizens consider that a legal act of the Union is required'.[70] The inclusion of Article 11 TEU, which invites direct citizen participation in policy-making, is a novel way for the Union to engage with citizens and bypasses traditional EU institutional dominated procedures of policy formulation and democratic input by excluding national parliaments, executives and even, at the outset, the European Parliament.[71] Its inclusion in the Treaty should, though, be kept in context. It is a largely symbolic development which per se is unlikely to improve either the quality of EU legislation or EU democracy, especially if it becomes a vehicle for well-funded interest groups or tabloid newspapers to pursue narrow policy agendas. Yet its inclusion should not go without comment, if for no other reason that it sends out a subliminal but pertinent message

---

[69] See COM (2008) 237 6.5.2008, *Final Commission Annual Report 2007 on Relations Between the European Commission and National Parliaments* at paragraph 2.3. The Commission states that 'In accordance with the Treaty and their constitutional roles and practice the national parliaments do not take part in decision-making at European level.'

[70] Article 11 (4) states that the procedures and conditions required for the Citizen's Initiative shall be determined in accordance with Article 24 (1) TFEU. Regulation (EU) No. 211/2011 on the Citizen's Initiative came into force on 1 April 2012 and contains the procedure for the operation of the Citizen's Initiative. This has been supplemented by Commission Implementing Regulation (EU) No. 1179/2011, which lays down technical specifications for the collection of online petitions. For a positive analysis of the Citizen's Initiative and how it may contribute to improved participatory democracy see Puntscher Riekman, S. (2010) 'Constitutionalism and Representation'.

[71] The Citizen's Initiative is not a new concept and already operates in several Member States. At the national level the Citizen's Initiative is used in inter alia Austria, Italy, Poland and Portugal. Regional and local Initiatives also operate in Germany, Austria, Spain and Sweden.

about the state of EU democracy, and that its inclusion in the Treaty reinforces the understanding that EU integration has been achieved at the expense of a parliamentarisation.

The Citizen's Initiative constitutes a tacit acknowledgement by the EU of the need for improved democratic input into the decision-making process, and which should be sourced from a multiplicity of stakeholders, including the citizen. Article 11 TEU dovetails with the complementary competences in Articles 5 and 6 TFEU which are intended to promote policy co-ordination between Member States by engaging with a broad group of stakeholders and actors. However, when this development is considered alongside those for national parliaments it is further evidence that the Treaty of Lisbon, as with previous Treaties, does not pursue parliamentarisation in the decision-making process. The Initiative contributes nothing to the improvement of executive accountability to national parliaments, nor does it re-centre national parliaments within the EU's decision-making process. While it may be perceived as an idea that will promote popular participation in decision-making, it is unlikely to improve either the quality or legitimacy of legislation. The primary criticism that can be levelled at Article 11 TEU is that it retains a very traditional understanding of the EU's institutional architecture. As was the case under the pre-Lisbon provisions, the participation of 'outsiders' in EU decision-making is limited to what can be defined as non-decision areas.[72]

The Community method, under which the Commission has the monopoly of initiative and the process of decision-making, which is formally undertaken by the Council and the European Parliament, is left unchanged. The Treaty also maintains the constitutional status quo of the Member States, which retain the power of agreeing any future Treaty reform, without any need to directly confer with the citizen. The Convention method used to initially agree the Constitutional Treaty, the majority of whose provisions are contained within the Treaty of Lisbon, is a model of citizen participation and dialogue which attempted to create a sense of ownership for EU citizens in the content of the Treaty. It is, however, unlikely that this form of direct democracy will be an integral part of EU governance in the coming years or that it has even set a precedent for any future Treaty reform. For example, the 2012 Fiscal Treaty was agreed by the Member States without any direct consultation with EU citizens. In this vein, the Treaty of Lisbon falls significantly short

[72] See further Magnette, P. (2007) 'European Democracy between Two Ages' at 27.

of introducing any compulsory, permanent or effective forms of direct democracy at the core of which would be a parliamentary system of governance which is accountable to EU citizens. Moreover, the Treaty does not include other direct mechanisms for engaging with the citizen, for example through the use of EU-wide referenda. Though referenda can be viewed as an unpredictable method for engaging with citizens, they are used as a formal part of the governance procedures in several Member States to ascertain the consent of citizens. The Citizen's Initiative offers only modest opportunities for improved legislative accountability and democracy and for bringing the EU closer to its citizens, but one key value of the Citizen's Initiative stands out which, at the very least, recognises what remains absent from the EU decision-making process. The purpose for the Initiative's inclusion is to contribute to the further democratisation of decision-making by encouraging input from a broader base of stakeholders to fashion a European public agenda which fosters a cross-border debate about EU policy issues and which brings together citizens, as a form of EU *sui generis*, who may be in agreement on a specific issue. The overriding requirement is that the manner by which EU citizens can become involved is standardised in terms of process and that it is inclusive. In such circumstances, it is not inconceivable that citizens *may*, by virtue of the Citizen's Initiative, become more engaged in EU policies and, as a consequence, the institutional and political processes of the EU. The Citizen's Initiative and Article 11 TEU more generally have been hailed by the Economic and Social Committee as a 'milestone on the road to a people's Europe that is real and feasible'.[73] This is a highly optimistic assessment of the impact which one rather vague Treaty provision may have upon the democratisation and accountability of EU decision-making. In particular, Article 11 TEU is an extremely ambitious attempt to bring within one Treaty provision a diverse range of participatory mechanisms, many of which are not necessarily concerned with improving citizen involvement. The use of consultations and dialogue with civil society, which is part of the agenda of improving the input and output legitimacy of legislation, is more concerned with maximising the quality and effectiveness of EU decision-making than with improving the participation of the citizen. Furthermore, and perhaps most crucially, such consultations bypass the accountability function and mechanisms of national parliaments with

[73] Economic and Social Committee (2010) *Opinion on the Implementation of the Lisbon Treaty* at paragraph 5.1.

which citizens closely identify and do not help to bridge the gap between the citizens and the EU institutions.

7. CONCLUDING REMARKS

Despite substantial periods of reflection and debate since the Treaty of Maastricht and four new Treaties, the criticisms of a democratic deficit in the EU have not been put to bed. The discussion in this chapter highlights that improved accountability and legitimacy in the EU cannot be achieved without reference to the democratic traditions and practices of national parliaments. Direct citizen participation, though welcome, does not by itself remedy the shortcomings of the EU polity. The primary criticism that has been consistently levelled at the EU has been that, unlike the Member States, the EU does not possess a fully developed parliamentary system of governance, at the core of which are EU citizens and which provides clear constitutional guarantees of accountability.[74] The supra-national and technocratic nature of EU integration has marginalised EU citizens and it will take more than the limited opportunities offered by the Citizen's Initiative to bridge the legitimacy gap that exists. The democratisation of the EU and the role for national parliaments in this process are complicated issues because they transcend the vertical levels of governance that constitute the EU's multi-level governance framework. In particular, how can national parliaments exert influence over a decision-making procedure which has transferred significant power from the parliament to be exercised by the executive within the Council? Moreover, how can national parliaments co-operate with the European Parliament to improve accountability, particularly in the context of the ordinary legislative process where the European Parliament is a co-legislator with the Council? This itself raises fundamental questions about the capacity of Protocol 2 to consistently secure effective scrutiny and ensure compliance with the principle of subsidiarity. In Chapter 2 the challenges presented to national parliaments by EU integration are discussed in more detail, as well as how these have marginalised national parliaments within the EU polity. Particular emphasis is given to how integration and the process of Europeanisation have affected the ability of national parliaments to influence their executives and how the criticisms of deparliamentarisation have impacted upon national parliaments to secure the accountability of EU decision-making.

---

[74] Judgment of *Bundesverfassungsgericht* at paragraph 351.

2. European integration and deparliamentarisation

1. INTRODUCTION

European integration, or what is commonly referred to as 'Europeanisation',[1] has resulted in the transfer of legislative competence from the national arena to the EU, with the EU assuming responsibility for regulating key economic and social policies. Europeanisation has created a shared policy and legislative agenda which Member States are bound to implement and which has resulted not only in new laws, but also in new practices for Member States and their institutions. The use of 'hard' law as a tool of harmonisation has, in recent years, been accompanied by the increased use of 'soft' law and policy co-ordination following the adoption of the Lisbon Agenda in 2000 and the more recent Agenda 2020 Programme. This less formal decision-making, which encompasses an exchange of policy ideas between Member States, has become an important instrument of Europeanisation through which non-mandatory policies have developed. Soft law has advanced Europeanisation because it enables the EU to embrace spontaneous realignment of national policy to correspond to a single EU model by facilitating peer-learning between some or all Member States. Europeanisation has necessitated a distinct governance framework at the centre of which is the ordinary legislative procedure. The main effect of this governance structure has been to transfer legislative powers to the EU institutions and restrict the capabilities of national institutions and actors.[2] The legislative powers of the European Parliament have been enhanced and the technocratic nature of EU decision-making means that it is national ministers within the Council who agree legislation and not national parliaments. This governance structure has created what is termed a 'deparliamentarisation'

---

[1] See generally Bulmer, S. and Lequesne, C. (eds) (2005) *The Member States of the European Union.*

[2] See Kassim, H. (2005) 'The Europeanisation of Member State Institutions' at 293–298.

within the EU arising from the absence of national parliamentary participation in EU decision-making and the erosion of executive accountability in EU affairs.[3] National parliamentary scrutiny mechanisms are intended to secure ministerial accountability, but these individual scrutiny activities vary in degree and effectiveness across the Member States, operate independently of the EU legislative process and are no substitute for the loss of legislative competence. In this context it may be more accurate to determine that Europeanisation has caused a 'de-national-parliamentarisation' due to the omission of a specific role for national parliaments within the Treaties. To address this deficit the Treaty of Lisbon 2007[4] included a number of new provisions concerning national parliaments, including a revised Protocol 1 on National Parliaments[5] and a new Article 12 TEU which states that 'national parliaments contribute *actively* to the good functioning of the Union'. This suggests that national parliaments will collectively and proactively engage, where appropriate in co-operation with the European Parliament, in more than just the individual parliamentary scrutiny of EU affairs. An 'active contribution', arising from the subsidiarity monitoring procedures of Protocol 2,[6] creates an expectation that, collectively, national parliaments will provide democratic legitimacy to EU legislation and foster a parliamentary system of governance.

2. DEPARLIAMENTARISATION WITHIN THE EU MEMBER STATES

2.1 The Loss of Legislative Competence

Since 1957 national parliaments have relinquished legislative competence and this has been identified by some authors as the overriding reason for deparliamentarisation,[7] with Norton[8] and Maurer and Wessels considering

[3] See Kiiver, P. (2006) *The National Parliaments in the European Union* at 41–42.

[4] See further Dougan, M. (2008) 'The Treaty of Lisbon 2007' at 657–661.

[5] Protocol 1 of the Treaty of Lisbon on the Role of National Parliaments in the European Union.

[6] Protocol 2 on the Application of the Principles of Subsidiarity and Proportionality. See also Article 12 TEU and Protocol 1.

[7] See, for example, Maurer, A. (2001) 'National Parliaments in the European Union Architecture'.

[8] See Norton, P. (1996) 'Introduction: The Institution of Parliaments' at 1.

national parliaments as 'victims' of EU integration.[9] By contrast Raunio and Hix,[10] though accepting these arguments, have also suggested that integration is only one, albeit important, constituent part of a wider deparliamentarisation. Domestic factors, such as strong executives, the growth of devolution and regional governments, the increased use of delegated legislation and the development of agencies to deliver policies have all contributed to the loss of competence by national parliaments. The conclusions of Norton and Maurer and Wessels reflect the discourse prior to the Laeken Declaration, the Convention on the Future of Europe and the Treaty of Lisbon. It may be argued that these views have been overtaken by the Treaty of Lisbon and are confined to a period of integration in which the Treaties did not sufficiently recognise national parliaments. In particular, it is important to consider the potential impact of new Article 12 TEU, Protocol 1 and Protocol 2 of the Treaty of Lisbon and other provisions such as Article 47 TEU, which provides for improved control by national parliaments of *Passerelle* clauses. To what extent do these changes address the argument that Europeanisation has marginalised national parliaments and do these provisions create a foundation for a progressive parliamentarisation of EU decision-making? Before considering this issue it is necessary to consider how Europeanisation and the increased exercise of competences at the EU level have contributed to deparliamentarisation.

Proponents of a deparliamentarisation thesis[11] suggest that the transfer of competences may be identified as the overwhelming factor which restricts the ability of national parliaments to control the executive and overshadows any domestic realignment. According to Moravcsik,[12] EU integration has domestically strengthened the executive and consequently, at the EU level, the Council. This has been primarily achieved at the expense of national parliaments and arises from the technocratic nature of EU decision-making which has restricted the accountability of the executive to national parliaments. Within this technocratic form of decision-making it is ministers who have assumed overall responsibility in those areas which have been 'Europeanised'. Maurer and Wessels

---

[9] See Maurer, A. and Wessels, W. (eds) (2001) *National Parliaments on their Ways to Europe* at 432.

[10] See Raunio, T. and Hix, S. (2003) 'Backbenchers Learn to Fight Back' at 145.

[11] See for example Norton, P. (1996) 'Introduction: The Institution of Parliaments' and Wessels, W. and Romestch, D. (1996) 'Conclusion'.

[12] Moravcsik, A. (1998) 'Introduction: The Choice for Europe' 11.

argue[13] that in parallel to Europeanisation the Treaty-makers responded to criticism of a 'democratic deficit' by pursuing EU democratisation through increased legislative powers for the European Parliament to secure both input and output legislative legitimacy.[14] Consequently, democratisation occurred without reference to national parliaments and Maurer identifies this political evolution as the primary evidence for deparliamentarisation.[15]

The appeal of a more formal presence for national parliaments in the EU Treaties is understandable and this was advocated for many years as part of a process of improving legislative legitimacy.[16] Though national parliaments were part of the Community and EU institutional architecture and were mentioned in ratification clauses, national legislatures were barred from influencing the EU's inner workings and most crucially from direct input into the legislative process. This peripheral constitutional position has reinforced the notion of deparliamentarisation. Broadly speaking, national parliaments have largely been bystanders in the process of EU integration, with the exception of ratifying the Treaties. Democratisation of the EU has improved the legislative position of the European Parliament to being that of equal co-legislator with the Council and national parliaments have, for the most part, used their internal scrutiny procedures to try and control the activities of their own minister within the Council. This domestic scrutiny of EU affairs through seeking to exert accountability over ministers was first recognised by an informal Declaration in the Treaty of Maastricht. Gradually, and with each new Treaty, national parliaments have had their domestic scrutiny activities further recognised and today, under the provisions of the Treaty of Lisbon, national parliaments have been allocated specific additional

13 See Maurer, A. (2001) 'National Parliaments in the European Union Architecture' at 28.

14 See generally Scharpf, W.F. (1999) *Governing in Europe* and Scharpf, F.W. (2010) 'Legitimacy in the Multi-Level European Polity' at 89. As seen in Chapter 1, Scharpf argues that output legitimacy, or 'government for the people', connects the legitimacy of a political system with its (perceived) performance. It attributes legitimacy to a political system based upon capacity to achieve citizens' goals (a measure of effectiveness) and to provide solutions for their problems. Scharpf's primary point is that, in at least some cases, the EU action can be considered as legitimate by reference to its output even if input legitimacy is largely lacking.

15 Maurer, A. (2005) 'The Convention and the National Parliamentary Dimension', *Arena Working Papers*, available at http://www.arena.uio.no/publications/papers/wp05_01.pdf (accessed 16 November 2009).

16 Ibid.

powers to review legislative proposals for compliance with the principle of subsidiarity. However, this has not prevented calls for further reforms and the creation of a specific forum, at the EU level, through which national parliaments can express a clearer collective voice.[17]

In the course of the post-Laeken debate suggestions for reforms ranged from the creation of a chamber of national parliamentarians next to the European Parliament[18] to an assizes-type Congress of Parliaments.[19] The European Union Committee in the House of Lords considered whether either type of forum could form an operational second legislative chamber in the EU and more generally whether there was any desirability for such an institution.[20] The House of Lords concluded, correctly, that even if such a second chamber could function, it was doubtful whether there was any appetite among national parliaments to transfer the tasks of legislative scrutiny or competence monitoring to such an institution. A second chamber made up of representatives of national parliaments was rejected by the Constitutional Convention.[21] The arguments against such a constitutional step far outweigh the benefits and reinforce the view that scrutiny of Council decision-making should occur within national parliaments under their own parliamentary procedures. The introduction of any second chamber at the EU level, and thus an additional actor, would not, per se, improve parliamentary control over EU affairs. Moreover, it would compound the lack of transparency at the national level with regard to the EU legislative process, and add further delays to the legislative process.[22] Furthermore, it is inconceivable that national parliaments would surrender the scrutiny function completely and not wish to participate in some form of review. The primary purpose of national parliamentary scrutiny has traditionally been to secure ministerial

---

17 See, for example, Passos, R. (2008) 'Recent Developments Concerning the Role of National Parliaments in the European Union' at 33–38; Kiiver, P. (2011) 'The Early Warning System for the Principle of Subsidiarity' 98.

18 See HL 48 (Session 2001–2) *A Second Parliamentary Chamber for the EU.*

19 CONV 84/02 Contribution from Ms Anne Van Lancker, Member of the Convention: Socio-economic Governance in the Constitutional Treaty.

20 See HL 48 (Session 2001–2) *A Second Parliamentary Chamber for the EU.*

21 See CONV 353/02 Working Group IV The Role of National Parliaments, at paragraph.33.

22 CONV 81/02 Contribution from Mr Caspar Einem, Member of the Convention: National Parliaments; CONV 82/02 Contribution from Members of the Convention Representing the Finnish Parliament on the role of National Parliaments in the European Union Structure.

accountability. The detrimental effect on the efficiency of this accountability could not be justified by means of any additional input from a second chamber. In any system of parliamentary democracy it is highly likely that the views of a parliamentary majority coincide with the views of the government which is represented in the Council. If there is a divergence of views between the parliamentary majority and the government such conflicts are better resolved within the domestic parliamentary forum. This interpretation further strengthens the argument that national parliamentary involvement in EU affairs primarily reflects domestic priorities rather than the pursuit of a wider collective agenda with other national parliaments. That is not to say that national parliaments do not share collective concerns in relation to EU decision-making; the Amsterdam and Lisbon Protocols demonstrate that they do. But it is the principle of ministerial accountability, at the heart of which is the idea that national parliaments remain largely individual actors in EU affairs which, notwithstanding Protocol 2 of the Treaty of Lisbon, remains the preoccupation for the majority of national parliaments, especially in the context of the ordinary legislative procedure. This issue is explored in more detail in Chapter 6.

2.2 The Causes of Deparliamentarisation

A defining feature of EU integration has been the constitutionalisation of the EU[23] and the creation of what the European Court of Justice referred to as a 'new legal order'.[24] Together with the Europeanisation of policy, the centre of gravity for legislative action has shifted from the national arena to the EU. One consequence of this has been the peripheral role which national parliaments have held throughout the integration process, particularly with regard to decision-making.[25] EU decision-making remains dominated by the institutions and seeks to balance the supranational (Commission), the inter-governmental (Council) and the multinational (European Parliament). The present Treaty framework does not assign a role to national parliaments within the EU decision-making process, as formal ratification of legislative acts is not necessary. This lack of participation in EU decision-making must be distinguished from

---

[23] See generally Poiares Maduro, M. (1998) *We the Court.*

[24] Case 25/62 *Van Gend en Loos* v *Nederlanse Administratie der Belastingen* [1963] ECR 1.

[25] See Maurer, A. (2001) 'National Parliaments in the European Union Architecture' .

the scrutiny activities of EU legislative proposals carried out by individual national parliaments. The objective of this scrutiny is, first and foremost, to provide domestic accountability of ministers for decisions taken within Council, and arguments that this focus has changed because of Article 12 TEU or Protocol 2 can be rebutted.[26] Meanwhile, the formal task of national parliaments to implement directives leaves little scope for discretion and underlines their limited involvement in EU decision-making. In the case of implementation *any* failure by a national parliament of timely and proper implementation of directives constitutes a violation of EU law, the consequence of which may result in the payment of damages by the offending State.[27]

Despite their tangential role in EU decision-making, national parliaments remain the primary legislative chambers within the Member States and provide the principal form of political representation for EU citizens. National parliaments are an embodiment of political sovereignty; they are directly elected and have the function of controlling the executive. Furthermore, national parliaments are an expression of cultural identity and their composition broadly reflects the socio-cultural values of each Member State. Yet, notwithstanding this view there is no doubt that EU membership and the process of integration, which at its core necessitates the transfer of legislative competences, have transformed the constitutional status of national parliaments. However, it would be inaccurate to conclude that EU membership and Europeanisation alone are responsible for deparliamentarisation. One constitutional development that can be witnessed in many Member States is the process of the modernisation of government and public administration. The changes brought through the growth of regional parliaments, the increased use of non-governmental agencies and privatisation have all contributed to the progressive alteration of the position of the State which includes national parliaments. As part of these changes national parliaments have been portrayed as reactive institutions casting modest influence on policy initiatives coming from the executive.[28] For example, the reorganisation of government and administration in the UK, through changes such as devolution and the extended use of agencies, has been highlighted as a significant change in

[26] See Raunio, T. (2010) 'Destined for Irrelevance?'.

[27] Joined Cases C-6 and 9/90 *Francovich* v *Italian State* [1991] ECR I-535. This judgment established the principle of State liability for failure by a Member State to implement within the transitional period.

[28] See Raunio, T. and Hix, S. (2003) 'Backbenchers Learn to Fight Back' at 145.

the relationship between the executive and Parliament.[29] As a result, Raunio and Hix argue that these developments demonstrate that European integration is not per se responsible for the decline in influence of national parliaments. They state that: 'notwithstanding the transfer of constitutional, executive and legislature powers to the European level, the overall impact of European integration on parliamentary government in the domestic area has actually been rather modest'.[30] By contrast, proponents of what is referred to as the 'deparliamentarisation' thesis[31] suggest that Treaty developments have, almost exclusively, restricted national parliaments and pursued an objective of EU democratisation rather than seeking full parliamentarisation of the EU. Consequently, the preferred reform has been to grant increased powers to the European Parliament. Though the Treaties have recognised the presence of domestic legislatures, this has only ended with them being required to monitor subsidiarity once a legislative proposal is drafted rather than to participate directly in the process of decision-making.

The United Kingdom has not been unique among Member States to introduce constitutional and administrative changes that have extended the powers of non-governmental agencies.[32] If these developments are considered alongside the Europeanisation of law and policy within the Member States, it may be argued that national parliaments are fighting a rearguard action to maintain their influence both at the EU and domestic level. Europeanisation and constitutionalisation of the EU reflect the depth of integration and how much of domestic government policy is influenced or directed by EU objectives. To address the specific point of Raunio and Hix, while there undoubtedly does exist a domestic political, legislative and constitutional agenda within the Member States, this cannot be considered in isolation from the principles of EU law. Accordingly, any legislative proposal, even if dealing with purely domestic issues, may infringe the general principles of EU law. Furthermore, the development of soft law and the open method of co-ordination have

[29] See generally Norton, P. (1996) 'Introduction: The Institution of Parliaments'.

[30] See Raunio, T. and Hix, S. (2003) 'Backbenchers Learn to Fight Back' at 143.

[31] See for example Norton, P. (1996) 'Introduction: The Institution of Parliaments' and Wessels, W. and Romestch, D. (1996) 'Conclusion'.

[32] Since the Treaty of Maastricht, internal constitutional reorganisation has been a feature in many Member States, for example the reorganisation within the United Kingdom, Spain and Italy that has created much greater regional autonomy. See further the discussion in Chapter 7.

made additional inroads into domestic competence and through a process of 'creeping competences'[33] mainstreamed additional policy areas within the EU. The open method of co-ordination has strengthened the leadership role of the European Council, which takes the lead in policy co-ordination, with the Commission[34] adopting a strategic role by setting objectives and issuing guidelines and recommendations to national governments. The European Parliament remains on the periphery of this process, as do national parliaments. At the national level the open method falls predominantly within the activities of civil servants who possess expertise on the issues, and in this sense shares many of the features of the comitology process. As the open method is primarily intergovernmental in character, national parliaments should be in a constitutionally strong position to influence the proceedings. However, the difficulty lies in finding the parliamentary time to conduct the necessary scrutiny. Furthermore, reviewing often abstract guidelines or targets which are set by the Commission is not a priority for national parliaments within a busy parliamentary timetable. The new legal order, referred to by the Court in *Van Gend en Loos* is, today, contained within the comprehensive Treaty framework and recognises the presence of an omni-competent EU. This process of constitutionalisation and Europeanisation has not rendered national parliaments completely irrelevant. On the contrary, national parliaments maintain a pivotal role within the EU, not least that it is from their membership that the executive of each Member State is composed, and which ultimately provides the members of the Council. Furthermore, the Laeken Declaration[35] and the Convention on the Future of Europe both recognise that national parliaments are integral to an EU constitutional settlement. However, it is unquestionable that, irrespective of the Treaties, national parliaments continue to view EU integration from a largely domestic perspective and measure its effect in terms of impact upon their competences that they have 'surrendered'.

---

33 Hodson, D. and Maher, I. (2001) 'The Open Method as a New Mode of Governance' at 719. For the application of the open method of co-ordination to EU social policy see Szyszczak, E. (2001) 'The New Paradigm for Social Policy' at 1125. For its application to asylum and immigration policy see Bogusz, B. (2004) 'Modes of Governance for an EU Immigration Policy'.

34 The role of the Commission in the open method varies considerably between policy areas, with the Council often adopting the leading function instead of the Commission.

35 Laeken European Council, 15 December 2001, available at http://www.europa.eu.int/futurum/documents/offtext/doc151201_en.htm (accessed 26 July 2011).

3. THE EUROPEANISATION OF PARLIAMENTARY COMPETENCES

Harding has referred to the process of Europeanisation as creating a 'European legal space'.[36] As a part of this process, EU integration is accompanied by co-operation in, inter alia, the protection of human rights through the European Convention on Human Rights (ECHR). Though different in legal character from the EU, the norms of the ECHR are accepted by all Member States and are broadly reflected in the Charter of Fundamental Rights. Furthermore, the Treaty of Lisbon provides that the EU will now have the legal capacity to become, in its own right, a signatory to the ECHR.[37] While these developments have weakened the power of national parliaments it is important to note that they too come within the concept of the 'European legal space'. The key feature of all these Treaties and Conventions is that national legislatures must ratify them, and in the absence of any rejection it could be concluded that national parliaments have accepted the process of Europeanisation.[38] The primary impact of EU membership is that it has transformed the legislative competence of Member States across a diverse range of policy fields. National parliaments are no longer the primary legislators, with legislative competence being exercised by the EU institutions. Though Europeanisation is undoubtedly a primary cause of deparliamentarisation, the manner in which Europeanisation has impacted upon Member States and their legislative institutions varies significantly and depends, in large part, upon domestic constitutional arrangements. In particular, the consequences of Europeanisation for Member States with federal or devolved constitutional arrangements, such as Germany, Spain and the United Kingdom, will be different from

[36] Harding, C. (2000) 'Exploring the Intersection of European Law and National Criminal Law' at 375.

[37] This issue was first raised in Opinion 2/94 [1996] ECR I-1759. Advocate General Jacobs stated that the EU lacked the institutional capacity to become a signatory of the ECHR.

[38] It is important to distinguish between a rejection by the electorate in a referendum and that by a national parliament. The latter has so far not occurred throughout a ratification process. In the case of the Danish rejection by a referendum in 1992, the Maastricht Treaty remained unaltered except for the addition of a specific Protocol to address the concerns of the Danish electorate. The Irish 'no' vote in 2001 was once again as a result of a referendum and not a rejection by the Irish parliament. In the context of the Treaty of Lisbon see Louis, J.-V. (2008) 'The Lisbon Treaty: The Irish "No"' at 429.

those in Member States where there is a unitary constitutional structure, such as the Netherlands. The following discussion examines the effect of 'competence creep', which has resulted from deeper EU integration. It also considers the dual impact of Europeanisation upon national parliaments, namely the ever growing intervention of the EU in the legislative competence of national parliaments and gradual developments in other competences.[39] In the latter case, the consequence of the increased use of new modes of governance and soft law can be identified as a significant limitation of national competences.

3.1 Governance and Harmonisation

The limits placed upon the legislative competence of national parliaments are perhaps the most direct consequence of EU membership, but the precise extent of this transfer of competence cannot readily be measured. In particular, with the growth of complementary competences and the use of soft law as a tool of integration, the scope for legislative autonomy of the Member States has significantly diminished. The direct consequence of Europeanisation is that EU decision-making, in whatever legislative form, has reduced the decision-making capacity of national parliaments. This reduction in decision-making has arisen notwithstanding Article 5 TEU. However, Article 5 TEU leaves significant leeway for interpretation, meaning that exercise of legislative competence by the EU becomes a political as well as a legal question.[40] Under the pre-Lisbon Treaty structure, which is overwhelmingly responsible for the current extent of EU integration, the classification of exclusive and non-exclusive competences was not so clearly differentiated by contrast to the present statement in Article 4 TEU. Under the EC Treaty there were a number of flexible provisions, for example Articles 94 EC, 95 EC and 308 EC together with the doctrine of implied powers, which created a legal framework for intervention in many policy fields. In particular, the EU developed the 'flanking policies' of, inter alia, transport, the environment and consumer protection where EU legislative action overtook that of the Member States.

The EC Treaty conferred no general competence to harmonise national laws.[41] Article 5 (1) EC merely stated that the EC was competent only

---

[39] See further Pollack, M. (1994) 'Creeping Competence' at 95.

[40] See Weatherill, S. (2005) 'Better Competence Monitoring' at 25 and Craig, P. (2012) 'Subsidiarity' at 78–79.

[41] See Weatherill, S. (2002) 'Pre-emption, Harmonisation and the Distribution of Competence to Regulate the Internal Market' at 73.

where so provided by the EC Treaty. 'Non-economic' activities were to remain outside the legislative scope of Community law and should remain within the Member States, for example the provision of State education and healthcare services, although this did not shield those areas where the non-discrimination principle contained in Article 12 EC or the citizenship provisions of Articles 17 and 18 EC applied. Similarly, where there was an identifiable economic activity, the EC Treaty provisions regularly applied, for example the application of the free movement and competition rules to sport or healthcare, even though the EU did not have *legislative* competence in either field. In circumstances where Member States' laws and policies were divergent, this divergence posed a threat to the efficient functioning of the Internal Market and the EC Treaty allowed for *positive integration* to take place. The effect of this was to create Community policies which harmonised the Member States' divergent practices and led to the re-regulation of markets. The spillover effect from what is a functionally broad programme of harmonisation was to extend Community and/or EU law competence into a number of areas which are today seen as distinctive EU law disciplines: private law, consumer law, environmental law, social policy law, labour law, healthcare law, family law. In some instances these disciplines have been raised to the status of values within the EU and are to be mainstreamed through all EU policies. For example, the provisions of Article 3 (2) EC, now found in Article 8 TFEU, mainstreamed equality between men and women; Article 6 EC, now Article 11 TFEU, mainstreamed environmental concerns and Article 127 EC, now Article 147 TFEU, states that a 'high level of employment' shall be taken into consideration in the formulation and implementation of Union policies and activities. Thus the integration programme, which is presented as an exercise in securing market freedoms through the creation of an Internal Market, has not only explicitly recognised the need for horizontal or flanking policies to support the four freedoms but has inevitably spilled over into a number of broad policy areas and has committed the EU to a sustained commitment to rule-making at the EU level.[42]

This has occurred at the expense of national competences and restricted the legislative capacity and autonomy of national parliaments. The growth of flanking policies which has enabled a broader reach for Internal Market regulation into non-economic policies has further underscored the practical legislative consequences that have accompanied

---

[42] See generally, Egan, M. (2001) *Constructing a European Market*.

deparliamentarisation. Article 95 EC did not vest the Community legislator with 'a general power to regulate the Internal Market'.[43] Any measures based upon Article 95 EC should only have been permitted where they genuinely contributed to eliminating obstacles to trade and removing distortions of competition. In theory, this placed a self-restraint upon unlimited exercise of Community competence and jurisdiction.[44] The recognition of the need for horizontal or flanking policies to support the Internal Market project, as well as the desire by some Member States to harmonise rules relating to social policy, migration, the environment, agriculture, health and safety, and consumer protection, created tensions within the EU as to how far non-economic objectives could also be the subject of harmonisation within the EU using Article 95 EC rather than a specific sectoral legal base for such measures. Under the EC Treaty some areas specifically rejected the use of harmonisation, for example health (Article 152 (4) (c) EC)[45] and employment (Article 129 EC), thereby implying that national parliaments retained competence. In the *Tobacco Advertising* case the Court held that in circumstances where there were two competing legal bases for a measure[46] the principal rule is that the Internal Market base should be used where the aim is to improve the functioning of the Internal Market. Where the aim was to achieve another policy goal (for example, the protection of the environment, social policy or public health) then the Court held that the appropriate specific legal base should be used. This choice of legislative base was significant for national parliaments because it dictated the legislative procedure to be

[43] Case C-376/98 *Germany* v *European Parliament and Council (Tobacco Advertising)* [2000] ECR I-8419 at paragraph 83.

[44] Case C-436/03P *European Parliament and Commission* v *Council* [2006] ECR I-1025.

[45] Health issues have, historically, been particularly problematic for the EU (see Article 152 (4) EC). As a result of the Treaty of Lisbon 2007 Article 168 (4) TFEU provides that measures should be adopted in the area of public health '*in order to meet common safety concerns*' but it will be possible for the Union to harmonise standards of quality and safety in relation to medicinal products and devices (Article 168 (4) TFEU) where the Internal Market legal base of Article 95 EC was previously used. The Union is also able to adopt incentive measures in relation to cross-border threats to health, and tobacco and alcohol abuse (Article 168 (5) TFEU). But incentive measures should not be harmonisation measures. In contrast, Article 168 (7) TFEU expands Article 152 (5) EC. Member States are responsible for the definition of health policy and the delivery of health services. Member States shall include the management of health services and medical care in the allocation of resources assigned to them.

[46] Ibid.

used and consequently defined the influence of national parliaments. Under sectoral Treaty bases such as Article 129 EC unanimity was required and the European Parliament was not a co-legislator, leaving national parliaments with increased opportunities to exert control over their ministers. However, where there was no EU competence for the additional policy goal then the Internal Market legal base could be used irrespective of whether the Internal Market was ancillary to the objective being sought. Thus Internal Market issues could not be disregarded when pursuing other ancillary goals that were necessary for market integration, and this strategy, which enabled ancillary policies to be agreed through the use of qualified majority voting, had a significant impact upon national parliamentary competences. This clearly had major repercussions for the exercise of legislative competence by national parliaments and led to criticism that the spillover of competence from Internal Market integration led to the incidental expansion of Community competences into new areas of regulatory activity.

This became labelled 'competence creep'.[47] Weatherill categorised the governance approach to the use of Community powers as one based upon *ex ante* restraint by the political institutions, which includes the parliamentary scrutiny activities of national parliaments as well as *ex post* review by the Court. However, this has not proved to be either an effective or acceptable constitutional mechanism to delimit the powers of the EU against the Member States and the constitutional principles governing the EU. For example, pre-Lisbon the impact of the fundamental free movement and competition provisions was being felt in a number of areas where the EU did not have legislative competence. Equally the process started in the 1970s, of introducing a wider range of values into EU law alongside the economic aims of integration, was recognised in the Court's case law but not articulated fully in the basic EC Treaty. Again, such non-Treaty developments had the effect of further undermining national competences and ultimately national parliaments. The Treaty of Amsterdam 1997 did not address the competence issues of the EU squarely and the issues were not resolved in the Treaty of Nice 2000. The Declaration attached to the Treaty of Nice 2000 instigated the process that continued with the Laeken Declaration in December 2001 and the Convention on the Future of Europe, culminating in the failed Constitutional Treaty. The Constitutional Treaty, rejected in 2007, was set

---

[47] See Weatherill, S. (2006) 'Why Harmonise?' at 22 and Weatherill, S. (2002) 'Pre-emption, Harmonisation and the Distribution of Competence to Regulate the Internal Market'.

the task to clarify and reorganise the EC Treaty rules governing competence and also to embrace new political actors, particularly the national parliaments, to monitor the exercise of Community powers. The Treaty of Lisbon now sets out in even greater detail and clarity the competences of the Union in Articles 4 and 5 TEU and Articles 2–6 TFEU. Now competences fall into three distinct groups: exclusive competence, non-exclusive competence and a third group where the Union shall carry out actions to support and co-ordinate the actions of the Member States provided for by Articles 5 and 6 TFEU. However, irrespective of any ostensible improved delineation of competences, the challenge of monitoring the exercise of shared EU competences by political institutions, and especially by national parliaments, remains the same, if not even more acute, under the Treaty of Lisbon. In the context of non-exclusive competence where the EU shares the exercise of competence with the Member States, the limits have been drawn by the application of the dynamic and politically sensitive principles of subsidiarity and proportionality which have always made the delimitation of the EU's competences even more complicated. As a result of the imprecise nature of these principles the scope of any legislative act is determined either by the EU's political institutions or by the Court of Justice.[48] It could also be argued that until the Treaty of Lisbon, which formally introduced subsidiarity monitoring by national parliaments into the decision-making process, the views of national parliaments on the exercise of EU competences were largely a peripheral consideration. This criticism explains why some form of 'collective' parliamentary voice, in the guise of subsidiarity monitoring, was suggested by the Constitutional Convention as a means of addressing the need to have national parliaments heard directly on the question of the exercise of competences. The scope and effect of Protocol 2, which provides the process for subsidiarity monitoring by national parliaments, is considered in Chapter 6.

3.2 EU Governance and the Transformation of National Parliaments

In the previous section the effect of the 'spillover' of EU competences was highlighted, illustrating how the effect of EU integration has gone beyond the borders of the Treaty and impacted upon what could be considered as domestic law, policy and procedures. With the benefit of hindsight it is inconceivable that EU integration would not have had this effect upon national parliaments and their capacity to legislate and to

48 See Craig, P. (2012) 'Subsidiarity'.

exercise their residual legislative functions.[49] The restrictions placed upon national parliaments have been categorised in two ways: either as 'passive' or 'active' restrictions.[50] Passive restrictions are those which restrict the ability of Member States to only legislate within non-exclusive competence, considering the overall scheme of EU law and the operation of constitutional principles such as supremacy. By contrast, active restrictions place a positive burden upon national authorities to undertake specific legislative and regulatory actions. Within the integration process and the legislative outcomes that this produces there is increased pressure upon national parliaments from passive restrictions. This restriction does not necessarily arise because of increased legislative activity on the part of the EU, with the number of legislative initiatives proposed annually remaining constant. The primary development that has occurred in recent years concerns the range of regulatory acts which are open to the EU, and in particular the increased reliance upon soft law and policy co-ordination rather than directives and regulations as tools of integration. It is the increased use of soft law that can be singled out for not only increasing the regulatory output of the EU, but also the process through which competence creep can be most clearly identified. Most recently, it is the ambitious Agenda 2020 Programme for which soft law and policy co-ordination are the primary methods of regulation.[51] In addition, the European Court of Justice has also played a significant role in shaping the EU legal order through its integrationist reasoning and expansive interpretation of Treaty provisions concerning, for example, citizenship of the Union, and especially the application of Articles 20–23 TFEU. Taken together, these political and judicial developments have caused a gradual, but nevertheless a constant, expansion of EU regulation and an erosion of domestic legislative competence. Active restrictions on legislative competences do as the name suggests, and arise from circumstances where Member States are required to legislate or take administrative measures in order to ensure conformity with EU obligations. This may require Member States to adjust existing national legislative provisions to ensure conformity with EU regulations, and involve Member

---

49 See Auel, K. and Benz, A. (2005) 'The Politics of Adaptation' at 372. See also Auel, K. (2007) 'Democratic Accountability and National Parliaments' at 494–497.

50 See Töller, A.E. (2006) 'How European Integration Impacts on National Legislatures' available at http://aei.pitt.edu/9283/1/toller.pdf (accessed 23 November 2011).

51 See further, Armstrong, K. (2011) 'The Character of EU Law and Governance' at 179.

States transposing EU directives into national law or making any necessary legislative or administrative amendments in response to a judgment from the European Court of Justice. Other circumstances where Member States will be required to act include introducing legislation to give effect to changes to the Treaty, for example in circumstances of the accession of new Member States, or to respond to any other policy changes which may be presented by the Commission. The overriding issue with regard to these active restrictions is that they are both prescriptive and place limits upon national parliamentary autonomy. They also illustrate the 'uncharted' constitutional and procedural implications upon national parliaments that arise from EU membership which have resulted from the Europeanisation of national legislative and administrative procedures. In substance, these restrictions constitute no more than giving effect to the principle of supremacy of EU law and essentially form part of any Member State's obligations to give effect to the provisions of Article 4 (3) TEU, which requires that: 'Member States shall take any appropriate measures, general or particular, to ensure the fulfilment of the obligations arising out of the Treaties or resulting from the acts of the Institutions of the Union.' Article 4 (3) TEU further requires that: 'The Member States shall facilitate the achievement of the Union's tasks and refrain from any measure which could jeopardise the attainment of the Union's objectives.'

The reference to Member States in Article 4 (3) TEU must by implication include the activities of the national parliaments of the Member States which undertake the legislative function of the Member States. Moreover, unlike the equivalent pre-Lisbon provision in Article 10 EC, Article 4 (3) TEU makes reference to giving effect to obligations arising out of the Treaties *or* resulting from the acts of the institutions of the Union. In the case of the latter this includes soft law and policy co-ordination and would appear to place a requirement upon national parliaments to give effect to regulatory acts which have not been agreed through the ordinary legislative process, but which come about because of the exercise of either executive powers by the Commission or through the technocratic law-making procedure of comitology. In such circumstances the obligation to give effect to these regulatory acts raises fundamental questions of accountability both at the EU and national levels because Member States are required to implement, without any effective safeguards, legislation which itself has been decided through a largely unaccountable and undemocratic process. The active restrictions that have been placed upon national parliaments and the degree to which these have caused deparliamentarisation have been the subject of much academic discussion which has sought to provide some quantitative evaluation of the extent to which there has been Europeanisation of national legislation.

This, however, is very much an imprecise science because the experiences of the Member States differ with regard to the amount of parliamentary legislation that is introduced, and this in turn is dependent upon a number of variables including the legislative procedures that are used to transpose directives and whether regional institutions assume responsibility for implementation. Notwithstanding these obstacles, it is possible to show a measurable impact of EU law through the Europeanisation of national legislation. For example, in 2009 König and Mäder[52] suggested that 'European impulses' affected, in an average parliamentary year, 24 per cent of all bills laid before the *Bundestag*. This figure went to a much higher proportion of 80 per cent in one legislative term, but while these statistics may dispel criticism that EU legislation is dominating the national legislative agenda, there is still a high proportion of 'hard' EU legislation which a national parliament must implement. Though legislative transposition can be more easily monitored it is very difficult to measure the effect which soft law has had in recent years on domestic legislation despite becoming a more prominent tool of integration. This is especially the case as regional parliaments and administrative bodies are becoming more prominent actors in the process of soft law governance.[53] According to the Commission's 2010 Report, *28th Annual Monitoring of the Application of EU Law*,[54] the *acquis* consisted of circa 8400 regulations and nearly 2000 directives,[55] each of which required between 40 and over 300 measures, for transposition into national and regional legislation. This is in addition to the primary law within the Treaties which requires significant parliamentary time and detailed amendments of existing legislation. This volume of EU legislation undoubtedly constitutes a significant proportion of the legislative composition of all Member States, and with approximately 800–1000 regulatory proposals per year emanating from the EU it is beyond question that the work of national parliaments is increasingly being influenced, or even dominated, by the EU policy agenda. Such a volume of legislation being produced through a policy-making and legislative

---

[52] König, T. and Mäder, L. (2009) 'The Myth of 80% and the Impact of Europeanisation on German Legislation'.

[53] See Weatherill, S. (2005) 'The Challenge of the Regional Dimension in the European Union' 1 at 3. See also the discussion in Chapter 7 of this book.

[54] SEC (2011) 1093 final. *28th Annual Monitoring of the Application of EU Law*.

[55] Ibid at 3.

process from which national parliaments are, de facto, detached cannot lead to any other conclusion than the EU legislative process is the primary cause of deparliamentarisation. Moreover, the volume of regulatory acts indicates a significant transfer of competence which has progressively restricted legislative autonomy of national parliaments. The extent to which this development has contributed to deparliamentarisation may be debated, especially in the light of the other domestic constitutional changes which have taken place. But what is beyond question is the pressure placed on national parliaments, both in terms of time and resources, to process this volume of EU legislation. In particular, there is a real risk that some national parliaments may simply operate in a functional rather than systematic way that will have major implications for the effective functioning of the Protocol 2 requirements of subsidiarity monitoring. If this is the case, and the discussion in Chapter 6 considers this issue in more detail, then it may be suggested that the Treaty of Lisbon has failed to successfully address the question of national parliaments being classified as either 'strong' or 'weak' actors in EU affairs.[56] It may be concluded from the above that EU integration places 'active' restrictions upon the power of national parliaments to set their own legislative agenda. For example, evidence presented by Auel and Benz[57] indicates that in the Finnish parliament, the *Eduskunta*, the number of EU-related items that are placed on the agenda of parliamentary committees has doubled with accession.[58] Now this can be considered as an uncontroversial finding and indicates that the Europeanisation of national parliaments impacts upon the work of committees beyond those dedicated exclusively to EU affairs committees or specific EU scrutiny committees. The primary observation that can be made is that, with some notable exceptions, in particular the House of Lords EU Affairs Committee, the majority of EU committees can be categorised as being passive and reactive and not necessarily controlling their own agenda. This arises, in great part, because it is the Commission and the

---

56 See Goetz, K. and Meyer-Sahling, H. (2008) 'The Europeanisation of National Political Systems', available at http://www.livingreviews.org/lreg-2008-2 (accessed 10 August 2009). 'Weak' parliaments are those where there is a lack of resources, information exchange and co-ordination across policy levels, ministries and agencies. Harlow suggests that participation in EU affairs by national parliaments is determined by the extent of control over foreign affairs by parliaments. See Harlow, C. (2002) 'A Plethora of Parliaments' at 85.

57 See Auel, K. and Benz, A. (2005) 'The Politics of Adaptation' at 374.

58 See also Raunio, T. and Wiberg, M. (2009) 'How to Measure the Europeanisation of a National Legislature?' at 74.

European Parliament which set the legislative and policy agendas and national parliaments have no direct input. Scrutiny activities are by their nature reactive and while many committees will scrutinise the Annual Work Programme of the Commission, and some such as the House of Lords Committee will hold oral evidence sessions with Commissioners or Commission officials, this only occurs *ex post* after the Programme has been published. Auel and Benz correctly surmise that EU law and policy are dominated by the Commission and domestic institutions can only have any impact when they react to EU initiatives.[59] To this end, though Protocol 2 engages national parliaments in subsidiarity monitoring and embeds them within the legislative process, this activity is one which is, for the most part, carried out towards the end of the legislative process.

3.3 From Legislative Sovereignty to Scrutiny as Substitute Sovereignty

The primary effect of EU integration for national parliaments is that they no longer legislate in areas where the EU has exclusive competence. Even where competence is shared, the Commission's interpretation of the justification for EU legislation and why the principle of subsidiarity should not be applied has led to the EU legislating in the overwhelming majority of, if not all, cases, when competence is shared. Moreover, this choice of EU legislative action has been consistently upheld by the Court, which has accepted the Commission's dual justifications of 'necessity' and 'effectiveness'.[60] The constitutional change which the reduction of legislative competences has had in some 'stronger' national parliaments is that they have developed their internal scrutiny mechanisms accordingly in response. The primary purpose for these national parliaments is to secure the full accountability of the executive. More precisely, this has historically been to secure the accountability of the minister to the national parliament in their capacity as a member of the Council. The process of detailed and vigorous national parliamentary scrutiny of EU affairs can be considered as a cathartic exercise for

[59] See Auel, K. and Benz, A. (2005) 'The Politics of Adaptation' at 378.

[60] See for example Case C-58/8 *Vodafone Ltd, Telefonica O2 Europe plc, T-Mobile International AG, Orange Personal Communication Services Ltd* v *Secretary of State for Business, Enterprise and Regulatory Reform* [2010] ECR I-4999 and Case C-49/01 *R* v *Secretary of State for Health ex parte British American Tobacco and Imperial Tobacco* [2002] ECR I-11453, in particular paragraphs 177 and 185.

national parliaments and gives an impression of 'control'. Yet, given the challenge of limited political control and influence over the EU legislative process, then national parliamentary scrutiny processes can be assessed as constituting merely some form of substitute sovereignty.[61] That is to say, from a domestic parliamentary perspective the more scrutiny that occurs then the more this is deemed to make up for the loss of legislative competence and the less politically impotent national parliaments feel. In many strong national parliaments the rigorous scrutiny process corresponds in large part to the exacting scrutiny that occurs of domestic legislative proposals and may be viewed as the parliamentary chamber merely discharging its duty of pursuing executive accountability.

Despite these practical limitations, the requirement of executive scrutiny should not be understated. It is a crucial task, and remains the only direct control over the executive throughout the entire EU legislative procedure. To this extent, and as argued earlier in this chapter, national parliaments do not want a new institution representing them at the EU level and performing this scrutiny function on their behalf. Though it may constitute no more than substitute sovereignty, it still requires individual ministers to be directly answerable to their parliament and this political process should not be underestimated. Parliamentary scrutiny can change the direction of governments and has been known to make or break ministerial careers. For this reason alone – that national parliaments are exercising constitutional control over ministers – it would be inappropriate for any existing EU institution to seek to influence or determine how national parliaments undertake these scrutiny activities. Yet despite this scrutiny, whether of the minister or in the guise of subsidiarity monitoring, it can only be effective if it is pre-legislative and based upon the *timely* provision of all available documentation. Pre-Lisbon, national parliaments were largely reliant upon their governments to provide EU documentation that formed the basis of their scrutiny activities. To this end many parliaments developed scrutiny reserves in order to restrain ministers from voting on a legislative measure in Council, prior to completion of the scrutiny process. The objective of the scrutiny reserve, the precise scope and operation of which varies in the national parliamentary chambers, has been to provide a minimum guarantee that some form of inquiry can take place prior to the final vote. Though the Treaty of Lisbon provides for more direct transmission of

---

[61] See the example of the United Kingdom Parliament by Cygan, A. (2007) 'EU Affairs before the United Kingdom Parliament' at 75.

documents to national parliaments straight from the Commission, the challenges of timely scrutiny remain. However, the existence of scrutiny reserves reinforces the argument that scrutiny procedures within domestic parliaments are substitute sovereignty because they allow a national parliament to review a legislative proposal, the substance of which has largely been agreed.[62] The status and operation of scrutiny reserves in the Treaty and how national parliaments operate their scrutiny activities are considered in detail in Chapter 3.

4. NATIONAL PARLIAMENTS AND THE EU'S BETTER LAW MAKING AGENDA

The growth in EU legislative activity and the limited control over it by national parliaments has been accompanied by an increased awareness on the part of the Commission that EU legislation and policy must have improved legitimacy amongst EU citizens and, above all, be relevant.[63] Since 2005 the Commission has sought to address both the substance and quantity of legislation through the Better Law Making Agenda,[64] which has, in particular, sought to improve the quality of EU legislation. The Better Law Making Agenda is, increasingly, of interest to national parliaments because an integral part of the Commission's strategy is to use EU legislation to address socio-economic challenges posed by the financial crisis and the economic difficulties that have plagued the EU since 2008. The primary effect of this is that under the guise of improving economic performance and employment, the EU, through programmes such as Agenda 2020, will be exercising more competence at the expense of the Member States. To reflect this increased dynamic of EU legislation and the urgency of the EU action the Commission has

---

[62] In evidence to the House of Lords EU Select Committee, Professor Damian Chalmers notes that the eight week period for review is inadequate and equates to the same period granted to private parties to make written observations to the Commission under its consultation process. See HL 62-II (2007–8) *The Treaty of Lisbon* at 333. See also HL 62-I (2007–8) *The Treaty of Lisbon: An Impact Assessment: Report* at 243, paragraph 11.42 and HC 563 (2007–8) *Subsidiarity, National Parliaments and the Lisbon Treaty*, 33 at paragraph 44.

[63] See COM (2001) 428 *European Governance – A White Paper* at 5.

[64] See COM (2005) 97 final *Communication from the Commission to the Council and the European Parliament*. The primary purpose of this document was to act as mid-term review of the Lisbon Strategy and set out new regulatory principles and mechanisms through which better regulation could be achieved and ultimately help to deliver the objectives of the Lisbon Strategy.

rebranded 'better regulation' to become 'smart regulation', but for national parliaments this change of nomenclature makes no material difference and does not disguise the fact that this is yet another example of deparliamentarisation.

4.1 Better Law Making and the Principle of Subsidiarity

It is beyond question that an increase in EU legislative activity has created challenges for national parliaments. This challenge arises especially in relation to the question of whether the EU is correctly exercising the competences granted under the Treaty. In the view of the Commission the aim of smart regulation is to design and deliver regulation that respects the principles of subsidiarity and proportionality and is of the highest quality possible. This must be done throughout the policy cycle from the moment the legislation is designed to when it is revised and then implemented.[65] A key component of better regulation, which is crucial for national parliaments if they are to undertake a comprehensive subsidiarity review, is that in the course of the policy-making process the Commission has conducted a thorough Impact Assessment of the legislative proposal.[66] This is particularly important because if subsidiarity monitoring is to be a collective exercise conducted simultaneously by all parliaments under the procedures of Protocol 2, then they must all work from the same documentation. The Commission has put in place an Impact Assessment system to prepare evidence for political decision-making and to provide transparency on the benefits and costs of policy choices.[67] A key element of this system is the Impact Assessment Board,[68] which provides independent quality control of the Commission's Impact Assessments. Since it was created in 2006 the Board has produced over 400 opinions, all of which are available to national

---

[65] See COM (2010) 543 final, *Smart Regulation in the European Union* at 3.

[66] See COM (2005) 97 final *Communication from the Commission to the Council and the European Parliament* at 4–5 where the Commission highlights that better regulation cannot be achieved without meeting the principle of subsidiarity and that the Commission has an obligation within Impact Assessments to ensure that the principle is adhered to.

[67] See http://ec.europa.eu/governance/better_regulation/impact_en.htm (accessed 11 October 2011).

[68] See Baldwin, R. (2005) 'Is Better Regulation Smarter Regulation?' at 485, who highlights that Impact Assessments are considered as the pivotal tool of better regulation by the Commission.

parliaments.[69] The purpose of Impact Assessments is that they should quantify benefits and costs when possible, but there are undoubtedly limits with regard to what can be precisely quantified within twenty-eight Member States. Inevitably, data are frequently limited, and the impact of EU legislation often depends on how it is implemented by national administrations. This also means that aggregating figures for benefits and costs of EU legislation over time, as some stakeholders have requested, would not be a meaningful exercise.[70]

Recent evidence suggests that the Commission is, on occasion, failing to provide the necessary quantitative information within Impact Assessments in order for national parliaments to make an informed decision concerning the compatibility of a proposal with the principle of subsidiarity. For example, in relation to the draft Regulation on a Common Sales Law for the European Union[71] the EU Scrutiny Committee in the House of Commons, amongst several other national parliaments, highlighted the shortcomings of the Commission's Regulatory Impact Assessment process and the limited quantitative and qualitative indicators and impact information which it provided. As a result the EU Scrutiny Committee concluded that the incomplete and inaccurate Impact Assessment impeded effective subsidiarity monitoring. The EU Scrutiny Committee correctly highlighted that, by virtue of Article 5 of Protocol 2, any draft legislative act should contain a 'detailed statement' making it possible to appraise its compliance with the principles of subsidiarity and proportionality. This statement should contain:

- some assessment of the proposal's financial impact;
- in the case of a directive, some assessment of the proposal's implications for national and, where necessary, regional legislation; and
- qualitative and, wherever possible, quantitative substantiation of the reasons 'for concluding that a Union objective can be better achieved at Union level'.[72]

---

[69] Available at http://ec.europa.eu/governance/impact/ia_carried_out/cia_2010_en.htm (accessed 12 February 2011).

[70] See Radaelli, C. (2007) 'Whither Better Regulation for the Lisbon Agenda?' at 192–193.

[71] COM (2011) 635 final *Proposal for a Regulation of the European Parliament and of the Council on a Common European Sales Law.*

[72] See the Reasoned Opinion of the EU Scrutiny Committee of the House of Commons on Common European Sales Law, of 23 November 2011 at 1, available

The detailed statement should also demonstrate an awareness of the need for any burden, whether financial or administrative, falling upon the EU, national governments, regional or local authorities, economic operators or citizens, to be minimised and to be commensurate with the objective to be achieved. Thus the Impact Assessment must also address the principle of proportionality. The EU Scrutiny Committee concluded that neither the Commission's explanatory memorandum nor the Impact Assessment contained a 'detailed statement to make it possible to appraise compliance with the principle of subsidiarity'[73] (and proportionality), as required by Article 5 of Protocol 2. The Committee concluded that a failure to provide this information by the Commission constituted an infringement of an essential procedural requirement of Protocol 2. This judgment was based upon the limited justifications given by the Commission for the need for such legislation. In its explanatory memorandum the Commission's Impact Assessment addressed subsidiarity in the following terms:[74]

> This initiative complies with the principle of subsidiarity for a number of reasons. The objectives of facilitating the expansion of cross-border trade for business and purchases by consumers in the internal market cannot be fully achieved as long as businesses and consumers cannot use a uniform set of contract law rules for their cross-border transactions. The current legal framework is not sufficient, as it lacks a single set of uniform substantive rules which cover comprehensively the lifecycle of a cross-border contract. Furthermore, as market trends evolve and prompt Member States to take action independently (e.g. in regulating digital content products) regulatory divergences grow. They lead to increased transaction costs and legal complexity for business, as well as uncertainty, affecting businesses and consumers involved in cross-border transactions. A number of stakeholders acknowledge that the existence of differences in contract laws have led to legal fragmentation which can affect the functioning of the internal market; this may entail additional transaction costs and legal uncertainty for business and a lack of consumer confidence. The Union is best placed to address obstacles to the functioning of the internal market as these obstacles have a clear cross-border dimension. More specifically, it is best placed to address contract law related obstacles by developing a single set of uniform substantive contract law rules. It will add value to the existing legal framework by creating such rules for consumers and businesses that engage in cross-border transactions.

---

at www.parliament.uk/business/committees/committees-a-z/commons-select/european-scrutiny-committee/scrutiny-reserve-overrides/ (accessed 3 December 2011).

[73] Ibid. at 1.

[74] See COM (2011) 635 final *Proposal for a Regulation of the European Parliament and of the Council on a Common European Sales Law* at 9.

While the Commission provides a robust justification of the principles behind this legislative proposal, it is questionable whether an Impact Assessment containing this form of generalist justification demonstrates conclusively that the EU legislation is either necessary or that there is a clear value added to be gained. Moreover, such a justification, as provided in the case of the European Sales Regulation, arguably fails to meet the Commission's own criteria for Impact Assessments, which state that in order to improve Impact Assessments the Commission will conduct a 'more rigorous analysis of subsidiarity'[75] which includes, inter alia, 'more quantitative evidence and analysis'.[76] In particular, in the case of the European Sales Regulation the EU Scrutiny Committee was most critical of the Commission for ignoring its own statistical evidence which strongly indicated that there was no overwhelming necessity or value added to be gained from EU legislation.[77] There are other examples where similar arguments of the Commission not executing rigid Impact Assessments have been put forward by national parliaments, for example in relation to the proposed Seasonal Workers Directive[78] and the proposed Deposit Guarantee Schemes Directive.[79] What is evident is that, notwithstanding the absence of consensus with regard to the precise subsidiarity implications, a number of national parliaments have highlighted that the proposed legislation merely replicated existing national laws. This strongly suggests that the Commission is failing to effectively review the impact of the proposed legislation upon existing national law, which should form a fundamental part of the Impact Assessment and which forms a procedural requirement under Article 5 of Protocol 2. This raises serious question marks concerning whether the Commission is using the justifications of necessity and value added very loosely and without direct reference to the precise legislative position of the Member

[75] See COM (2009) 15 final *Third Strategic Review of Better Regulation in the European Union* at 8.

[76] Ibid.

[77] For example, the Commission's Consumer Market Scoreboard (March 2011) found the major reasons for a lack of cross-border trade to be practical: 62 per cent of consumers cited fears of fraud, 59 per cent were worried about what to do if problems arose and 49 per cent were concerned about delivery. In the Commission's qualitative Eurobarometer survey on obstacles for citizens in the Internal Market (September 2011), the most prominent reason why consumers do not buy cross-border was that they prefer to buy locally.

[78] See COM (2010) 379 final *Proposal for a Directive on the Conditions of Entry and Residence of Third Country Nationals for the Purposes of Seasonal Employment.*

[79] See COM (2010) 368 (recast) *On Deposit Guarantee Schemes.*

States which, if unchecked, may have significant impact upon the exercise of parliamentary competences more generally. The problem, however, is further compounded by procedural limitations. The weakness of Protocol 2 is the difficulty of securing the necessary thresholds to raise a subsidiarity objection which may require the Commission to revisit the proposal. Though many national parliaments may express concerns about a proposal which they raise directly with the Commission, this does not constitute a formal subsidiarity objection within the meaning of Protocol 2. Thus, for example, seeking clarification from the Commission, or merely highlighting that existing national legislation may already exist, is not the same as formally raising a subsidiarity objection. This issue is explored in more detail in Chapter 6, but what is apparent is that though the Commission provides more information and directly to national parliaments post-Lisbon, it retains full control of the information that national parliaments receive. This means that poorly drafted Impact Assessments, which fail to adequately provide a clear justification of the need for EU action, cannot be considered as a good starting point for national parliaments to consider whether the proposal infringes the principle of subsidiarity.

4.2 The Need for Co-ordinated Action

The purpose of the Better Regulation Agenda is to develop a one-size-fits-all approach to regulation and one which is based upon a presumption that all legislative proposals will have a similar impact across all Member States. While it may be correct to suggest that the obligations imposed by EU legislation should be the same on each Member State, this fails to acknowledge both the extent of existing national legislation and whether EU legislation is the most appropriate means by which to regulate. National parliaments are pivotal to monitoring the precise scope of EU legislation primarily because they are responsible for monitoring subsidiarity. However, this can only be effective if national parliaments share the same concerns about the need and scope of EU legislation, but neither the process of Impact Assessments nor the procedures of Protocol 2 guarantee this shared understanding. Indeed, the absence of uniform agreement concerning whether a measure is compatible with subsidiarity remains a problem, and this undoubtedly reinforces the perception of deparliamentarisation in circumstances when legislation has not been fully justified by the Commission and national parliaments have failed to collectively raise an objection. Though subsidiarity monitoring provides some basic minimum standard of scrutiny for all national parliaments,

Protocol 2 has not introduced any standardisation, let alone harmonisation, of procedure or practice. This will mean that when digesting an Impact Assessment there are likely to be divergent views amongst national parliaments. It may be argued that the Commission produces Impact Assessments which are, on occasion, vague and imprecise because it does not expect or want a co-ordinated response from national parliaments which could formally challenge the assumptions that are being made, and takes a political advantage from the limitation of Protocol 2. Thus Impact Assessments run the risk of being mere formalities rather than providing the primary justification for legislative action by the EU, including the question of the legal base being used as well as compliance with subsidiarity and proportionality. The questions of whether national parliaments can address this issue and how, if at all, they may adopt a more co-ordinated stance towards subsidiarity monitoring in general are considered in Chapter 6.

5. NEW MODES OF GOVERNANCE AND NATIONAL PARLIAMENTS

So far this chapter has focussed on how the transfer of competences from Member States to the EU and the accompanying legislative harmonisation have been responsible for deparliamentarisation. However, the use of 'hard' law as a tool of harmonisation has in recent years been accompanied by the use of soft law as a tool through which to achieve harmonisation in an EU of twenty-eight Member States. The primary criticism of the Community method is that it is a State-centric top-down legislative process which excludes interested parties and stakeholders and is distant from the citizen. In recognition of these shortcomings, the EU has increasingly utilised alternative modes of soft law governance, such as the open method of co-ordination (OMC) to pursue Europeanisation. The OMC is, by comparison with the prescriptive nature of the Community method, considered to be inclusive[80] through the involvement of an increased and diverse range of stakeholders participating in policy formulation.[81] Yet despite these inclusive qualities the OMC may be criticised for developing into an alternative form of neo-centralism through which top-down Europeanisation is being pursued.

---

[80] See COM (2001) 428 *European Governance – A White Paper*.

[81] Zeitlin, J. (2005) 'The Open Method of Co-ordination in Question' 19; Smismans, S. (2005) 'Reflexive Law in Support of Directly Deliberative Polyarchy' at 99.

5.1 The Need for Soft Law

National parliamentary scrutiny of soft law and policy co-ordination has been problematic.[82] Treaty Protocols which recognised scrutiny reserves did not apply to soft law processes such as the OMC. On this issue the Treaty of Lisbon makes no significant change and this can be considered a weakness of the new arrangements. While the growth of EU competence and the extension of the ordinary legislative process have brought more legislative proposals within the scope of Protocol 2, this has been accompanied by an increased use of soft law which has created difficulties for national parliaments in monitoring under existing terms of reference and practices. EU enlargement and the consequential problem of managing diversity amongst twenty-eight Member States make a one-size-fits-all approach to legislative regulation increasingly difficult, necessitating a greater utilisation of soft law. An analysis of how the Commission envisaged that the OMC would operate indicates that it would be used to supplement existing decision-making through the use of quantitative and qualitative benchmarks and indicators as well as peer-review procedures.[83] These mechanisms provide a degree of accountability for decisions under the OMC, but as the OMC is primarily concerned with policy co-ordination the main scrutiny consequence for national parliaments is the absence of a structured legislative process which culminates in a 'hard' legislative proposal. The OMC permits differentiated levels of participation for Member States and, by contrast with the output of the ordinary legislative procedure, Scrutiny Committees have been less concerned with proposals for policy co-ordination which may only be relevant to a particular region or to a small group of Member States. However, despite the primarily non-binding and intergovernmental nature of policy co-ordination, it is important that the application of soft law processes is considered within the overall context of competence between the EU and its Member States.

---

[82] See Raunio, T. (2006) 'Does the OMC Really Benefit National Parliaments?' 130. For an opposing view see Duina, F. and Oliver, M. (2006) 'To the Rescue of National Parliaments: A Reply to Raunio' 132.

[83] See COM (2001) 428 *European Governance – A White Paper* at 8–9.

5.2 The OMC: More Democratic and Accountable Decision-Making?

Article 5 TFEU requires policy co-ordination on core integration policies including economic[84] and employment[85] policies and encourages the co-ordination of Member States' social policies under Article 5 (3) TFEU.[86] Article 6 TFEU extends EU competence and envisages policy co-ordination to 'supplement the actions of Member States' in new areas such as sport and tourism. Article 6 TFEU 'Europeanises', albeit in an informal manner, policy areas which had hitherto remained outside the scope of the Treaties. While there is a legitimate debate concerning whether the EU should be seeking to regulate areas such as sport,[87] inclusion within the Treaty will require national parliaments to be aware of policy proposals. However, political and legal priorities, together with limited time and human resources, are likely to determine that national parliaments will focus on hard law, leaving soft law proposals without appropriate review and reinforcing the perception of deparliamentarisation.[88] One feature of the OMC is that it encourages participation by a diverse range of stakeholders in policy formulation and seeks to improve input legitimacy. Unlike the ordinary legislative procedure, the Commission does not have a monopoly on proposals. When considered with the broad range of stakeholder input this makes the OMC difficult for national parliaments to monitor under existing scrutiny arrangements. Being inter-governmental in nature, the OMC also strengthens the role of the Council and European Council which should, constitutionally, place national parliaments in a stronger position to influence and exercise

---

[84] Article 5 (1) TFEU states that 'The Member States shall coordinate their economic policies within the Union. To this end the Council shall adopt measures, in particular broad guidelines to these policies.'

[85] Article 5 (2) TFEU states that 'The Union shall take measures to ensure coordination of employment policies of the Member States, in particular by defining these guidelines.'

[86] 'The Union may take initiatives to ensure coordination of Member States' social policies.'

[87] See Weatherill, S. (2008) 'On Overlapping Legal Orders' at 55.

[88] Both the House of Commons and House of Lords have recognised the importance of the OMC and regularly considered proposals brought forward. This is particularly the case where the proposal has implications in the provision of social welfare public services. See, for example, HC 34-xviii (2005–6) *Progress of European Scrutiny* and HL 137 (2005–6) *A European Strategy for Jobs and Growth*.

control over ministers.[89] However, in practice it is civil servants and not ministers who take the lead in policy formulation, making parliamentary control under established scrutiny procedures inappropriate. The Commission views the OMC as one method through which to expand EU competence in the face of resistance from some Member States as expressed in the Federal Constitutional Court's *Lisbon judgment*.[90] Despite the growth of soft law, the empirical evidence demonstrates that national parliaments have devoted little time to the review of OMC proposals.[91] It is not clear whether this is a result of a lack of awareness or voluntary non-participation, but there is some evidence to suggest that a failure to grasp the purpose and effect of soft law which produces tangible results through different regulatory procedures is part of the reason. Armstrong[92] argues that the OMC is developing as a mode of governance which is 'acting outside the traditional scrutinising structures of representative democracy'. He identifies that traditional parliamentary procedures of ministerial review and accountability are geared towards the scrutiny of hard law and that governance techniques which seek domestic influence are 'slipping through the scrutiny net'.[93] On this basis there is no reason to suggest that, taking the examples of the United Kingdom and German parliaments as the benchmark of 'strong' actors in EU affairs, the position will be significantly improved within those parliaments which are considered to be 'weak' actors. The primary reason for this limited participation in the scrutiny of the OMC arises from the dissemination of information. As OMC documents are non-legislative the information rights granted to national parliaments have been generally weaker. If governments are not obliged to send a document to their parliaments, then it is left to national MPs to request the documents. The Barosso Initiative for the provision of documents to national parliaments[94] has, in part, addressed the issue through the furnishing of consultation documents directly to national parliaments.

---

[89] See Duina, F. and Raunio, T. (2007) 'The Open Method of Coordination and National Parliaments' at 492–493; Raunio, T. (2007) 'National Parliaments and OMC', available at http://swp-berlin.org/en/get_document.php?asset_id+4124 (accessed 12 February 2010).

[90] Judgment of 20 June 2009 *Bundesverfassungsgerich*t, BVerfG, 2 BvE 2/08.

[91] See Duina, F. and Raunio, T. (2007) 'The Open Method of Coordination and National Parliaments' and Armstrong, K. (2006) 'How Open is the United Kingdom to the OMC Process of Social Inclusion?' at 302.

[92] Ibid.

[93] Ibid.

[94] For a detailed discussion of the Barosso Initiative see Chapter 3.

This includes documents which set out proposals for policy co-ordination. The problem is that national parliaments have limited time and the issue is one of priority in the face of 'information overload'. National parliaments are likely to conclude that the task of subsidiarity monitoring requires them to prioritise time for the review of hard supra-national legislation rather than non-binding policy proposals. Despite the difficulties with reviewing soft law, national parliaments should be encouraged to reconsider their internal scrutiny mechanisms and how these may be adapted to ensure accountability for this inter-governmental form of decision-making. An increased use of soft law should not be accompanied by the development of a new democratic deficit. Articles 5 and 6 TFEU formalise policy co-ordination in specific areas to complement existing competences operating under the ordinary legislative procedure. Though these Treaty provisions may be considered vague, it remains open to national parliaments to use their own procedures to maximise accountability and transparency of decision-making under these Articles. The main issue that arises for national parliaments and any review they may undertake of the OMC is whether they have the capacity to assume this task. At the very minimum national parliaments should use, and where necessary develop, established scrutiny techniques and processes of information-gathering and inquiry to reflect the variation of decision-making under the OMC. There are two reasons for this. First, it may indirectly improve the quality of domestic legislation through the incorporation of policy ideas from other Member States. Secondly, it could strengthen parliamentarians, and arguably promote parliamentarisation, by providing information to parliaments that can be used to challenge the government. This underlies the purpose of the OMC, which is to expose national politicians and civil servants to new ideas from other Member States with the primary purpose of policy improvement. In this context it has the capacity, though not the guarantee, to empower and strengthen those parliaments considered 'weak'. The Treaty of Lisbon may provide a clearer status for soft law, but a gap remains with respect to how national parliaments participate in its creation and monitor its consequences, whether individually or collectively. The Barosso Initiative may provide an opportunity to be 'in the loop' earlier for the purpose of policy formulation, which could inform more detailed discussions of associated or relevant hard law proposals. Ultimately it is a question of choices for national parliamentarians and 'weak' parliaments will probably be even weaker when it comes to the review of policy co-ordination, giving greater credence to the assertion that a parliamentarisation of EU decision-making processes is not a realistic proposition.

6. CONCLUDING REMARKS

There is no doubt that Europeanisation and closer integration, especially through the process of legislative harmonisation, are primarily responsible for the loss of legislative competence by national parliaments. It will be recalled that the Commission's justification of necessity for EU legislative action raises particular concerns because, at least until the Treaty of Lisbon, there was no formal Treaty mechanism by which the Commission's exercise of legislative competence could be examined. Subsidiarity monitoring provides new constitutional opportunities for national parliaments, but it is extremely unlikely that these procedures can act as an adequate regulatory buffer to prevent EU legislative action in the context of the Internal Market. This issue is considered in more detail in Chapter 5. The next chapter evaluates the status of national parliaments in the EU Treaties and considers their position as institutional actors within a multi-level polity. In particular, Chapter 3 explores their contribution as political actors and how effective the opportunities presented under the Treaty are at allowing national parliaments to exert influence over EU policy and decision-making. To this extent Chapter 3 examines whether the post-Lisbon Treaty arrangements indicate that national parliaments are becoming more prominent and relevant political actors and that there is some move towards a parliamentarisation within the EU.

3. National parliaments in the EU Treaties

1. INTRODUCTION

There is a degree of irony with the Treaty of Lisbon including a number of substantial changes aimed at improving the participation of national parliaments in EU affairs. It could be argued that the Treaty-makers have belatedly recognised that national parliaments have a distinct role to play in an enlarged EU.[1] It is also politically expedient for incumbent governments to demonstrate to their domestic electorates that national parliaments are not irrelevant actors in an enlarged EU. Accordingly, Article 12 TEU and Protocols 1 and 2 of the Treaty of Lisbon assign to national parliaments the task of subsidiarity monitoring through which they monitor the application of EU competences, and by doing so are expected to help bridge the democracy gap between the citizen and the EU.[2] The irony in this arises from the fact that national parliaments, with their traditions and principles of democratic scrutiny and accountability, have remained a constant throughout a period when the supra-national EU was developing in a less than democratic fashion. As seen in Chapter 2, Europeanisation and the emphasis upon institutional democratisation can be identified as the primary causes of deparliamentarisation. Against this background, why should domestic legislatures now be considered integral to legitimising EU legislation? At a time when the EU consisted of six, or even twelve Member States, and when their influence and contribution could arguably have been greater, national parliaments were peripheral to the development of European integration and their democratic features were largely ignored. Yet with an EU of twenty-eight Member States, national parliaments are expected to contribute to spreading the message of a more democratic, accountable and transparent EU.

---

[1] See generally Barrett, G. (ed.) (2007) *National Parliaments and the European Union.*

[2] As acknowledged in CONV 353/02 Working Group IV The Role of National Parliaments, Final Report of Working Group IV on the Role of National Parliaments at paragraph 4.

Despite this expectation some national parliaments, such as the United Kingdom Parliament and Scandinavian legislatures, have recognised they have a limited role in EU policy and decision-making and have tended to focus on securing ministerial accountability.[3] This is recognition that within the process of Europeanisation, the national parliaments fulfil a different role from the traditional one of supreme legislator.[4]

The primary effect of integration is that national parliaments have surrendered legislative competence to supra-national EU institutions, which is the primary reason for deparliamentarisation. As a result, national parliaments have been described as 'victims' of Europeanisation[5] because the technocratic characteristics of EU decision-making have strengthened executives and the Council at the expense of national parliamentary practices.[6] Furthermore, the regulatory tools of Europeanisation have not been restricted to directives, regulations and decisions. The EU has extensively utilised soft law, such as the open method of co-ordination, and the Court of Justice has also driven forward integration. These regulatory techniques have delivered a gradual, but consistent, expansion of EU competences, primarily at the expense of national parliaments. The Treaty of Lisbon included a number of substantive amendments designed to improve the participation of national parliaments in EU decision-making, the most important of which is the allocation of subsidiarity monitoring.[7] This development is intended to address the criticism of 'deparliamentarisation' and that EU legislation often lacks legitimacy amongst its citizens. This chapter examines the status of national parliaments within the EU Treaties. It analyses the changes made by the Treaty of Lisbon for the participation of national parliaments in EU decision-making and whether improved arrangements for information transmission and competence monitoring have repositioned national parliaments as key actors within the EU polity.

---

[3] See HC 152 xxxiii-I (Session 2001–2) *Democracy and Accountability in the EU and the Role of National Parliaments.*

[4] See Cygan, A. (1998) *The United Kingdom Parliament and European Union Legislation* and Cygan, A. (2001) *National Parliaments in an Integrated Europe*.

[5] See Norton, P. (1996) 'Introduction: The Institution of Parliaments' at 1.

[6] See Moravcsik, A. (1998) 'Introduction: The Choice for Europe' at 9.

[7] See Peters, J. (2009) 'The Role of National Parliaments' at 33.

2. RECOGNITION WITHIN THE EU TREATIES

A key theme that arose from the debate surrounding the failure to ratify the Constitutional Treaty is that deeper EU integration requires the consent of EU citizens.[8] In practice this requires the consent of national parliaments. The *Bundersvervasungericht* (Federal Constitutional Court (FCC)) considered the question of the legitimacy of EU integration in the *Maastricht Treaty Case*.[9] German ratification of the Maastricht Treaty was challenged because it threatened the constitutionally guaranteed principles of German democracy. Specifically the issue related to the position of the federal States under Article 20 of the *Grundgesetz*. This Article provides that Germany is a democratic federal State, and that all State authority is derived from the citizens. Furthermore, under Article 38 of the *Grundgesetz* German citizens are guaranteed the right of participation in elections, the purpose of which is to provide ultimate democratic control over the government. The argument was that these two provisions of the Constitution would be infringed through a large scale transfer of competences to the EU. This would be unacceptable if that left national parliaments unable to control the integration process, or if the EU pursued closer integration but failed to develop an adequate system of institutional checks and balances. In particular, it was contended that central to this framework of accountability should be national parliaments. The FCC found that on the substantive issue of the challenge the Treaty of Maastricht did not infringe the principles within Articles 20 and 38 of the *Grundgesetz*. The primary reasoning for this was that the EU could not act beyond the powers which it had been granted by the Member States. Consequently national parliaments were not deprived of any powers in addition to those which they had voluntarily ceded, and in any case the Maastricht Treaty provided safeguards for future integration. The FCC concluded that ultimately Germany, and all other Member States, must ratify any new Treaty. In practice the FCC argued that this would give national parliaments an influential, or even a decisive, voice in the integration process. Two decades later can the FCC's conclusions be considered as being too optimistic? Yes the EU has recognised the need for improved accountability, but several issues must be considered which have materially affected the constitutional position of national parliaments since this

---

[8] See Besselink, L.M. (2006) 'National Parliaments in the EU's Composite Constitution' at 119.

[9] *Brunner* v *European Union Treaty* [1994] 1 CMLR 57. See also Cullen, P. (1995) 'Competing Legitimacy at European and National Levels' at 61.

judgment. First, since the Treaty of Maastricht there have been three further Treaties, all of which have addressed the position of national parliaments in the EU and how their influence can be extended. Simultaneously, these Treaties have also increased the competences of the EU and brought more decision-making within the ordinary legislative procedure. Despite the improved recognition of national parliaments under the Treaty, it would be incorrect to conclude that the Treaties have repositioned national parliaments as pivotal actors within the EU polity. For example, the greater use of qualified majority voting (QMV) has had significant implications for national parliaments and their ability to secure ministerial accountability within the legislative process. Secondly, a thread that can be traced through all Treaties going back to the Treaty of Maastricht is that national parliaments have only benefited from new provisions to the extent that these cannot stop the ordinary legislative process.[10] This is true even of the Treaty of Lisbon because, under the 'yellow card' procedure of Protocol 2, the ultimate decision with regard to whether to continue with the legislative process in the event of the threshold being attained by national parliaments is one which is outside the control of national parliaments and lies in the hands of the Council and European Parliament. On this analysis, Treaty reform can be defined as improving procedural opportunities for national parliaments rather than their constitutional status within the EU polity.

2.1 The Treaty of Maastricht

The Treaty of Maastricht was the first formal recognition within the Treaties that national parliaments should have some status within the EU polity. The Treaty included two non-legally binding Declarations relating to the role of national parliaments and in particular their individual scrutiny activities. Declaration No. 13 stated that 'it is important to encourage greater involvement of national Parliaments in the activities of the European Union'. This objective was to be achieved mainly through improved access to information which was highlighted as the main restriction to improved national parliamentary scrutiny. The provision of adequate and timely information continues to be crucial to national parliaments to this day. At the time the Treaty was drafted the problem of access to information was further compounded because national parliaments were dependent upon the provision of information from third

---

[10] See Kiiver, P. (2006) *The National Parliaments in the European Union* at 41–42.

parties, and in particular their national governments. Declaration 13 merely stated that: 'governments of Member States will ensure, inter alia, that national Parliaments receive Commission proposals for legislation in good time for information or possible examination'. This meant that within the framework of differing national parliamentary procedures for examining EU affairs there was no consistency concerning the provision of information to EU affairs committees. Only some parliaments, for example the United Kingdom Parliament, had introduced comprehensive scrutiny reserves which tried to improve the flow of information to the EU committees. Such Reserves also sought to exert some element of constraint over the minister in Council if the documents had not been forthcoming and parliamentary scrutiny was incomplete. The Treaty-makers recognised at Maastricht that there was a need for increased involvement by national parliaments but this could in no way be described as constituting parliamentarisation. What the Treaty did was to build upon existing informal practice of the *Conférence des organes spécialisés dans les affaires communautaires* (COSAC), where there was very limited co-ordination of national scrutiny activities and exchange of ideas. Moreover, central to achieving this closer co-operation between national parliaments was the European Parliament. In particular, this required that the democratic credentials of national parliaments be emphasised, and also the importance of these qualities to further EU integration. From this it can be seen that re-engaging with the EU citizen through the proxy assistance of national parliaments, which is a core objective of the Treaty of Lisbon, has its roots in the Treaty of Maastricht. Secondly, and perhaps more importantly, the Treaty of Maastricht introduced the principle of subsidiarity.[11] In the post-Lisbon EU it is now clear that this principle, which regulates the exercise of non-exclusive EU competences, also encapsulates the control which national parliaments were trying to exert over ministers through parliamentary scrutiny. In particular, subsidiarity expresses formally a question which several national parliaments had been regularly asking ministers in the course of parliamentary scrutiny; namely, does the EU really need to act?

Subsidiarity, whether in the form expressed in Article 5 EC or in its current guise in Article 5 TEU, remains a political concept. The primary aim of the subsidiarity principle is to ensure decision-making at the

[11] See Toth, A.G. (1994) 'A Legal Analysis of Subsidiarity' at 37; Steiner, J. (1994) 'Subsidiarity under the Maastricht Treaty' at 49; and Craig, P. (2012) 'Subsidiarity: A Political or Legal Analysis' at 72–73.

lowest possible level of governance. Given this objective, the principle is one whose application is ripe for review by national parliaments. Thirdly, the Edinburgh guidelines[12] on the application of the subsidiarity principle, which were intended to practically flesh out the provisions of Article 5 EC, recognised that the subsidiarity provisions of the Treaty of Maastricht were too vague. If national parliaments were to raise questions concerning the exercise of competence, the monitoring of subsidiarity by national parliaments would be ineffective without a clearer statement of what the principle meant in practice. Notwithstanding its inclusion in the Treaty of Maastricht, it is not until the Protocol of the Treaty of Lisbon that the Treaty formally acknowledges how subsidiarity is to be monitored.

2.2 The Treaty of Amsterdam

The Protocol on the Role of National Parliaments introduced by the Treaty of Amsterdam provided a clearer and more formal status for national parliaments by comparison with Declaration No. 13 of the Treaty of Maastricht. In particular, the Protocol recognised the importance of scrutiny reserves for national parliaments as being a necessary requirement to enable national parliaments to subject the legislative proposal to meaningful scrutiny prior to the adoption of the Council's common position. Additionally, the Treaty of Amsterdam incorporated into a Protocol on the Application of the Principles of Subsidiarity and Proportionality the Edinburgh subsidiarity guidelines.[13] This development signposted to national parliaments that their scrutiny activities should not just be focussed on national priorities of ministerial accountability, but that such scrutiny should also encompass a broader objective in which the exercise of EU competences was considered by national parliaments. While both Protocols created legally binding obligations with regard to transmission of information to national parliaments, and formally recognised the right of national parliaments to enforce scrutiny reserves, there remained an absence of a process through which national parliaments could enforce their decisions. Moreover, the Protocol failed to motivate national parliaments and engage them in EU affairs in a manner which went beyond the basic individual function of securing ministerial

---

[12] Agreed by the Member States at the Edinburgh European Council, Annex 1 to Part A, EC Bulletin 12-1992, at 14.

[13] See paragraphs 4 and 5 of the Amsterdam Protocol on National Parliaments. See also Cygan, A. (2001) *National Parliaments in an Integrated Europe* Chapter 2.

accountability. This was undoubtedly a weakness of the Amsterdam arrangements.

2.3 The Constitutional Treaty

The Constitutional Convention addressed the issue of how subsidiarity monitoring could improve accountability and the Constitutional Treaty included provisions, the majority of which were retained in the Treaty of Lisbon, to improve participation by national parliaments in EU affairs. The primary development was to implement the findings of Working Group IV and include the provisions that national parliaments would undertake review of EU legislation for its compliance with the principle of subsidiarity. Under Article I-11 (3) of the Constitutional Treaty national parliaments were to ensure compliance with the principle of subsidiarity in accordance with the procedure set out in the accompanying Protocol. The primary criticism of Article I-11, and why the corresponding provision was amended in the Treaty of Lisbon, was that national parliaments had to conclude this process within the maximum six week period available. In the light of the challenges faced by national parliaments when conducting scrutiny, especially given the incompatibility between national parliamentary timetables and the EU legislative process, this period was extended to eight weeks under the Treaty of Lisbon

3. NATIONAL PARLIAMENTS AFTER THE TREATY OF LISBON

It is one of the explicit aims of the Treaty of Lisbon, set out in its Preamble, to enhance the 'democratic legitimacy of the Union' and it is unquestionable that national parliaments are considered as prominent actors that are necessary to achieve this paradigm. This objective of improved democratic legitimacy was a constant theme of the process leading up to the Treaty of Lisbon, beginning with the Laeken Declaration in December 2001. Thus the Treaty of Lisbon includes a new Title II, *Provisions on Democratic Principles*, which spells out the principles of good governance upon which the EU is based. This is expanded upon in Chapter 2 of the TFEU, where the provisions for EU citizenship and new provisions designed to improve the connection between the EU institutions and society at large are set out. In this context of improving democracy and participation in the EU legislative process, the Treaty of Lisbon presents substantially new provisions for national parliaments both at the macro level of participation in EU affairs and the micro level of improving the legislative process through the scrutiny of the ordinary legislative procedure. On a macro level the Treaty includes some general statements about national parliaments in Article 12 TEU and states that 'National Parliaments contribute actively to the good functioning of the Union' in specific ways which are laid out within the Treaty. This includes monitoring the process of Treaty revision and the use of *Passerelle* clauses by the Council. On a micro level the Treaty provides that 'National Parliaments ensure compliance with the principle of subsidiarity' in accordance with Protocol 2. This highly involved and technical task of ensuring subsidiarity compliance enables national parliaments to participate in the legislative process, albeit towards the end of that process. The specific details concerning the post-Lisbon arrangements for subsidiarity monitoring by national parliaments will be discussed in Chapters 5 and 6. The inclusion of Article 12 TEU is a departure from previous Treaties because it provides a constitutional recognition of national parliaments and their democratic credentials and indicates that national parliaments are constitutionally relevant to EU integration. However, though referring to national parliaments and giving them certain prerogatives, the Treaty does not define 'national parliaments' nor does it refer to them in an EU institutional context. Moreover, absence of a definition of national parliaments leaves significant scope for interpretation with regard to what this actually encompasses and what the parameters of the role should be.[14] Unlike previous Treaties – where the role of national parliaments was confined to inclusion in a Declaration or Protocol and addressed primarily procedural questions concerning the transmission of information and the operation and status of scrutiny reserves – Article 12 TEU, ostensibly at least, mainstreams the values of parliamentary democracy into the EU. However, though this is a positive statement within the Treaty, it stops well short of a parliamentarisation of the EU, or that national parliaments acquire a formal status in EU governance that has elevated them to a single cohesive bloc of institutional actors.

3.1 General Oversight of EU Affairs by National Parliaments

Overseeing general EU policy and integration has always been an important function for national parliaments, even before the Treaty of

---

[14] For a useful discussion of the impact of Article 12 TEU see Wyrzykowski, M. et al. (2011) 'General Report: The Role of National Parliaments in the European Union' Vol. 1, at 12–14.

Maastricht recognised the scrutiny activities of national parliaments. Though this general task of observing EU policy has only been formally included within the Treaty of Lisbon, debates concerning ratification of new Treaties, enlargement and the EU budget have regularly taken place in all national parliaments. In this context, this more general oversight of EU policy and affairs, rather than specific scrutiny of EU legislative proposals, forms part of the broader aim of national parliaments to protect their sovereignty. This process of parliamentary oversight is another example of the substitute sovereignty discussed in Chapter 2 whereby scrutiny of EU affairs in national parliaments is seen as a political counterbalance to the transfer of legislative competence. National parliamentary oversight of general EU affairs is therefore not a new animal. As already indicated, ratification of every new Treaty has, de facto, required the consent of national parliaments. Though the pre-Lisbon versions of Articles 48 and 49 TEU referred to all new Treaties being ratified by *Member States* this was in reality a power that was formally exercised by the national parliament. But, and this is an undoubted criticism of the pre-Lisbon procedure, the ratification by national parliaments was at the end of the revision or accession process and constituted no more than a 'take it or leave it' option. This may offer at least a partial explanation of why all Treaty reforms since the Treaty of Nice have faced difficult ratification procedures. The Convention process,[15] out of which the Treaty of Lisbon was conceived, offered an opportunity for national parliaments to participate directly in the process of Treaty revision. The creation of the Constitutional Convention was a reaction to the rejection of the Treaty of Nice by Irish voters[16] and the controversy surrounding the Inter-Governmental Conference that led to the agreement of the Treaty of Nice. Though there was no Treaty obligation, the establishment of the Convention has created a precedent by which national parliaments engage directly in the process of Treaty revision and one which should therefore be formally acknowledged. The Treaty of Lisbon has extended and formalised the powers of national parliaments in circumstances of Treaty revision or accession. Under Article 48 (2) TEU, which covers the ordinary revision procedure of the Treaties, national parliaments are specifically identified as institutions, alongside the European Council, and are to be 'notified' directly by the

---

[15] The use of the Convention method for securing more inclusive decision-making was first used in the drafting of the Charter of Fundamental Rights.

[16] The Irish referendum for the Treaty of Nice took place on 7 June 2001 with a result of 53.9 per cent to 46.1 per cent against ratification of the Treaty. The turnout for the referendum was only 30 per cent.

Council of any proposed Treaty amendments. The precise scope of this is unclear, as 'notified' could range from receiving the full documentation to perhaps simply being informed directly of the Council's Press Release, but this formal recognition gives rise to a specific Treaty right which should be justifiable. However, how this right is to be procedurally enforced is less than clear and what information national parliaments receive will clearly be dependent upon how 'notified' is to be interpreted. The Treaty also includes several other revision procedures which give rise to certain rights for national parliaments and which when taken together create an ostensible perception that national parliaments are more engaged in EU affairs.

3.2 National Parliaments and Treaty Revision: The Ordinary Revision Procedure

As already noted, the Treaty, under Article 48 (2) TEU, enables national parliaments to be 'notified' by the Council of Treaty amendments proposed under the ordinary revision procedure and requires Member States to ratify them according to their national requirements. As with the pre-Lisbon position, the reference within the Treaty to ratification by 'Member States' should not be considered as anything other than the use of a euphemism for 'national parliaments'. Indeed this is an inescapable conclusion because under Article 48 (4) TEU the proposed amendments are said to come into force after they have been ratified by Member States 'in accordance with their constitutional requirements'. Though the Treaty does not explicitly refer to national parliaments at this point, it does nevertheless, through the use of the phrase 'constitutional requirements', strongly imply that national parliaments, and where appropriate sub-national parliaments, are integral to this ratification. Moreover, even in cases of a referendum, primary legislation will be required for the referendum to take place, and even if a referendum is binding upon a national parliament, as is the case in Ireland, the legislation is likely to include clear procedures for the parliament to follow after the referendum, including any obligations to be placed upon the government.[17] This raises an important, and perhaps hypothetical, question concerning the interpretation of Article 48 (2) TEU. In the light of wording of Article 48 (2) TEU, can a national parliament be said to have the capacity to block a Treaty amendment? In short, the answer is probably 'no' because

---

[17] See Dougan, M. (2008) 'The Treaty of Lisbon 2007' at 658–659.

rejecting a Treaty amendment would ultimately be the formal responsibility of the minister in the Council or within the Inter-Governmental Conference and not one which is within the domain of the parliament. However, what is particularly significant under this Treaty provision is the domestic constitutional context and how the relationship between parliament and the minister is regulated. This will include the constitutional impact of a parliamentary vote and whether by taking this vote it creates a binding obligation upon the minister.[18] In addition, this raises the question of how, if at all, can the national parliament enforce this procedurally, not least because the political pressure in the Council may cause a minister to depart from the parliament's position. There is at least the potential that future Treaty reform, in some Member States, could have constitutional repercussions concerning the relationship between parliament and the executive. Though the national parliament does not cast the vote in the Council, it is at least conceivable that in the case of some Member States, for example Denmark or Latvia, the parliament could, de facto, determine the Member State's position, which is binding upon the minister. The innovation of the Treaty of Lisbon is that, under Article 48 (3) TEU, national parliaments can now be involved upstream and more directly in Treaty amendment at the stage of the Convention, but real questions marks remain over the extent to which national parliaments may be able to influence the Convention. Though national parliaments may propose amendments this does not create any specific legal obligations upon the Council, especially because the Convention is the discussion phase of Treaty revision rather than the decision-making phase. Under Article 48 (4) TEU final decisions with regard to the adoption of the amendments are for the conference of representatives of governments of the Member States and convened by the President of the Council of which national parliaments are not members. Thus, under the new arrangements, national parliaments may be considered as key stakeholders in the Convention process, but it is the Member States, as the contracting parties, which through their nominated representatives take the final decisions with regard to the content of the revised Treaty. On this analysis it is therefore possible, and even highly likely, that national parliaments will be isolated within, or even excluded from, the actual amendment process. On the presumption that the Council will approve the amendments and the European Parliament will similarly assent to the revised Treaty, the ball is then back in the court of Member

[18] See Wyrzykowski, M. et al. (2011) 'General Report: The Role of National Parliaments in the European Union' at 27–29.

States to ratify the Treaty in accordance with their constitutional requirements. Given that, in the overwhelming majority of instances, this will necessitate parliamentary ratification, it may be that national parliaments ultimately have the final say with regard to the Treaty and may choose to reject it. Though national parliaments may be excluded from the Convention this is, politically, a dangerous decision on the part of the President of the Council given that the Treaty expressly confers the powers of participation on national parliaments and the eventual risk that they can reject the Treaty. However, as with many powers that have been conferred upon national parliaments by the Treaty of Lisbon, the problem lies with enforcement. As already noted, it is difficult to determine exactly how national parliaments could protect this prerogative, and the process of Treaty revision is very much left up to horse-trading and bargaining. The irony with this situation is that if national parliaments are left on the outer reaches of this process this is, in part, as a result of a Treaty that they themselves have ratified.

3.3 National Parliaments and Treaty Revision: The Simplified Amendment Procedure

Under Article 48 (6) TEU, which sets out the procedure for Treaty revision under the simplified procedure, national parliaments have fewer powers by comparison with the ordinary revision procedure. The primary reason for this is that the simplified revision procedure applies only in those circumstances where there are revisions undertaken to Part 3 of the TFEU concerning internal policies and action of the EU, and this is only in those circumstances when a revision does not expand EU competences. By comparison with Article 48 (2) TEU, Article 48 (6) TEU does not oblige national parliaments to be informed of amendments, but it is inevitable that national parliaments will discover these proposals with relative ease and they are likely to be debated within parliaments. However, unlike under the ordinary revision procedure, the Convention is not convened and thus no outlet or forum exists for national parliaments to directly voice their objections. Moreover, there is no Conference of representatives of governments which is convened which similarly reduces the scope for national parliamentary input. In practice the responsibility for proposing and negotiating amendments rests solely with the Council, and any control of individual ministers will be based upon domestic scrutiny arrangements or specific constitutional restraints that may exist in such circumstances. The only, and rather limited, opportunity for national parliaments to voice their concerns arises at the end of the Simplified Amendment Procedure. Under Article 48 (6) TEU any amendments must be approved by the Member States in accordance with their 'constitutional requirements', but this provides no specific guarantees of changes being made to any proposed amendments. In reality the only opportunity rests with national parliaments rejecting a proposed Treaty amendment, but this is neither particularly constructive nor likely to be well received by other Member States.

3.4 National Parliaments and *Passerelles*

Passerelles are provisions within the Treaties which enable the European Council to unanimously decide to replace unanimous voting in the Council with QMV in specified areas, following the consent of the European Parliament. This changes the voting procedure from a special voting procedure to the ordinary legislative procedure, and the justification for the use of *Passerelles* is generally one of efficiency. The key point for national parliaments is that such a change is outside the ordinary and simplified revision procedures found in Articles 48 (2)–(6) TEU. The general *Passerelle* procedures are found in Article 48 (7) TEU, but there have also been some sector-specific *Passerelle* clauses which existed prior to the TEU which have been retained by the Treaty of Lisbon. The powers of national parliaments to review the use of *Passerelles* depend exclusively on the type of *Passerelle* clause being used. Depending upon the *Passerelle* clause at issue, the powers of national parliaments vary from being able to issue what essentially constitutes a 'red card' to stop the process to no powers of influence at all in several sector-specific *Passerelles*. The incorporation of a general *Passerelle* clause in Article 48 (7) TEU is one of the key changes brought about by the Treaty of Lisbon[19] and its inclusion is intended to improve legislative efficiency and promote deeper integration in a given policy area. It provides a convenient way to, de facto, alter the operation of parts of the Treaty, but without the need for complete Treaty revision or the disputes to which this could lead. As with all Treaty provisions, the

[19] The FCC in the *Lisbon Treaty judgment* acknowledged the significance of *Passerelles* with regard to the improved position of national parliaments under Article 48 TEU, but noted that positive action would be required by the *Bundestag* and *Bundesrat* to ensure that rights would be protected. See Judgment of 20 June 2009 *Bundesverfassungsgerich*t, BVerfG, 2 BvE 2/08 at paragraphs 319 and 413. See also Halberstam, D. and Möllers, C. (2009) 'The German Constitutional Court says "Ja Zu Deutschland!"' at 1243–1244, and Wyrzykowski. M. et al. (2011) 'General Report: The Role of National Parliaments in the European Union' at 29–31.

general *Passerelle* clause has been ratified by Member States and so the issue today is not about its existence, but concerns the question of how the use of *Passerelles* is monitored, in particular by national parliaments. This monitoring by national parliaments is crucial as their influence over the minister is likely to be reduced through any shift from unanimity to QMV in the Council, and the use of a *Passerelle* also constitutes a transfer of legislative power to the European Parliament which amounts to a further restriction upon the competences of national parliaments.[20] *Passerelles* therefore not only provide for flexible methods of modification of EU decision-making, but can also alter institutional relationships and the distribution of powers, raising constitutional questions of legitimacy and accountability. For these reasons such autonomous amendments require very close supervision to ensure that they are not being used to circumvent legitimate accountability. The broad scope of the application of *Passerelle* clauses necessitates the effective monitoring of their use, and Article 48 (7) TEU itself refers to national parliaments as the 'guardians' of this process. Crucially, national parliaments have been given a right of veto which provides some guarantee that EU policy and legislation correspond broadly with the interpretation of integration that is to be found in twenty-eight Member States. Unlike subsidiarity monitoring, decisions by national parliaments with regard to the use of a *Passerelle* will be independent, with no requirement of horizontal co-ordination between parliaments. In this sense a national parliament's decision is very much based upon the national interest. Moreover, in principle the veto is in substance different from the 'yellow card' issued under Protocol 2 because it refers to a procedure which can change the operation of the Treaty, rather than being concerned with the scrutiny of a specific document. Thus national parliaments will use their own parliamentary procedures to determine exactly how this decision-making process should be executed. Article 6 of Protocol 1 on the Role of National Parliaments in the EU requires that every proposal to amend the voting procedure under a *Passerelle* must be communicated to a national parliament 'at least six months in advance of the final decision'. The effectiveness of this procedure arises from the use of the veto. In particular, once a veto has been raised by a national parliament the procedure comes to an end and there is no alternative method by which the decision can be reversed. The six months for national parliaments to

---

[20] See Peers, S. (2005) 'Transforming Decision-Making on EC Immigration and Asylum Law' at 285 for an analysis of how this worked in the area of justice and home affairs after the Treaty of Amsterdam.

consider the proposal to use a *Passerelle* is quite generous and should in most cases offer sufficient opportunity for an informed debate to take place.

The primary point to note is that national parliaments must voice their opposition, as silence will be construed as consent on their part. One issue, which the Treaty fails to address, is that by referring to 'national parliaments' as the guardians of this process it is suggesting the existence of some form of homogeneous group of institutional actors that exist across the EU. This is far from the case, and moreover the Treaty does not offer any definition of what actually constitutes a 'national parliament' for this purpose. Unlike subsidiarity monitoring, where there is a reference to chambers and the 'yellow card' threshold recognises the bicameral nature of most EU Parliaments, Article 47 TEU does not make this distinction or indicate how, or which chamber, or if both chambers for that matter, should make the decision on behalf of a national parliament. This is not altogether surprising, given the heterogeneous nature of the Member States' Constitutions, but this lack of a definition of a 'national parliament' adds significant weight to the argument that within the EU there is no cohesive single bloc of national parliaments. This also counters the premise that by fulfilling some important, yet narrow functions, national parliaments have acquired some measure of quasi-institutional standing. With regard to sector-specific *Passerelles*[21] the procedure is broadly in line with the general provisions, but national parliaments only have a similar veto in the area of cross-border regulation of family matters, which is covered by Article 81 (3) TFEU. National parliaments are, with this sole exception, generally excluded from the other, more minor *Passerelle* procedures. Under Article 81 (3) TFEU it is possible to switch decision-making in this area from the ordinary legislative procedure to the special legislative procedure which will shift the decision-making power to the Council with the European Parliament only having a right of consultation. The policy behind this is to speed up decision-making in a sensitive area of EU co-operation where domestic rules and practices relating to family law issues need to be aligned and quick decisions are often required. The peripheral role of the European Parliament, which is to all intents and purposes sidelined by the operation of this *Passerelle*, highlights these factors, but the shift to

[21] Other *Passerelles* can be found in Article 31 (3) TEU, Article 31 (2) TFEU, Article 153 (2) TFEU and Article 192 (2) TFEU but in none of these cases do national parliaments have any right of veto. All these *Passerelle* clauses pre-date the Treaty of Lisbon. See further Peers, S. (2005) 'Transforming Decision-Making on EC Immigration and Asylum Law'.

the Council of exclusive legislative power does arguably improve the accountability of the minister to the national parliament by comparison with that available under the ordinary legislative procedure where QMV and European Parliament amendments would restrict this. Once again, national parliaments have six months to achieve this and there is no indication of how this is to be resolved in the context of bicameral parliaments.

4. EU ACCOUNTABILITY AND THE LIMITS FOR NATIONAL PARLIAMENTS

The two main sources of democratic legitimacy in the EU are national parliaments and the directly elected European Parliament. For the overwhelming majority of EU citizens it is the executive, accountable to their national parliament, that is the central element of democratic legitimacy.[22] Yet this view does not readily correspond with the supra-national character of the EU and the practical difficulties that exist when seeking effective accountability of ministers who take decisions in the Council of Ministers. In particular, it will be government ministers, sitting in the Council, who act in a legislative capacity without the application of most of the procedural or constitutional safeguards that will exist in a parliamentary democracy. That should not suggest that accountability is not achievable; merely that accountability must be pursued through some other constitutional mechanisms that take into account the supra-national characteristics of the EU legislative process. To this end the Treaty of Lisbon provides, in Article 12 TEU, that 'national parliaments contribute *actively* to the good functioning of the Union'.[23] This 'active contribution' arises from the provisions of Protocols 1 and 2 which assign to national parliaments the tasks of general oversight of EU affairs and the subsidiarity monitoring of all legislative proposals. A question explored within Chapters 5 and 6 is whether subsidiarity monitoring offers sufficient constitutional and regulatory safeguards against the incorrect exercise of EU competence by the EU institutions and whether it sufficiently protects the legislative prerogatives of national parliaments.

---

[22] See Van Dijk, J. (2009) 'National Parliaments and Political Accountability in Europe' at 85; Kiiver, P. (2012) *The Early Warning System for the Principle of Subsidiarity* at 14–16.

[23] Emphasis added. Article 12 TEU is the first ever reference to national parliaments in the main text of the Treaty.

4.1 The Challenge of Securing Accountability

Though the consent of the European Parliament is required under the ordinary legislative procedure,[24] the Council of Ministers will still operate independently when agreeing its common position towards a legislative proposal. Within the ordinary legislative procedure the Council and the European Parliament, though equal co-legislators, may adopt different positions. In particular the Council, composed of national ministers who remain accountable to their national parliaments, may have a different perspective on the nature and extent of the legislative proposal. This is because the Council and the European Parliament represent two different constituencies within the decision-making process. This largely influences their distinct positions with regard to whether EU action may be required and what constitutes the appropriate boundaries of input legitimacy. The legislative process provides for compromise between the Council and European Parliament when disagreements arise. This compromise can usually be achieved through the Conciliation Committee, but the question of compliance of a legislative proposal with the principle of subsidiarity which national parliaments are supposed to undertake, and whether this provides output legitimacy, is one that is less clear.[25] Furthermore, this Council autonomy has over the years been compounded by the secrecy and lack of transparency of Council proceedings.[26] While the Council is not collectively accountable, in a political rather than legislative sense, to any other institution, Council members remain, in theory at least, individually politically accountable to domestic legislatures.[27] In practice, sufficient control over individual Council members has been difficult, given the use of QMV in the Council.[28] The criticism of this levelled by some national parliaments is that it has proved to be, on occasion, difficult for a national parliament such as the

---

24 See Article 289 TFEU.

25 The constitutional and procedural questions raised by subsidiarity monitoring are discussed in Chapters 5 and 6.

26 HC 152 xxxiii-I (Session 2001–2) *Democracy and Accountability in the European Union* at paragraph 20.

27 See further Norris, P. (2007) 'Representation and the Democratic Deficit' at 273; Curtin, D. (2009) 'The Council of Ministers' at 125.

28 See CONV 353/02 Working Group IV The Role of National Parliaments, Final Report of Working Group IV on the Role of National Parliaments at paragraph 7, which recommended that effective accountability of decision-making could only be achieved if there was much greater transparency within the Council. The commitment to transparency must be questioned with the increased use of Trilogues within decision-making. See further the discussion in Chapter 4.

United Kingdom Parliament, which uses a document-based scrutiny system, to know how, or why, the minister voted with regard to a legislative proposal. Moreover, even when the minister informs parliament, this explanation is given *ex post*, making it difficult to secure effective accountability in all cases. Direct accountability of the Council to the European Parliament can be identified as one institutional mechanism through which to remedy this deficit. In some respects, for example through the exercise of its veto within the ordinary legislative procedure, the European Parliament has more power than national parliaments. The ability to formally block legislation goes beyond the scope of what national parliaments can do. If we take the example of a strong document-based scrutiny process such as the House of Commons, then under existing arrangements, the European Scrutiny Committee merely scrutinises the Council's agreed common position on a legislative proposal. This scrutiny, which includes monitoring the legislative proposal for subsidiarity compliance, does not automatically take into account any amendments introduced by the European Parliament, but Protocol 1 does provide an opportunity to do this, albeit a very short one.[29] Furthermore, such scrutiny would not guarantee that the views of any parliamentary chamber are represented in the final legislation, as other Member States in the Council may reject the amendments. With the use of QMV and restriction of the national veto, the only effective control over the content of a legislative proposal and the input legitimacy this brings would appear to lie in the hands of the European Parliament. Despite this pivotal position, there remains little popular support for the European Parliament amongst EU citizens. Turnout at elections is low by comparison with national parliamentary elections[30] and there is little knowledge of its activities amongst the electorate, who tend to be motivated by national, rather than EU issues.[31] The effect of this is that political parties and individual MEPs are not held fully accountable for their actions and decisions at EU level.

[29] See Article 4 Protocol 1.

[30] See Special 320 Eurobaromoter Post Electoral Survey 2009 at 6.

[31] See HC 152 xxxiii-I (Session 2001–2) *Democracy and Accountability in the European Union* at paragraph 15.

4.2 Expressing the Limits of Collective Parliamentary Monitoring: The FCC *Lisbon Treaty Judgment*

A key objective of the Treaty of Lisbon is to improve representative democracy within the EU.[32] In the decision-making process this representative democracy is complemented by elements of participative, associative and direct democracy, and in the case of the latter this includes the Citizen's Initiative. Article 10 (2) TEU highlights that representative democracy arises from two tracks of legitimation; namely the European Parliament, which directly represents citizens, and the Heads of State represented in the European Council and the Member States' members of government represented in the Council. In the case of the European Council and the Council, accountability is to national parliaments and ultimately the citizen. The question of EU legislative legitimacy post-Lisbon was considered by the German FCC's *Lisbon Treaty judgment*[33] and whether, inter alia, subsidiarity monitoring by national parliaments provides adequate guarantees against the alleged infringement of democracy arising from a transfer of competence to the EU and whether in the EU decision-making process the Council provides sufficient legitimacy. The FCC judgment is noteworthy because it provides a domestic judicial perspective on the scope of application of the subsidiarity principle and whether the fulfilment of subsidiarity monitoring maintains the chain of legitimacy to national parliaments. In this judgment the FCC stressed that, notwithstanding Europeanisation, the Member States must retain a significant degree of political control over economic, social and cultural matters. This means in practice that national parliaments must retain a prominent role in securing accountability of EU affairs. In policy areas such as family law, where limited Europeanisation has occurred, the FCC considered that a 'fully homogeneous Union approach' is not possible or even desirable.[34]

The FCC held that the transfer of powers to the EU level should only occur where there is a *genuine* cross-border dimension which necessitates co-ordinated and harmonised EU action and that national parliaments would need to be vigilant to guard against unnecessary EU legislation.[35] To this extent the FCC recognises that national parliamentary oversight is essential to prevent competence creep. In what can be described as an

---

[32] See Article 10 (1) TEU.

[33] Judgment of 20 June 2009 *Bundesverfassungsgericht*, BVerfG, 2 BvE 2/08.

[34] Ibid., paragraph 351.

[35] Ibid., paragraph 251.

ambiguous judgment the FCC walks a tightrope between laying out the criteria for securing legitimacy, at least as it is understood under the German constitutional framework, and not obstructing the political desire of deeper integration. The FCC seeks to delineate clearly the boundaries of EU competence beyond which Member States remain free to regulate those areas which, in its view, remain outside the scope of the Treaty. The FCC states that in circumstances where there is an absence of adequate legal protection at the EU level, it reserves the right to review whether legal instruments adhere to the principle of subsidiarity.[36] Notwithstanding this 'line in the sand', the FCC is also at pains to state that it does not view the protection of fundamental political and institutional structures in Germany, or similar judicial protection by other national courts within Member States, as a contradiction with the principle of loyal co-operation. By stressing the Basic Law's 'openness' towards European integration the FCC argues that safeguarding national constitutional identity under the German Constitution and the EU Treaty go 'hand in hand'.[37] Though the FCC accepts the primacy of EU law it is questionable whether, on this reasoning, the 'circle can be squared'. This is particularly so when the EU institutions determine that, in cases of non-exclusive competence, the adoption of common rules to regulate the Internal Market can *only* be achieved by EU action, thereby creating a presumption that a legislative proposal is both necessary and justified, making it subsidiarity compliant.

The FCC concludes that the requirement of democratic legitimacy in, for example, family law can *only* arise from the legislative activities of national parliaments.[38] An implication of this is that in such sensitive policy areas the FCC does not consider subsidiarity monitoring as a universally adequate substitute for the exercise of exclusive Member State competence which is reviewed by the national parliament. This argument reinforces the importance of the individual scrutiny function of national parliaments, and the judgment questions the effectiveness and desirability of collective subsidiarity monitoring in relation to these sensitive policy areas. The FCC would appear to reserve a right of exclusive parliamentary control for the *Bundestag* in such policy areas,

---

[36] Ibid., paragraph 240.

[37] Ibid.

[38] Ibid., paragraph 101. See further, Steinbach, A. (2010) 'The Lisbon Judgment of the German Federal Constitutional Court' at 376; Doukas, D. (2009) 'The Verdict of the German Federal Constitutional Court on the Lisbon Treaty' at 887; Kiiver, P. (2012) *The Early Warning System for the Principle of Subsidiarity* at 45.

notwithstanding that the EU institutions may consider the existence of a cross-border dimension that requires EU legislation and which would trigger the operation of Protocol 2. The judgment, by suggesting that it is the *Bundestag* that is best placed to determine what EU legislative proposals infringe German constitutional competence, displays a degree of mistrust towards other national parliaments. The FCC suggests that they may not take subsidiarity monitoring seriously, the effect of which will be to permit EU legislation in policy areas where, the FCC believes, Member States should retain competence. Furthermore, in the overall context of accountability under the Treaty, the FCC seems sceptical about the representative functions of the European Parliament within EU decision-making, and suggests that the absence of a parliamentary system within the EU necessitates a prominent role for national parliaments to monitor subsidiarity to prevent 'competence creep'.[39] The judgment leaves the presence of an imprecise threat hanging over exactly *how* the FCC will act in future disputes when it considers that EU law breaches the subsidiarity principle. Perhaps this is deliberate and the judgment is intended to act as a deterrent to any further legislative or judicial competence creep.

While the Treaty of Lisbon provides institutional recognition for national parliaments as guardians of subsidiarity, they cannot be considered 'EU institutions'. Their uncertain status, as directly elected institutions on the margins of an EU decision-making process which seeks to improve participatory democracy, is an irony that was not lost on the FCC. The FCC states that this limited form of 'institutional recognition' in the Treaty cannot compensate for the continuing legitimation deficit that arises from the representation provided by the European Parliament and which the FCC considers as being insufficient.[40] This argument is not without merit when, for example, electoral turnout for European Parliament elections is compared with that in national parliamentary

[39] It is important to note Article 48 (7) TEU, which provides that the Council may decide to adopt legislative acts using the ordinary legislative procedure notwithstanding the Treaty's requiring the use of a special legislative procedure. In such circumstances national parliaments shall be notified and any national parliament may object to this change of legislative process. This gives national parliaments a right of 'veto' and can prevent the use of QMV. This power is exercised individually not collectively by national parliaments, and provides them with a longer time period within which to determine their position by comparison with the eight weeks afforded under Protocol 1 for national parliaments to collectively agree that a legislative proposal infringes the principle of subsidiarity.

[40] See paragraph 213.

elections.[41] Since the Single European Act the status of national parliaments as legislative institutions has been considerably curtailed. The extension of EU competence and the demise of the national veto in Council make national parliamentary control of ministers more difficult. Ministers who are mandated to vote in a particular way in Council (as in the case of Latvia and Denmark) can employ the justification that they were outvoted, notwithstanding their opposition, with the threat of minimal domestic censure. This undermines the political control of ministers which is identified in Article 10 (2) as one of the two tracks of participatory democracy. The question which the FCC addressed is whether the procedural strengthening of subsidiarity monitoring 'shifts existing political rights of self-determination to procedural possibilities of intervention and legally assertable claims of participation'.[42] The FCC is not totally dismissive of the worth of subsidiarity monitoring and collective action by national parliaments to act as a buffer against competence creep and agrees that securing output legitimacy is an important task. Perceptively, the FCC identifies that while subsidiarity monitoring per se is not a substitute for legitimacy arising from direct elections or the broader representative functions of national parliaments, this activity has the potential to improve legitimacy when performed by *all* Member States under a uniform set of criteria. Thus the FCC identifies that there is a place, albeit limited, for subsidiarity monitoring to prevent competence creep and that horizontal co-ordination and co-operation between national parliaments will be of assistance. However, the judgment doubts whether horizontal co-ordination can be consistently achieved or that it will provide a viable alternative to effective political procedures which secure national parliamentary control of ministers.

4.3 The Fiscal Treaty Judgment: The Individual Parliamentary Role Confirmed?

The scope of German parliamentary control over the executive in EU affairs was once again considered by the FCC in the circumstances of applications for the issue of temporary injunctions to prevent the signing of the European Stability Mechanism (ESM) Treaty until such time that the FCC had heard the full hearing of a challenge to the legality of this

41 See Special 320 Eurobaromoter Post Electoral Survey 2009 at 6.

42 Judgment of *Bundesverfassungsgericht* at paragraph 294.

Treaty under the German Constitution.[43] The FCC held, in dismissing the applications, that the ESM Treaty could be ratified if at the same time it is ensured under international law that the limitation of liability set out under Article 8 (5) sentence 1 of the ESM Treaty limits the amount of all payment obligations arising to the Federal Republic of Germany from this Treaty to its designated share.[44] Furthermore, the FCC held that no provision of the ESM Treaty may be interpreted in a way that establishes higher payment obligations for the Federal Republic of Germany without the agreement of the German representative. Finally, the FCC held that the provisions of the ESM Treaty concerning the inviolability of the documents of the ESM[45] and the professional secrecy of all persons working for the ESM[46] do not stand in the way of the comprehensive information of the *Bundestag* and of the *Bundesrat*. The FCC's reasoning draws upon the principles of accountability and democracy it laid out in previous judgments such as the *Lisbon Treaty judgment*. In particular, the ESM judgment places significant emphasis upon the need for prior parliamentary approval and control in the operation of the ESM Treaty. In the FCC's view, as elected representatives of the people, the Members of the *Bundestag* must retain control of fundamental budgetary decisions, even in a system of inter-governmental decision-making where the objective is to create financial stability within the Eurozone. Thus the *Bundestag* would be prohibited from establishing mechanisms of considerable financial importance without the prior mandatory approval of the *Bundestag*. In this context, the *Bundestag*, as the legislature, is also prohibited from establishing permanent mechanisms based on international treaties because this would be tantamount to accepting liability for decisions by free will of other Member States. This reasoning resonates strongly with the FCC's view in the *Lisbon Treaty judgment* that monitoring legislative proposals for their impact upon Germany is best achieved through German parliamentary control. The scepticism expressed about collective subsidiarity monitoring is more directly expressed with regard to the operation of the ESM Treaty where any burden placed upon the German people to show solidarity with other Member States must be subjected to rigorous parliamentary control. This highlights more directly that for the FCC it is the control of ministers by

---

43 Judgment of June, 12 September 2012 *Bundesverfassungsgerich*t, BVerfG, 2 BvE 1390/12.

44 In the case of the Federal Republic of Germany the authorised capital stock of the ESM is EUR 190 024 800 000.

45 See Article 32 (5), Article 34 and Article 35 (1) ESM Treaty.

46 See Article 34 ESM Treaty.

the German parliament which remains crucial. What the FCC's reasoning demonstrates is that EU integration and decision-making may only go ahead with the formal consent of the German parliament, and this at the very least implies that such accountability should be pursued by *all* national parliaments. This position can be considered as the FCC protecting the general oversight activities that national parliaments fulfil under Articles 48 and 49 TEU which in this case of the ESM Treaty concerns both the exercise of the Treaty and the protection of monetary union. In this case, the FCC considered that the ESM Treaty and the interests of Germany in protecting monetary union were aligned. The FCC held that, to this end, a future democratically legitimised change of the stability requirements under the ESM Treaty is not from the outset incompatible with Article 79 (3) of the Basic Law. The Basic Law does not guarantee the unchanged further existence of the law in force, but those structures and procedures, which in the context of a continuous development of monetary union necessary to secure economic stability, keep the democratic process open and at the same time safeguard the *Bundestag*'s overall budgetary responsibility.

5. SECURING MINISTERIAL ACCOUNTABILITY: THE OPERATION OF SCRUTINY RESERVES

The discussion in this chapter has so far focussed on securing ministerial accountability to national parliaments. However, if national parliaments are to engage in EU affairs to the extent identified in Article 12 TEU and make a contribution to promoting democracy and ensuring that competences are correctly exercised, then it is essential that the appropriated climate and resources are available for them to fulfil these inter-related tasks. The two key issues for national parliaments, which have consistently inhibited the scrutiny activities of national parliaments, are the need for adequate time and the prompt provision of the necessary information which forms the basis of scrutiny.[47] The overriding objective of the scrutiny process is to influence the minister *prio*r to the Council adopting its definitive common position. The dependency of national parliaments on governments for the provision of information has been consistently highlighted as a significant weakness of the scrutiny arrangements that

[47] See HC 152 xxxiii-I (Session 2001–2) *Democracy and Accountability in the European Union* at 22, paragraph 33.

were put in place by the Treaty of Amsterdam.[48] Kiiver[49] and Tans[50] identified that executive dominance and control of information was the norm in the majority of Member States and consequently impaired the process of securing executive accountability. In the Constitutional Convention, the single most highlighted restriction to effective parliamentary review that was universally identified was the late provision of the relevant documentation that forms the basis of scrutiny.[51] What may be described as an 'information deficit' raised question marks over the success of co-ordinated horizontal subsidiarity monitoring by national parliaments.

5.1 The Amsterdam Protocol on National Parliaments

Recognising the improved provision of information to national parliaments as a prerequisite for effective scrutiny has been a constant. Declaration No. 13 annexed to the Treaty on European Union and Protocol 13 annexed to the Treaty of Amsterdam both purported to involve national parliaments to a greater extent in EU matters. Declaration 23 annexed to the Treaty of Nice invited national parliaments to participate in the debate on the future of the Union and the Laeken Declaration proposed specific questions about the role of national parliaments that the Convention should tackle. Working Group IV on the role of national parliaments had identified some basic factors influencing the effectiveness of scrutiny and acknowledged that national parliaments did not always make use of the powers they had to scrutinise their governments.[52] In addition to recommendations on the provision of documents directly to national parliaments, more time for parliamentary scrutiny and regular exchanges of information between the European Parliament and

---

[48] See HC 563 (Session 2007–8) *Subsidiarity, National Parliaments and the Lisbon* Treaty at 4.

[49] See Kiiver, P. (2006) *The National Parliaments in the European Union* at 58.

[50] Tans, O. (2007) 'Conclusion: National Parliaments and the European Union' at 229.

[51] See CONV 353/02 Working Group IV The Role of National Parliaments, Final Report of Working Group IV on the Role of National Parliaments at paragraphs 9–15.

[52] Ibid., at paragraph 9.

national parliaments, the Group had also suggested that national parliaments should be involved early in the legislative process and in possession of all the relevant information, using a simple mechanism that would not delay the legislative process unnecessarily.

In February 2005 the Commission adopted a ten-point plan which aimed to involve all relevant parties, particularly national parliaments, in European integration. This was developed in 2006 as part of 'Plan D', as a result of which Commissioners attended over a hundred meetings with national parliaments. Commissioners also participated in inter-parliamentary meetings between the European Parliament and national parliaments. In its Communication, 'A Citizens' Agenda: Delivering Results for Europe',[53] the Commission stated that it would 'transmit directly all new proposals and consultation papers to national parliaments, inviting them to react so as to improve the process of policy formulation'. This commitment was welcomed by the European Council in June 2006, and the Commission began to provide national parliaments directly with non-legislative and consultative documents and its new legislative proposals (except classified documents) in September 2006 under what has become known as the Barosso Initiative. Scrutiny reserves, which have existed in some form in the majority of national parliaments, were recognised by the Amsterdam Protocol.[54] This Protocol's recognition of individual scrutiny activities is important, but cannot be considered as a constitutional counterbalance to the gradual de-parliamentarisation that has accompanied integration and serves mainly to promote the individual scrutiny activities of national parliaments. Scrutiny reserves are individual to each parliament, reflect national priorities and do not create a framework for horizontal co-operation. This Protocol amounted to no more than a rudimentary acknowledgement of individual parliamentary procedures within Member States. Furthermore, on the substantive question of document provision and adequate time for the completion of scrutiny the Amsterdam Protocol was subject to several deficiencies.

Under the Amsterdam Protocol the primary role of national parliaments in EU affairs had been to scrutinise the activities of the minister in the Council. This scrutiny, which sought to influence the minister prior to the final adoption of the measure by the Council, encompassed a review of the Council's draft common position. However, this had minimal

---

[53] COM (2006) 211 *A Citizen's Agenda: Delivering Results for Europe*.

[54] For a comprehensive overview of the functioning of scrutiny reserves in the Member States see generally Tans, O. (2007) 'Conclusion: National Parliaments and the European Union' .

impact outside national capitals and essentially focussed upon the domestic impact of the proposed legislation. Furthermore, this scrutiny was not without difficulty, not least because of the weaknesses with the Amsterdam Protocol for national parliaments in relation to the transmission of documentation to national parliaments. Under the Amsterdam Protocol parliaments were wholly dependent upon their governments for the provision of information[55] and the systematic late provision of a limited number of documents impaired executive accountability.[56] In relation to legislative proposals the Amsterdam Protocol was weak because it required the Commission to make these available in 'good time' for governments to distribute them to parliaments 'as appropriate'. This inconsistent access to documents across the Member States reinforced the inconsistency between weak and strong parliaments and created an 'information deficit' within many legislatures. Yet despite this information deficit national parliaments have not been hampered to the point of impotence in their individual oversight of EU activities. By contrast, rather than remaining passive and isolated institutions, many national parliaments have, at least in the context of information transmission, taken the initiative and improved their internal parliamentary procedures by which they have secured ministerial accountability. In particular this has arisen through obtaining guarantees from the executive in relation to parliamentary scrutiny of EU affairs. The most common way that this was achieved was through the introduction of scrutiny reserves, the existence of which can be considered as the 'cornerstone' of the scrutiny process within the Member States.[57] This is primarily because the scrutiny reserves include binding guarantees from the executive and recognised within the Treaty, that no agreement will be given to a legislative proposal in Council until the domestic scrutiny process is complete, save in cases of 'urgency'.

---

[55] See HC 563 (Session 2007–8) *Subsidiarity, National Parliaments and the Lisbon Treaty*, at 4.

[56] See CONV 353/02 Working Group IV The Role of National Parliaments, Final Report of Working Group IV on the Role of National Parliaments at paragraphs 21–36. See also Tans, O. (2007) 'Conclusion: National Parliaments and the European Union' .

[57] See Cygan, A. (2001) *National Parliaments in an Integrated Europe* at 63. See generally on the importance of scrutiny reserves in the Member States Maurer, A. (2001) 'National Parliaments in the European Union Architecture' at 432.

5.2 The Treaty of Lisbon Arrangements

Under the Amsterdam Protocol the obligation to supply documents directly to national parliaments extended only to Commission consultation documents. In relation to legislative proposals the Amsterdam Protocol was weak, requiring the Commission to make these available in 'good time' in order for governments to ensure that the national parliament received them 'as appropriate'. The Amsterdam Protocol left it to national governments to provide documents as and when they saw fit. By contrast, the Lisbon Protocol includes an extended right to receive a variety of documents directly from the Commission, or other originating institution, rather than being dependent upon the government to formally deposit. This is in addition to the improved provision of documentation under the Barosso Initiative. In a decision-making process where time is of the essence to arrive at a collective viewpoint on subsidiarity this is a noteworthy development. Under the Treaty of Lisbon, Protocol 1 requires the direct provision of documents to national parliaments to include draft legislative acts,[58] the annual legislative programme, Council agendas[59] and minutes, and the annual report of the Court of Auditors.[60] Of most significance is the commitment to transmit draft legislative acts *directly* to national parliaments. To fulfil the subsidiarity monitoring task assigned in Article 3 of Protocol 1 the early provision of the documentation is a prerequisite to facilitate the necessary horizontal discussion prior to any collective conclusion. In particular this is essential if the threshold under Protocol 2 to trigger the subsidiarity early warning mechanism is to be attained.[61] The improved provision of information is only part of the picture; the provision of information must also be *timely*. The slow provision of information has proved to be problematic for national parliaments primarily because their internal scrutiny procedures and the ordinary legislative procedure operate independently. Article 3 of the Amsterdam Protocol provided that 'a period of at least six weeks must elapse between publication of draft EU legislation in all languages and placing the matter on a Council agenda for a decision', to enable national parliaments to complete their scrutiny of the Council's proposed

---

[58] Article 2 of Protocol 1 on the Role of National Parliaments in the European Union. This includes draft legislation that originated from a group of Member States under Article 329 TFEU and would appear to cover proposals for policy co-ordination arising under Article 5 TFEU.

[59] Article 5, Protocol 1.

[60] Articles 1 and 2, Protocol 1.

[61] Article 7 (2), Protocol 2.

common position. Under the Treaty of Lisbon this is extended to eight weeks, with a further ten days elapsing between placing the proposal on the agenda and adoption of the provision under the ordinary legislative procedure. Though the additional two week period is longer than the equivalent proposal in the Constitutional Treaty,[62] in practice it is unlikely to make a significant difference.[63] A feature of decision-making, particularly after the 2004 enlargement, is that an increasing number of proposals are agreed by the European Parliament at the first reading stage of the legislative process.[64] The primary consequence of this is that if a national parliament only completes scrutiny towards the end of this eight week period, its views could only be incorporated if the subsidiarity warning mechanism had been triggered. Otherwise a national parliament's opinion may not be heard. The new provisions within the Treaty of Lisbon for information transmission are not a panacea and, independently, do not collectivise decisions by national parliaments on the question of subsidiarity. Though the Treaty allocates subsidiarity monitoring to national parliaments it has not standardised national parliamentary procedures. For this reason parliaments previously termed 'weak' for their EU oversight activities are still likely to be considered 'weak' actors in relation to their subsidiarity monitoring. Furthermore, the timely provision of information is insufficient to independently make a significant difference to improving national scrutiny procedures even if the guarantees in Protocols 1 and 2 are legally binding.

6. CONCLUDING REMARKS

What is evident from the Treaties is that the 'European function' of national parliaments in which they act as 'guardians' is one that is generally confined to the latter stages of either the legislative process or Treaty amendment. That said, the Treaty of Lisbon offers perhaps the

---

[62] The Constitutional Treaty maintained the six week period included within the Treaty of Amsterdam.

[63] See HL 62-II (2007–8) *The Treaty of Lisbon: An Impact Assessment: Evidence* at 333. See also HL 62-I (2007–8) *The Treaty of Lisbon: An Impact Assessment: Report* at 243, paragraph 11.42, and HC 563 (2007–8) *Subsidiarity, National Parliaments and the Lisbon Treaty*, 33 at paragraph 44.

[64] According to the European Parliament Report on the *Application of the Co-decision Procedure: Analysis and Statistics of the 2004–9 Legislature*, 72 per cent of legislative proposals were agreed at first reading. This is an increase from 33 per cent for the 1999–2004 parliamentary term. Available at http://ec.europa.eu?statistics/docs/report_statistics_public_draft.pdf (accessed 12 August 2011).

most viable arrangements for national parliaments to participate in EU affairs given that they have not acquired any formal institutional status. Opportunities for subsidiarity monitoring or reviewing the use of *Passerelles* do, to some extent, fulfil the provisions of Article 12 TEU and offer improved democratic input at the EU level and democratic legitimacy at the national level. However, these opportunities are limited by national constitutional and procedural requirements and it is this heterogeneous nature of parliamentary involvement which will undoubtedly limit the extent to which national parliaments make use of the new provisions. More generally, participation by national parliaments in EU affairs has historically been hindered by limited access to information and the short time for scrutiny. Though the Treaty of Lisbon, and to some extent the Barosso Initiative, address these problems, the detailed and complete involvement of national parliaments in EU affairs in which they become formal guardians of European policy and integration has yet to be achieved. It is suggested that this is unlikely to occur because it is not considered a political priority for national parliaments. Notwithstanding these new opportunities offered by the Treaty of Lisbon, much of the daily involvement of national parliaments in EU affairs and fulfilling some form of 'guardian' role is neither new nor Treaty dependent. Moreover, the extent to which subsidiarity monitoring refocusses national parliaments away from seeking to exert control over their ministers is questionable. The exercise of EU competences, the process of Treaty reform and the scrutiny of legislative proposals are parliamentary activities that arise from the normal parliamentary function of seeking accountability of the executive. In the case of the EU this accountability is split amongst twenty-eight Member States with vastly different constitutional traditions and in some parliaments the accountability of individual ministers will be better than in others. In Chapters 5 and 6 the principle of subsidiarity and subsidiarity monitoring will be examined in more detail and also whether the allocation of this task by Article 12 TEU to national parliaments cuts through the constitutional heterogeneity and creates a minimum uniform standard for participation by national parliaments in EU affairs. To this extent, Chapters 5 and 6 consider whether the task of subsidiarity monitoring achieves something which previous Treaty arrangements did not; namely the 'Europeanisation' of national parliamentary scrutiny. However, before considering this issue, Chapter 4 examines how the operation of ordinary legislative procedure has impacted upon national parliaments.

4. The ordinary legislative process and national parliaments

1. INTRODUCTION

Chapters 2 and 3 considered how EU integration has impacted upon national parliaments. Chapter 2 highlighted how the process of Europeanisation has resulted in the transfer of significant competences to the EU from the Member States. This has led to criticisms that Europeanisation is the primary cause of a deparliamentarisation in the EU which has contributed to the democratic deficit. Chapter 3 examined how Treaty development has progressively recognised the democratic credentials of national parliaments which, through their own internal scrutiny mechanisms, have sought to exert some control over the executive within the EU legislative process. This leads to the inevitable question of whether the more prominent role of national parliaments in the EU, and especially their more recent role of undertaking subsidiarity monitoring, have improved democratic control over the EU institutions and law-making process. This chapter examines the operation of the ordinary legislative procedure and what this means for national parliaments, both in terms of their ability to scrutinise the executive and, in particular, to use the scrutiny reserves effectively. The primary issue for national parliaments is that as part of their oversight activities they need to ensure that ministerial accountability is upheld while simultaneously engaging in subsidiarity monitoring. This creates both practical and substantive challenges for national parliaments because there will, on occasion, undoubtedly be a divergence between securing ministerial accountability and benchmarking a legislative proposal against the principle of subsidiarity.

This chapter focusses primarily on the questions of how, and to what extent, national parliaments can secure accountability of individual ministers in the Council, when the Council exercises its legislative powers, and fulfil the function of securing parliamentary scrutiny of the executive. The process of EU law-making has, historically, marginalised national parliaments.[1] The 'Community method' of decision-making has reflected the process of supra-national integration in which the interests of the EU, the Member States and EU citizens were represented through EU institutions. This inter-institutional relationship has always been significant and not just for the purposes of law-making. It is the nature of this relationship and the allocation of powers which have frequently been highlighted for demonstrating the presence of the democratic deficit.[2] The absence of a parliamentary model within the EU polity further supported the notion that EU integration had caused a deparliamentarisation because legislative powers had been taken from national parliaments and given to institutions which did not have corresponding methods through which to secure accountability.[3] Though the European Parliament has been granted additional powers by the Treaties, these have stopped well short of creating a parliamentary system of governance which includes robust procedures for independent review and scrutiny of the legislative process. Though national parliaments engage in scrutiny of the EU legislative process and review legislative proposals according to their own procedural criteria and constitutional requirements, and since 1992 have had their scrutiny reserves recognised within the Treaty, there is an overwhelming consensus that the EU legislative process remains distant and opaque. Democratisation had granted the European Parliament additional powers and since the Treaty of Amsterdam the Parliament has been a genuine 'co-legislator' with the Council. But, from the perspective of national parliaments this has only been of limited assistance, not least because through EU democratisation, the increased legislative powers granted to the Parliament have positioned it at the core of a legislative process which national parliaments are seeking to review. The European Parliament may be considered a 'parliament', but from the perspective of national parliaments the priorities and agenda are different in the context of the legislative process and its involvement in the ordinary legislative process as a co-legislator with the Council should not be considered as a parliamentarisation of EU decision-making.

---

1 See Cygan, A. (2011) 'The Parliamentarisation of EU Decision-Making' at 478.

2 See O'Brennan, J. and Raunio, T. (2007) 'Deparliamentarisation and European Integration' at 2–8.

3 See Scharpf, F.W. (2010) 'Legitimacy in the Multi-Level European Polity' at 89.

2. THE DEMOCRATISATION OF DECISION-MAKING

Europeanisation has necessitated a distinct governance framework at the centre of which is the ordinary legislative procedure. Under the ordinary legislative procedure legislative powers have been transferred to the Council and European Parliament at the expense of national institutions and actors.[4] This governance structure is a significant element of the 'deparliamentarisation' arising from the absence of national parliamentary participation in EU decision-making and the erosion of executive accountability in EU affairs.[5] In terms of monitoring the ordinary legislative procedure the primary issues have been that domestic scrutiny intended to secure ministerial accountability has varied in effectiveness across the Member States, operated independently of the EU legislative process and could not be considered as an appropriate substitute for the loss of legislative competence. The difficulty that has always faced national parliaments is that they are seeking to review and secure accountability of a legislative process over which they have only very limited influence and which is played out remotely from national parliaments.[6] In addition, national parliaments have no control over the timing of the legislative process, which is wholly determined by the time periods within the Treaty and the rules of procedure and practices that have been drawn up by the Council and the European Parliament. Moreover, changes to the legislative process have sought to increase its efficiency, which has further eroded the influence of national parliaments. Though the revised legislative process is now more 'results focussed' this has been achieved at the expense of, inter alia, a fully parliamentary approach to EU decision-making.

2.1 The Co-decision Procedure

The Treaty of Maastricht introduced the co-decision procedure. This was a development from the co-operation procedure introduced in the Single European Act 1986. Back then, the purpose of the co-operation procedure was twofold. First, it introduced the process of qualified majority voting (QMV), which replaced unanimity and limited the national veto, thereby making decision-making in Council easier. Secondly, the co-operation

---

[4] See Kassim, H. (2005) 'The Europeanisation of Member State Institutions' at 300–303.

[5] See Kiiver, P. (2006) *The National Parliaments in the European Union* at 41–42. See also Curtin, D. (2009) 'The Council of Ministers' at 125–133.

[6] See Harlow, C. (2002) 'A Plethora of Parliaments' at 85.

procedure brought the European Parliament within the decision-making process and gave it the power to propose amendments. The objective of this was to enhance the democratic qualities and legitimacy of legislation through direct input from the European Parliament. However, the power of amendment was limited because the Council retained the right to reject amendments and adopt the legislative proposal in its original form. The Maastricht version of the co-decision procedure remedied some of the defects of the co-operation procedure by protecting the power to propose amendments. Moreover, the co-decision procedure introduced a new stage, a so-called 'third reading', whereby a new joint body called a Conciliation Committee would be convened if the Parliament and Council failed to agree an amended proposal. The objective of the Conciliation Committee would be to agree, within six weeks of being convened, an amended legislative proposal which both institutions could support. Though an improvement over the co-operation procedure, co-decision was still subject to drawbacks, not least that the Council could still adopt the original proposal by unanimity if the Conciliation Committee could not agree a joint text. The co-decision procedure finally became real joint decision-making through changes introduced by the Amsterdam Treaty.[7] In 1997, the crucial development introduced by the Treaty of Amsterdam came at the stage when the Conciliation Committee was convened. Under the Treaty of Maastricht, Article 251 EC stated that if the Council and Parliament failed to agree the content of a measure in the Conciliation Committee then the Council could, using unanimity, agree its original common position. Significantly, under the post-Amsterdam version of Article 251 EC the opportunity for such unilateral Council action was prohibited. The effect of the Amsterdam amendments was to shift the centre of gravity, within the co-decision procedure, in favour of the European Parliament. Co-decision became the common legislative procedure for Internal Market measures introduced under Article 95 EC, and the Treaty of Nice extended the scope of Article 251 EC to cover additional policy areas.

2.2 The Ordinary Legislative Procedure

After more than fifteen years co-decision entered a new era with the Treaty of Lisbon and became known as the ordinary legislative procedure. The ordinary legislative procedure is based upon a principle of parity between the European Parliament and the Council, and by strengthening

[7] Shackleton, M. (2000) 'The Politics of Co-decision' at 325.

the role of the Parliament its purpose is to render the procedure more democratic and accountable. In particular, the two co-legislators agree legislation jointly and neither of them can adopt legislation without the agreement of the other. Under the Treaty of Lisbon the ordinary legislative procedure is, in substance, the same as the co-decision procedure first included within the Treaty of Amsterdam. Article 294 TFEU provides for up to three readings: first reading, second reading and third reading, with a conciliation process if the Council and European Parliament are unable to agree a compromise proposal. The procedure can, however, be concluded at any of these stages if the two co-legislators reach an overall agreement. As is explained below, agreement is now more commonly being reached at first reading, which itself has significant impact upon the scrutiny activities of national parliaments. If the Council does not approve all the amendments of the European Parliament at second reading then the third phase, which entails the convening of the Conciliation Committee, is entered into. With the Treaty of Lisbon the scope of the ordinary legislative procedure almost doubled to cover eighty-five legal bases[8] by comparison with the forty-four that were included in the Treaty of Nice. The major development is that co-decision is now extended to a significant number of policy areas where the European Parliament previously had a right of consultation or a simple assent. This change is particularly noteworthy because the primary consequence of a policy area coming within the ordinary legislative procedure is that QMV is the voting mechanism that will be used within the Council, which undoubtedly weakens the position of individual ministers in the Council who can no longer block a legislative proposal through use of a veto. Moreover, this has very significant spillover consequences for national parliaments and their ability to exercise control over the minister, and for the views of national parliaments to be taken into account in the Council deliberations. Though the operation of the scrutiny reserves may provide some restraint over the national minister, the primary problem is that, with the growth of the ordinary legislative procedure and the volume of legislative and regulatory activity emanating from the EU, there is a greater pressure for the

[8] The Treaty of Lisbon has also introduced QMV as the norm for Justice and Home Affairs issues, which is a consequence of the abolition of the pillar structure. This has brought decisions on issues such as cross-border crime, drug trafficking, illegal immigration and terrorism within the scope of the ordinary legislative procedure with the consequence that the loss of the veto has led to national parliaments having much less control over the exercise of decision-making in these policy areas.

Council and the European Parliament to achieve a compromise agreement at a much earlier stage of the legislative cycle. A key feature of decision-making after the 2004 enlargement is that an increasing number of proposals are agreed by the European Parliament and the Council at the first reading stage of the legislative process.[9] For national parliaments this means that they have a much shorter period of time to complete the scrutiny of the legislative proposal than the eight weeks which are provided for within Protocol 2. Not only does this weaken the accountability of the minister to the national parliament, but also if a national parliament only completes scrutiny towards the end of this eight week period, its views could only be incorporated if the subsidiarity warning mechanism had been triggered. This is dependent upon attaining the minimum one-third threshold required to raise the yellow card, but since its inception this has occurred on only one occasion.[10] In the light of the trend towards an earlier agreement between the Council and the European Parliament within the legislative cycle there will undoubtedly be some impact upon the efficacy of subsidiarity monitoring undertaken by national parliaments. This process of conciliation has gradually become formalised and the use of Trilogues as a forum for achieving agreement between the Council and the European Parliament has, arguably, fundamentally shifted the dynamic within the legislative process to reflect more clearly the supra-national character of the legislative process and will ultimately have the effect of weakening the scrutiny activities of national parliaments.

2.3 The Use of Trilogues

The underlying principle of the ordinary legislative process is that it reflects a compromise proposal agreed between the primary political actors. The role of the Conciliation Committee is to provide a formal forum within which such a compromise may be achieved. Given the short

---

[9] According to the European Parliament Report on the *Application of the Co-decision Procedure: Analysis and Statistics of the 2004–9 Legislature*, 72 per cent of legislative proposals were agreed at first reading. This is an increase from 33 per cent for the 1999–2004 parliamentary term, available at http://ec.europa.eu?statistics/docs/report_statistics_public_draft.pdf (accessed 12 March 2010).

[10] In May 2012, nineteen chambers raised subsidiarity objections in relation to COM (2012) 130 final *Proposal for a Regulation on the Exercise of the Right to take Collective Action within the Context of the Freedom of Establishment and the Freedom to Provide Services*. As a consequence, the Commission withdrew the proposal. See further the discussion in Chapter 6.

time frame of six weeks from first convening the Conciliation Committee to final agreement, the emphasis is upon securing an agreement efficiently, but one which also ensures that the legislative proposal has the necessary legitimacy. The Trilogues, as the name indicates, is a tripartite discussion which consists of the Council, Commission and European Parliament and occurs without any reference to national parliaments or the procedures contained within Protocol 2.[11] The Trilogue is convened at the point when the Council is ready to present its position with regard to any European Parliament amendments that have been proposed, even if the Council has yet to formally conclude the second reading. The Trilogue constitutes what can be defined as an executive form of deliberation under which representatives from each institution within the Conciliation Committee, together with the Commission, seek to agree a political compromise with regard to a legislative proposal which can then be presented to the conciliation committee as a joint text.

At the first Trilogue the Presidency representative outlines the Council's position on the Parliament's second reading amendments and the Council will usually accept some of these amendments but reject others.[12] The Parliament negotiating team responds to the Council's observations and the ensuing debate may lead to a new, and fundamentally different, legislative proposal. Trilogues sometimes conclude with a request that detailed drafting work be carried out by a small working party at 'political' level[13] or by civil servants at a 'technical' level. The consequence of the volume of legislation and the constricted time periods for the legislative process laid down by Article 294 TFEU is that Trilogue

---

[11] See Shackelton, M. and Raunio, T. (2003) 'Codecision since Amsterdam' especially at 177–179 and Kardasheva, R. (2012) *Trilogues in the EU Legislature*, SSRN Working Paper Series, available at http://ssrn.com/sol3/papers.cfm?abstract_id=2119912 (accessed 14 August 2012).

[12] Negotiations in Trilogues are based on what is known as a 'four-column working document' setting out the position of the Parliament and the Council. The first column sets out the Council's position at the first reading and the second column states the Parliament's second-reading amendment thereto. The third column indicates the Council's reaction to the relevant Parliament amendment – acceptance, rejection or the formulation of a possible compromise text. The updated position of the Parliament's delegation is shown in the fourth column. Thus while the first two columns remain unchanged throughout the conciliation procedure, the last two columns are subject to change to reflect the progress of the negotiations.

[13] This will usually comprise the Rapporteur from the relevant European Parliament Committee, the chair of the Council Working Group and a Commission representative.

meetings are becoming very much the norm within the legislative process.[14] This poses challenges for national parliaments to rigorously review a legislative proposal, and perhaps also more fundamental questions relating to the extent to which democratisation and transparency have been secured within the ordinary legislative process. In short, do the Trilogues undermine the very purpose for which the ordinary legislative procedure was first introduced in the Treaty of Maastricht as a means of addressing the democratic deficit? In the light of the modus operandi of Trilogues, their increased use is difficult to justify with the objective that the ordinary legislative process should provide more transparent and legitimate decision-making. Trilogues are meetings of restricted access which are held behind closed doors and which clearly raise concerns of both transparency and accountability.[15] The accusation can be made that deals reached behind closed doors within an executive committee undermine the notion of a transparent legislative process which is closer to the EU citizen. For national parliaments the implications of Trilogues are significant because the conclusion reached may constitute a legislative act which is fundamentally different from the proposal and which was first presented by the Commission. This proposal would have formed the basis of the scrutiny undertaken by national parliaments in advance of the Council adopting its common position prior to first reading and upon which the subsidiarity review would have been based. The use of Trilogues encapsulates, in a micro-cosmic form, the supra-national nature of EU decision-making by bringing into sharp focus the process of negotiation between competing political and institutional actors within the legislative process which, through the use of Trilogues, has become even more remote from national parliaments. This is because the Trilogue negotiations occur in a small executive committee rather than taking place as a transparent deliberative process. This reinforces the argument that Europeanisation and democratisation are together responsible for deparliamentarisation and that the EU citizen remains distant from this largely technocratic legislative process.

The Trilogues clearly target efficiency and to secure agreement on a legislative proposal in the light of the preparatory work that has been undertaken by all the actors and institutions which are involved. However, despite the justification of legislative efficiency, the use of Trilogues can be criticised for being in conflict with the principles of good

---

[14] See Farrel, H. and Héritier, A. (2004) 'Interorganizational Negotiation and Interorganizational Power in Shared Decision-Making' at 1191.

[15] See further, Häge, F. and Kaeding, M. (2007) 'Reconsidering the European Parliament's Legislative Influence' at 341.

governance and legitimate decision-making, both of which are values which were held up as paradigms for EU governance within the Commission's own White Paper on EU Governance[16] and in the Laeken Presidency Conclusions. Though the use of Impact Assessments and expansion of the ordinary legislative procedure ostensibly suggest improved consultation and democratisation of EU decision-making, the use of closed door negotiations to conclude the final legislative act undermines the values of transparency and openness and reinforces a perception that, notwithstanding Treaty reform, the democratic deficit continues to exist. In relation to national parliaments much of the discussion concerning the impact of Europeanisation and the use of the ordinary legislative process has focussed on deparliamentarisation. Arguments have been put forward[17] that the European Parliament is in a position to fill, at least in part, the parliamentary void and that its participation in decision-making embraces a parliamentary norm within the legislative process – namely that legislative acts are adopted by elected representatives, which helps to secure their legitimacy. Within the ordinary legislative process the legitimacy argument may also win support from the representation offered by the minister in the Council who is very likely to be an elected representative of a national parliament. Yet, ironically, in an attempt to secure improved legislative efficiency, even this argument of representation and transparency may be rebutted if closer consideration is given to the functioning of the Trilogues.[18] If the format of the Trilogues is considered then it may be suggested that flexibility and efficiency are achieved at the expense of transparency, legitimacy and democratic accountability. In particular, the executive nature of Trilogues removes the opportunity for deliberation in decision-making and restrains the ability of individual MEPs to propose amendments to legislation. This has a spillover effect upon national parliaments because – assuming that they and the European Parliament do, on occasion, share concerns about a legislative proposal which have been relayed to the European Parliament in the course of a COSAC meeting – the restricted opportunity for review by the plenary of the European Parliament restricts the opportunity for democratic input into

[16] See COM (2001) 428 *European Governance – A White Paper* at 8.

[17] See for example Shackleton, M. (2000) 'The Politics of Co-decision' at 325; Hix, S., Noury, A. and Roland, G. (2005) 'Power to Parties' at 209; and Scharpf, F. (1999) *Governing in Europe* at 7–20.

[18] Farrel and Héritier (2004) 'Interorganizational Negotiation and Interorganizational Power in Shared Decision-Making' at 1200–1204.

the legislative process.[19] Kardasheva points out that publicly available documents from the Council and the European Parliament[20] indicate that approximately 40 per cent of EU legislation that was passed between 2000 and 2008 went through a Trilogue. Furthermore, more than 76 per cent of ordinary legislative proposals were discussed at some type of informal meeting, and in policy areas including the environment, energy and transport, more than 70 per cent of the total legislative proposals were subjected to Trilogues. While the European Parliament may have gained additional institutional powers its influence will largely depend upon internal cohesion and co-operation between the various political groupings within it. The absence of a debate will, as in all parliamentary processes, remove an opportunity for opposition voices to be heard or amendments to be proposed. The move away from the Conciliation Committee, the operation of which itself raised questions of democratic accountability, to use of Trilogues which offer more informal inter-cameral conflict resolution, merely adds further weight to the argument that, notwithstanding the reforms of the Treaty of Lisbon, EU decision-making is undemocratic and not properly accountable, both at the EU level and at the national level.

3. QMV AND PARLIAMENTARY SCRUTINY

There is no doubt that the use of QMV in the Council has accelerated the pace of EU integration. It could also be argued that, as a direct consequence, the use of QMV within the Council for decision-making has also accelerated the pace of deparliamentarisation because the ordinary legislative procedure operates without reference to the decision-making procedures of national parliaments. Moreover, as more competences are transferred to the ordinary legislative procedure, so has the use of QMV been extended within the Council. Since the inception of QMV national parliaments have consistently found it difficult to secure effective accountability of the minister in the context of the legislative process. This is because national parliaments can only exert control over *their* own minister, and, secondly, the nature of majority voting means

---

[19] See Obholzer, L. and Reh, C. (2012) 'How to Negotiate Trilogues in the EU'.

[20] Appendix 1 and 2 in Kardasheva, R. (2012) *Trilogues in the EU Legislature*, SSRN Working Paper Series, available at http://ssrn.com/sol3/papers.cfm?abstract_id=2119912 (accessed 14 August 2012) at 25–31.

that ministers will, on occasion, be outvoted in the Council. In circumstances such as those under the Danish or Latvian model of mandating the minister, but equally in those instances when a parliament's view is expressed following an inquisitorial scrutiny process, how far can a minister be held accountable for a decision which was opposed, but for which other ministers voted in favour? Thus, it can be argued that while QMV is efficient and seeks consensus in EU decision-making, and is ostensibly more democratic through the involvement of the European Parliament, a new democratic deficit has been created at the national level under which individual ministerial responsibility may be restricted. This is because ministers who are subjected to national parliamentary scrutiny *prior* to a Council meeting cannot readily influence other ministers to change their voting position, especially if, as in the case of Denmark or Latvia, the minister is subject to a parliamentary mandate. It is at this point that the disconnect between national parliamentary scrutiny and the timetable of ordinary legislative procedure is most evident. Though subsidiarity monitoring seeks to address the problem of the disconnect between national parliaments and the ordinary legislative procedure, it is questionable whether formal consideration of this principle by national parliaments under the procedures of Protocol 2 provides sufficient guarantees. The precise scope and nature of Protocol 2 and subsidiarity monitoring is considered in more detail in Chapter 6, and though benchmarking against the subsidiarity principle by national parliaments was practised before the Treaty of Lisbon, there is strong evidence to indicate that since its inclusion in the Treaty of Maastricht, the Commission has remained generally ambivalent to the application of this principle in its pursuit of deeper integration. As the discussion in Chapter 2 showed, in its process of Impact Assessments the Commission has not necessarily given due consideration to subsidiarity as a fundamental regulatory principle of EU law and paid only lip service to its justification when determining whether EU legislative action is required. A direct consequence of this is that once the decision to legislate by the Commission has been made, a chain of events takes place under the ordinary legislative procedure which makes it very difficult for national parliaments to exert any effective control, unless they can reach some consensus on the application of the principle of subsidiarity using the procedures of Protocol 2.

3.1 QMV as a Tool of Integration

The process of decision-making by QMV has developed substantially since its inception in 1966 under the 'Luxembourg Compromise' in response to De Gaulle's 'empty chair' policy which began in June 1965. For De Gaulle, it was inconceivable that France would oppose a decision and still be obliged to carry it out. In an explanation of this policy the then French Minister of Foreign Affairs, Maurice Couve de Murville stated:[21]

> how could anyone imagine that one would, without our agreement and *a forteriori* against our will, dispose of our sovereignty? It is also a question of good sense: who could imagine that a policy measure would be made acceptable and applicable in a country that has refused it because it believes it goes against its political or economic interests?

The crisis was resolved by the use of the Luxembourg Compromise under which decisions could be taken by a qualified majority vote, and in circumstances where a Member State invoked its vital interests, the Council would endeavour to find a solution that could be adopted by all the Member States. France, however, continued to insist that where important national interests were at stake, the discussions must continue until a unanimous agreement was reached.[22] It is clear that references to sovereignty raised explicit concerns of an erosion of parliamentary competences, a corollary of which is the ability of a parliament to control the exercise of those competences. Even in an EU of only six Member States there were already concerns that the use of majority voting would prevent Member States rejecting unpopular policies which they then must justify to a domestic audience. This is a very rudimentary form of deparliamentarisation, but one which has grown as EU competences expanded and QMV became the primary form of voting in the Council. In this context, the issue surrounding QMV today remains very much the same; that is, Member States will, on occasion, have to adopt legislation which they do not necessarily want. This is the consequence of EU membership and reflects the obligations of the solidarity clause within Article 4 (3) TEU. With the growth of scrutiny of EU affairs in national parliaments, the deparliamentarisation debate now also embraces the broader impact of QMV upon national parliaments' ability to fulfil the basic requirements that exist under the separation of powers doctrine. That is, when acting in their capacity as directly elected legislatures, they

---

[21] See Couve de Murville, M. (1971) *Une Politique Etrangère 1958–1969* at 297 (the author's own translation is used).

[22] On the impact of the Luxembourg Compromise and how it was applied see generally Teasdale, A.L. (1993) 'The Life and Death of the Luxembourg Compromise' at 567; Vasey, M. (1988) 'Decision-Making in the Agriculture Council and the Luxembourg Compromise' at 725.

seek to exert accountability over the executive, irrespective of the circumstances, when the executive is legislating. In the context of the EU, national parliaments do this independently through the exercise of different procedural mechanisms under which they seek to scrutinise *their* own executive. This is a right that is recognised explicitly by Article 4 of Protocol 1. Though the scrutiny reserves provide for minimum time periods for the completion of scrutiny, all national parliaments, irrespective of their scrutiny procedures, still face significant challenges to ensure that effective scrutiny of ministers can be completed in what is a very short time frame and in the context of a legislative process over which they have no direct control. The pressure to create a European Internal Market by 31 December 1992 made the need for QMV a necessity. The completion of the Internal Market required the implementation of approximately 290 directives and it is highly questionable that this could have been achieved through the use of unanimity. That said, both the Single European Act 1986 and the Treaty of Maastricht 1992, while extending the use of QMV, maintained unanimity in a number of sensitive policy areas, such as direct taxation and social security.

The spirit of De Gaulle's opposition to the use of majority voting undoubtedly lives on and is still, to this day, reflected in both the political negotiations that take place at the Inter-Governmental Conference and in the negotiations to conclude the final Treaty. For example, the fractious negotiations that led to the Treaty of Nice were a catalyst for change that ended up with the Constitutional Convention being used as a more inclusive forum in which the concerns of a broader group of stakeholders, including national parliaments, could be heard. At the Intergovernmental Conference preceding the Treaty of Amsterdam 1997, the difficulty of arriving at a unanimous agreement following enlargement was recognised by the Commission, which stated that this difficulty would 'increase exponentially' as the number of Member States increases.[23] In addition, the language of the United Kingdom, which to some extent mirrored De Gaulle's sovereignty rhetoric of 1966, in the course of the BSE crisis indicated that *more* QMV was needed to avoid a future political impasse which might arise from the use of the veto.[24] In essence the more legislation agreed through QMV, the less control

---

[23] Commission of the European Communities (1996) 'Opinion to the Intergovernmental Conference 1996' at paragraph 2.2.1.

[24] In protest at what was seen as a mishandling of the BSE crisis by the Commission, the then United Kingdom Prime Minister, John Major, told the House of Commons on 21 May 1996 that his government could not continue to co-operate 'normally' in the Community's legislative process as long as there

available to individual Member States. While this may be seen as a 'necessary evil', which secures both legislative agreement and deeper integration, this has come at the expense of domestic accountability of ministers to their national parliaments. Post-Lisbon, this expediency that QMV brings can also have implications for subsidiarity monitoring for similar reasons; namely, that the one-third threshold required by Protocol 2 to raise a 'yellow card', though not representing a majority of votes, still requires a substantial degree of consensus amongst national parliaments. It is questionable if, on occasion, subsidiarity objections will not be pursued if it is apparent that either a qualified majority already exists in the Council, or if there are clear indications that a Trilogue will lead to the agreement of a text. The issue for national parliaments will be whether it is worthwhile dedicating resources to the scrutiny of a legislative proposal over which they are unlikely to be able to exert any effective influence.

3.2 QMV after the Treaty of Lisbon

QMV in the Council of Ministers traditionally functioned as follows. Each Member State received a number of votes on the basis of a political deliberation. A decision was adopted by qualified majority when a certain threshold was reached. Pre-2004, and when the EU constituted fifteen Member States, the total number of votes was eighty-seven and the qualified majority was set at sixty-two. The threshold has been amended with each enlargement, but was always intended to represent a threshold that constituted 71 per cent of the total votes.[25] In the operation of the original Community method, the smaller Member States, for example Belgium, were allocated a relatively higher share of the votes than the larger Member States. In an EU that consisted of fifteen Member States, Belgium, with a population of 10 million citizens, received five votes under the QMV formula applied prior to the 2004 Accession. By contrast Germany, with a population of 82 million, only received ten votes. This caused political tensions concerning the over-representation of smaller countries which led to a re-weighting of votes in the Treaty of Nice, the primary purpose of which was to rebalance the allocation of votes. Thus, since 1 November 2004 larger Member States such as Germany and the United Kingdom have been allocated twenty-nine votes and smaller

---

was no agreement on a framework allowing a progressive lifting of the export ban on British beef.

[25] See Matilla, M. and Lane, J. (2001) 'Why Unanimity in the Council?' at 31.

countries such as Belgium have received twelve votes.[26] The net effect of this change is that the larger Member States have almost tripled their votes. In relative terms, this has reduced the over-representation of the smaller Member States and arguably provides improved representation of the Member State in the Council. As a corollary, it can be said to offer some improvement to legislative legitimacy.

The Convention on the Future of Europe sought to simplify the process of QMV, especially in the light of the enlargement to twenty-eight Member States. What was proposed by the Convention and has been included in Article 238 (3) TFEU is a replacement for the Treaty of Nice provisions which seeks to bring a greater element of representation into the voting process. This seeks to anchor the decision-making with EU citizens by introducing an element of representation into voting by the Council. The aim of this is to provide a dual democratic legitimacy coming from both the political institutions that participate in the ordinary legislative process. The objective of democratising EU decision-making includes the creation of a governance framework in which the European Parliament and Council inject input legitimacy and representative democracy into the ordinary legislative process, and national parliaments through their domestic scrutiny activities and, in particular, subsidiarity monitoring, provide some form of output legitimacy. It is, however, questionable whether the arrangements in Article 238 (3) TFEU constitute a substantial improvement in representative democracy within the ordinary legislative process. First, the new arrangements are subject to lengthy transitional arrangements found in Protocol 36 which require that from the coming into force of the Treaty of Lisbon on 1 December 2010 to 31 October 2014 the Treaty of Nice allocation of votes in Council is used to determine a qualified majority in Council. In particular this means that a qualified majority requires 255 votes, which constitute 62 per cent of the population of the EU. Between 1 November 2014 and 31 March 2017 Article 238 (3) TFEU will apply unless under Protocol 36 (3) a Member State requests that the Treaty of Nice provisions are used to determine the qualified majority. Secondly, the provisions of Article 238 (3) require for a qualified majority at least 55 per cent of members of the Council, comprising at least 65 per cent of the EU's population. While this may appear, ostensibly, to be more representative, the presence of Protocol 36, albeit that its impact is time limited, illustrates that questions remain with regard to the precise parameters of what constitutes a decision which can be considered to be properly representative of

[26] See Protocol 36 Title II TFEU on Transitional Provisions.

EU citizens.[27] It can be conceded that the requirement within Article 238 (3) TFEU that 55 per cent of Council votes represents a minimum of 65 per cent of the EU's population strives to inject more representative principles into the EU's law-making process. In a process of supra-national decision-making it is difficult to see how such representation could be better achieved, but despite the efficiency and necessity arguments which justify the use of QMV in an EU of twenty-eight Member States, for national parliaments the problem of securing accountability of ministers remains unchanged from that which was first encountered post-Maastricht. That is, irrespective of how QMV operates in the Council, it reduces the capacity of the national parliament to exert effective control over a minister in circumstances where a qualified majority may approve a legislative proposal to which the national parliament is opposed. This applies equally to circumstances where the national parliament is scrutinising the individual minister or fulfilling the subsidiarity monitoring requirements of Protocol 2. In the case of Protocol 2, and as will be discussed in Chapter 6, the need for horizontal co-ordination amongst national parliaments has created a new dynamic which brings with it a new set of challenges to secure a significant degree of consensus amongst a considerable number of national parliaments within a short time frame. When these are examined in the context of QMV it is evident that there exists a procedural and substantive disjuncture between the process of subsidiarity monitoring and those decisions taken in the Council. In particular, subsidiarity monitoring is undertaken remotely from the political dialogue that exists between the EU institutions, and especially in the Conciliation Committee and the Trilogues.

4. THE CHALLENGE OF EFFECTIVE SCRUTINY

As already highlighted in this chapter, effective scrutiny of the ordinary legislative procedure is dependent upon a number of variables, not all of which are within the direct influence of national parliaments. The problems with the operation of QMV in the Council have already been identified, and especially how this reduces the capacity of national parliaments to exert influence over the minister. This problem can be alleviated, but the extent to which this occurs is dependent upon a number of factors, and most importantly this depends primarily upon the internal scrutiny mechanisms within the national parliaments. There is no

---

[27] See Best, E. and Settembri, P. (2008) 'Legislative Output after Enlargement' at 183.

doubt that the variable nature of scrutiny across the twenty-eight national parliaments will determine the extent to which national parliaments will review the operation of the ordinary legislative process, and for this reason parliaments have been historically classified as either 'strong' or 'weak' parliaments. Secondly, for national parliaments to engage in any form of scrutiny and for any purpose the timely provision of information is necessary to provide them with the raw materials for scrutiny. Thirdly, national parliaments must themselves take this task seriously and employ sufficient resources to review the operation of the ordinary legislative process, which in practice means that they must be prepared to use scrutiny reserves whenever necessary. The nature of the ordinary legislative process is that it is based upon securing a compromise and, as already seen, the use of Trilogues is fundamental to achieving this objective. The challenge for national parliaments is that the ordinary legislative process is an organic one which results in, often substantial, modifications to draft proposals during the legislative process itself. As already noted, national parliamentary scrutiny takes place at an early stage of the formal legislative cycle, and before first reading, but this is still towards the end of the decision-making process taken as a whole. Though national parliaments can react to legislative amendments, it is uncertain that sufficient time will be available on all occasions to review the proposed changes. Scrutiny by national parliaments is largely based upon assessments of the legislative proposal provided to EU committees by the government. For example, in the United Kingdom the responsibility lies with the Cabinet Office to issue detailed Guidance to Departments outlining how and when they should keep parliament informed of European proposals and the negotiations being held on them. By contrast, in France the information available to the parliament is much more extensive than that provided to the United Kingdom Parliament at corresponding points of the ordinary legislative procedure. For example, the *Sénat* is well informed on negotiations through 'receipt of diplomatic telegrams'.[28] In evidence provided to the EU Scrutiny Committee in the House of Lords Mr Léglise-Costa[29] clarified the position by stating that 'the reports of the Permanent Representation [to the Paris-based secretariat for European affairs] are transmitted' to the Parliament with very

[28] See HL 125 (Session 2008–9) *Codecision and National Parliamentary Scrutiny* at 90; and Jancic, D. (2013) 'The French Parliament' at 875.

[29] HL 125 (Session 2008–9) *Codecision and National Parliamentary Scrutiny* at 13. Mr Léglise-Costa, French Deputy Permanent Representative to the EU, was of the view that the content of the legislative proposal is broadly agreed in the Trilogue at which he stated that the 'real negotiation takes place'.

few exceptions.[30] In addition two members of staff from the French parliament are housed in the French Permanent Representation where they are able to access documents from the Council.[31] In circumstances where they consider that a Council document related to a proposal under the ordinary legislative procedure would be of interest to their parliamentary committees they are free to forward it to them. The key difference between the United Kingdom and French models is that, unlike the United Kingdom Parliament, its French counterpart is not dependent on the government for this information because it has moved upstream in the decision-making process to obtain the information directly from the source. This highlights one of the long-standing problems with securing effective scrutiny, which the Barosso Initiative recognises; namely the reliance upon national governments to provide information to parliaments, which if slow or vague will hamper effective scrutiny.[32]

4.1 The Barosso Initiative for Transmission of Documents to National Parliaments

Protocol 1 is an important development because it provides legally binding guarantees. However, national parliaments have, at least in practice, benefited more directly from the launch of the informal 2006 Barosso Initiative for direct dialogue with national parliaments. This Initiative, under which certain documents are sent directly to national parliaments, is, symbolically if not substantially, more important than the Treaty changes. Under the Initiative parliaments are invited to respond to proposals through the use of collective reasoned opinions which necessitate horizontal co-operation and dialogue. The Barosso Initiative can be considered as an institutional response to the failure to ratify the Constitutional Treaty whose provisions for national parliaments had been held up as a paradigm for improved accountability.[33] Under the Initiative the Commission committed itself to a more efficient provision of a wider set of documents than provided for in the Amsterdam Protocol and which de facto superseded the obligations under the Amsterdam Protocol. This

---

[30] Ibid.

[31] Ibid.

[32] Ibid. at 21, where the Committee criticised the government for being slow with the provision of documentation on several occasions which impacted upon the scrutiny process.

[33] See Barrett, G. (2008) '"The King is Dead, Long Live the King"' at 66, who notes that moving upstream within the legislative process is more likely under the Treaty of Lisbon.

included the transmission of all legislative proposals and consultation papers directly to national parliaments. This can be considered as a politically astute commitment on the part of Barosso because it gave national parliaments as much as, if not more than, what the Constitutional Treaty would have delivered through a Protocol and suggests a spirit of co-operation between the Commission and national parliaments.[34]

The Initiative also reduces the dependency of national parliaments on governments and simultaneously sends out a political signal that Treaty reform is not motivated by centralisation or competence grab. National parliaments have reacted positively to the Barosso Initiative. In many respects this is an uncontroversial response, as they have nothing to lose from the Initiative and have gained the opportunity to receive more documentation and at an earlier stage of the policy and decision-making cycles. In the annual report for 2011 on dialogue between the European Commission and national parliaments[35] the Commission noted that the total number of opinions received from national parliaments in 2011, including reasoned opinions under the subsidiarity control mechanism, reached a total of 622. This figure represents an increase of some 60 per cent compared with the number of reasoned opinions which were submitted in 2010,[36] which had already seen a 55 per cent increase over 2009.[37] This upward trend demonstrates an exponential increase into 2012/13 with more than 500 opinions received by December 2012.[38] The great majority of the 622 opinions received in 2011 contained substantive comments and questions with regard to the specific content of Commission proposals and initiatives which were not formally classified as 'reasoned opinions' within the meaning of Protocol 2. As has been the case since 2009, only a comparatively small number, amounting to a total of sixty-four opinions delivered, were formally designated to be reasoned opinions within the meaning of Protocol 2 and notifying a breach of the

---

[34] See Jancic, D. (2012) 'The Barosso Initiative' at 80–81.

[35] COM (2012) 375 final 10.7.2012, *Annual Report 2011 on Relations Between the European Commission and National Parliaments.*

[36] This was a total of 387 opinions. See COM (2011) 344 final 10.7.2012, *Annual Report 2010 on Relations Between the European Commission and National Parliaments.*

[37] This was a total of 250 opinions. See COM (2009) 343 final 7.7.2009, *Annual Report 2008 on Relations Between the European Commission and National Parliaments* at 4, paragraph 2.1.

[38] The information was obtained from the Interparliamentary Exchange (IPEX) website at http://ipex.eu, accessed 5 January 2013.

principle of subsidiarity.[39] But, as will be discussed in more detail in Chapter 6, these reasoned opinions included, for the first time since the Treaty of Lisbon came into force, sufficient reasoned opinions[40] on a legislative proposal to trigger the early 'yellow card' in relation to the draft Regulation on the Right to take Collective Action.[41] Finally, the number of reasoned opinions that have been submitted since 2009 could itself be small by virtue of technical mistakes made by national parliaments.

This is because there may be a lack of understanding with regard to what actually constitutes a reasoned opinion and what format it must take. It would appear that the Commission is looking for an explicit statement that a reasoned opinion is being issued by a parliamentary chamber. It is therefore not inconceivable that the number since 2010 may have been higher but for the failure by parliamentary chambers to use the correct nomenclature when communicating with the Commission. The political message from the Barosso Initiative is that the Commission wants to co-operate with national parliaments to improve democratic oversight and consequently output legitimacy through the use of established parliamentary procedures. The Treaty of Lisbon has formalised the practice of direct transmission of more documents, but the Initiative indicates more than just the one-way transmission of information and documentation; it envisages a *dialogue* between national parliaments and the Commission. An active vertical dialogue between the Commission and national parliaments may also facilitate co-operation and dialogue between national parliaments which may have some impact which 'Europeanises' their activities.[42] This horizontal dialogue is particularly important if the early warning mechanism in Protocol 2 is to function.[43] The early warning mechanism necessitates a vibrant horizontal dialogue through which national parliaments can establish a synchronised common interpretation of subsidiarity. Through interaction with the Commission, national parliaments will also engage in this horizontal dialogue, in

---

[39] See COM (2009) 343 final 7.7.2009, *Annual Report 2008 on Relations Between the European Commission and National Parliaments* at 4.

[40] The threshold was reached on 12 May 2012.

[41] See COM (2012) 130 final *Proposal for a Regulation on the Exercise of the Right to take Collective Action.*

[42] See the discussion in Kassim, H. (2005) 'The Europeanisation of Member State Institutions' at 297–303.

[43] Though Jancic does indicate that there may be scope for some competition between the Barosso Initiative and Protocol 2. See Jancic (2012) 'The Barosso Initiative' at 82–83.

addition to moving 'upstream', and benefit from obtaining documents directly from source. This move upstream may also facilitate a preliminary analysis of subsidiarity which national parliaments could use as a basis for future collective action via the early warning mechanism. However, national parliaments also require clear interpretative information from their own governments to determine the subsidiarity implications and make judgments concerning the necessity for or efficiency of EU legislative action. Accordingly, national parliaments will still require a detailed and timely Explanatory Memorandum from their own government to conduct their scrutiny. In this sense the documentation provided under the Barosso Initiative is only one part of a much larger information matrix that is necessary for effective and meaningful scrutiny.

4.2 Monitoring Changes to Legislative Proposals

Though the Barosso Initiative improves the transmission of documentation the Initiative is limited to *original* policy proposals and does not encompass the detailed changes which may occur during the legislative process. These arise from the legislative process and are based upon the amendments proposed by the European Parliament. National parliaments still need to have the government's position on the revised legislative proposal which may differ significantly or substantially from this and, as the example of the United Kingdom Parliament illustrates, constitutes the weak link in the scrutiny chain.[44] The other problem that exists is how to define when amendments should be deemed 'significant' or a difference 'substantial'. Connected to this is the question of how many updates on changes should be received. It is clear that a text may be reissued a very large number of times during negotiations and that the majority of these versions of a text would not necessarily be of use during a national parliament's scrutiny procedure. This inevitably creates a tension and it is not normally possible to say that a particular document matters and that another one does not and to be able to determine that objectively and in advance. The most objective criterion to determine whether additional information should be provided by a government to national parliaments should be by reference to whether the policy implications of the proposal

[44] See Kerse, C. (2007) 'Parliamentary Scrutiny in the United Kingdom Parliament and the Changing Role of National Parliaments in European Union Affairs' at 349.

had changed. But, independently, this is not sufficient because a government's decision that further information should be provided to parliamentary committees must also be accompanied by immediate action on the part of the government to deliver an accompanying Explanatory Memorandum.

The Guidance provided by the United Kingdom government on how to keep Parliament updated in the course of the ordinary legislative procedure states that it is made clear to 'Departments that it is their responsibility to consider carefully and proactively at every stage when an update to Parliament is needed'.[45] This obligation upon the government illustrates that scrutiny of EU affairs is no longer limited to a specific committee which considers the documentation in advance of the Council meeting. On the contrary, it recognises that EU legislation is dynamic and that it is likely to have a horizontal impact across a number of departments. For parliaments such as those in the United Kingdom and Germany, the ordinary legislative procedure has no doubt had an impact upon their modus operandi and has necessitated a move away from a purely document-based approach towards a significance-based approach; that is, that governments will need to inform and update Parliament that a particular piece of information/decision will be significant in the negotiations which necessitates that Parliament is updated.[46] However, it remains questionable whether such procedures can consistently provide the guarantees that national parliaments will require, either in terms of the information that is provided or with regard to the time available to review and comment upon the revised proposal. Finally, it is highly questionable what impact national parliaments can have at the stage of the Trilogue or Conciliation Committee when the legislation is to all intents and purposes a 'done deal'. Moreover, QMV is likely to make it difficult to raise any objections to the revised legislation. It is beyond question that informal Trilogues, while helpful to expeditious agreement of legislation, make effective scrutiny of the ordinary legislative procedure by national parliaments very difficult. There are two reasons for this. First, their informal and confidential nature is not transparent and as a result it is difficult for all national parliaments, irrespective of their scrutiny arrangements, to follow the course of negotiations and comment usefully to their government. Secondly, the Council is represented only by the Presidency, which tends to hold its cards close to its chest. As a

---

[45] See Cabinet Office (2009) *Parliamentary Scrutiny of EU Documents: Guidance for Department*, Cabinet Office, 20 April at paragraph 1.4.

[46] See generally, Cygan, A. (2001) *National Parliaments in an Integrated Europe*.

result it may be difficult for all governments other than the Presidency to follow the course of negotiations and to represent the views of their national parliament at the appropriate point. The increased use of informal Trilogues, to the point that they are now the primary form of negotiation between the European Parliament and the Council, has magnified the difficulties faced by national parliaments within the ordinary legislative procedure. As a result it is important that the system under which the governments keep national parliaments updated on negotiations is effective and operated uniformly and rigorously across the Member States. This is essential if the process of scrutiny, and especially that of subsidiarity monitoring, is to be meaningful. In particular, it is necessary if national parliaments are to raise subsidiarity objections following the conclusion of a Trilogue. However, such a co-ordinated response is unlikely because, despite the Treaty of Lisbon and emphasis upon national parliaments, those parliaments previously considered 'weak' actors in scrutiny will remain weak. Nothing in the Treaty of Lisbon changes the operation of internal scrutiny arrangements. Paradoxically, the Treaty of Lisbon has, notwithstanding its new provisions for national parliaments, exacerbated the difficulties faced by all national parliaments through the expansion of the ordinary legislative procedure into new areas of competence, most notably agriculture, fisheries, and justice and home affairs. In practice this means that even more legislation is now decided through the use of opaque, informal and confidential Trilogue meetings and brings into sharp focus the criticism that national parliaments remain peripheral actors in the EU legislative process.

5. CONCLUDING REMARKS

The ordinary legislative procedure is the practical embodiment of the loss of legislative competence that has accompanied EU integration. Though national parliaments have long engaged in scrutiny of this legislative procedure, their modus operandi has been heterogeneous and their influence has tended to be limited to the national minister only. Even this influence could be considered as broadly ineffective because it had no direct bearing on the legislative process. The growth in the use of QMV within the ordinary legislative procedure has significantly restricted the opportunities for national parliaments to secure ministerial responsibility because there is a strong likelihood that a minister will be outvoted. Moreover, notwithstanding the developments in the Treaty of Lisbon the discrepancy between strong and weak national parliaments remains because the Treaty has not harmonised national parliamentary scrutiny procedures. To this extent the Treaty of Lisbon has failed to deliver a coherent horizontal bloc of national parliaments which are simultaneously and to the same extent engaged in the scrutiny of EU legislative proposals. The main development for national parliaments in the legislative process is the task of subsidiarity monitoring. While monitoring subsidiarity is itself not a new concept the provisions of Protocols 1 and 2 are – and they do offer new opportunities for national parliaments. The main development with regard to subsidiarity monitoring, and perhaps the oversight of EU affairs more generally by national parliaments, is that Protocols 1 and 2 indicate that national parliaments function as some form of collective grouping by virtue of the fact that they all engage in subsidiarity monitoring at the same time using broadly the same documentation. In Chapters 5 and 6 the operation of Protocols 1 and 2 is considered in more detail, and whether through the process of subsidiarity monitoring national parliaments are, collectively, able to provide improved accountability and legitimacy to the EU legislative process.

5. Subsidiarity as a regulatory principle in EU law

1. INTRODUCTION

In the context of EU integration the principle of subsidiarity has, since its inception, been caught in a dilemma. On the one hand it has been held up as a crucial regulatory principle of multi-level governance which is used to determine the appropriate level at which legislative action should be taken.[1] On the other hand, the evidence indicates that the application of the principle at EU level has been generally inconsistent and political institutions within the EU which pursue deeper integration have usually been able to ensure that regulatory action is taken at the EU level.[2] This problem has proved difficult to resolve because of its relevance to the exercise of the competences allocated to the EU, and specifically when the EU shares competence with the Member States. In such circumstances, the Commission has, in the overwhelming majority of circumstances, been able to demonstrate an Internal Market imperative which justifies EU action. Part of the difficulty with subsidiarity operating as a regulatory principle is that it does not have a normative definition and, depending upon the context, the principle of subsidiarity may be seen as a purely political maxim or as a binding rule of law.[3] Either way, subsidiarity as expressed in Article 5 TEU is a vague formulation which is open to various interpretations across the Member States. For example, the application of the subsidiarity principle in Germany has caused

---

[1] See for example the Commission's explanation of this principle in COM (2012) 373 final *Report from the Commission on Subsidiarity and Proportionality* at paragraph 2.1.

[2] See further Chapters 2 and 6 on how the Commission has in particular interpreted the 'necessity for legislative EU action'.

[3] See Craig, P. (2012) 'Subsidiarity' at 72; Horsley, T. (2011) 'Subsidiarity and the European Court of Justice' at 1; Davies, G. (2006) 'Subsidiarity' at 63; Estella, A. (2002) *The EU Principle of Subsidiarity and its Critique*. Estella argues that, given the close nature of co-operation within the Internal Market, EU intervention will always be necessary, at 113–114.

internal constitutional difficulties which have not been witnessed in other Member States, where by contrast the discussion has tended to focus on the more direct questions of whether the EU should act. The original socio-philosophical principle of subsidiarity provided that tasks which a smaller unit can carry through should not be taken on by a bigger unit, unless the small unit depends on support ('subsidium') in certain areas. The principle of subsidiarity was influenced greatly by the social encyclical by Pope Pius XI, who noted that 'any community action' would be 'inherently subsidiary'.[4] Transferred to the State level, the principle of subsidiarity is formative for the federal systems of the Federal Republic of Germany and the Swiss Confederation, where it acts as a regulatory principle which guarantees the exercise of constitutional competences by federal States. At the European level, subsidiarity was anchored in primary law as a general principle by the Treaty of Maastricht 1992. The primary reason for this inclusion was to offer a regulatory buffer against the strengthening of the European legislator through the ongoing transfer of national competences. In this respect, the principle of subsidiarity exerts on the one hand a protective and defensive function for smaller units – the national, regional and local levels – and on the other hand it serves a legitimising function for an act of the larger unit – the EU. Through the Treaty of Lisbon, national parliaments have acquired a new role through which they seek to exert control over the legislative procedure by monitoring the principle of subsidiarity under Protocol 2 on the Application of the Principles of Subsidiarity and Proportionality. If the protective and defensive function of the principle is kept in mind, this new power is a logical development within a multi-level governance framework, because it is national parliaments who are most directly affected through the transfer of competences and as such they should have some opportunity to seek to influence the exercise of these competences. The operation of Protocol 2 as a mechanism through which subsidiarity is monitored by national parliaments is considered in detail in Chapter 6. This chapter focusses on the application of subsidiarity as a regulatory principle within decision-making and especially what kind of regulatory criteria should be used to determine whether integrative measures are to be taken at the EU level.

---

[4] Quadrogesimo Anno, Papst Pius XI (1931), point 79; see Marx, R. and Wulsdorf, H. (2002) *Translation of Quadrogesimo Anno, Papst Pius XI. (1931)* at 125.

2. FROM MAASTRICHT TO LISBON: SUBSIDIARITY IN THE TREATIES

Although the principle of subsidiarity had been mentioned in the Single European Act in the context of environmental legislation,[5] Article 3 (b) of the Treaty of Maastricht set out a general principle of subsidiarity with regard to EU competence vis-à-vis the Member States.[6] The current version of the principle of subsidiarity, contained within Article 5 TEU, regulates the exercise of concurrent competences. The principle of subsidiarity does not therefore apply in circumstances where the Treaty has granted the EU exclusive competence or where there is no EU competence. Through the inclusion of the subsidiarity principle in the Treaty of Maastricht the Member States underlined the need to ensure that decisions are made as closely as possible to the citizen, mainly for reasons of legitimacy, and that constant checks are made as to whether EU action is justified in the light of the possibilities for successful action at the national, regional or local level. The subsidiarity principle was put forward by the federal Member States, such as Germany and Belgium, whose regional entities refused to see rationalised competences move to the European level.[7] The subsidiarity principle was also espoused, but for very different reasons, by the United Kingdom government, which in keeping with its resistance to the deeper integration proposed by the Treaty of Maastricht, considered subsidiarity as means by which to restrict the scope of EU action, especially legislative harmonisation of social, consumer and environmental protection. For the then Conservative United Kingdom government, the approximation of laws within these policy areas constituted a move towards a 'European Superstate' that

---

[5] At the time, Article 130 (4) EC stated that 'the Community shall take action relating to the environment to the extent to which the objectives ... can be better attained at the Community level than at the level of the Member States'. It can be suggested that implicit within Article 130 (4) EC was the principle of proportionality of Community action.

[6] The term 'subsidiarity' would appear to have been introduced into EU parlance in the European Parliament's Draft Treaty on European Union in 1984. It has also become familiar in the context of the 1989 Social Charter. In its Action Programme relating to the Community Charter of Basic Social Rights for Workers (COM (1989) 568 final) the Commission, at paragraph 3 of the General Introduction, refers to subsidiarity, in the context of recognising that the regulation of social rights is a matter that 'lies with the Member States'.

[7] See Hrbek, R. (2003) 'The Role of the Regions in the EU and the Principle of Subsidiarity' at 59; Kokott, J. (1999) 'Federal States in Federal Europe' at 175.

would impact upon the United Kingdom's economic competitiveness.[8] The principle of subsidiarity as found within the Treaty of Maastricht created legally binding quasi-contractual obligations for the EU institutions to determine whether there was a justification for EU action. However, as already noted the principle of subsidiarity was vague and the precise scope of its application was unclear. To this end the Edinburgh European Council laid down comprehensive guidelines to clarify the application of the subsidiarity principle as well as the obligations to be placed upon the EU institutions.[9] Shortly after the Edinburgh Council, an inter-institutional agreement between the Council, the European Commission and European Parliament was signed, in which the Commission was committed to provide each of its submitted proposals with a justification concerning the principle of subsidiarity, and to create a yearly report about the observance of the subsidiarity principle.[10]

2.1 The Edinburgh Guidelines on the Application of Subsidiarity

The Edinburgh Council of December 1992 set itself the objective of clarifying how subsidiarity would operate in the EU legislative process.[11] Prior to the Edinburgh Council the Commission's Communication to the Council and the European Parliament made the following observations:[12]

---

[8] See United Kingdom, 'Growth, Competitiveness and Employment in the European Community', in Commission of the European Communities (1993) *Growth, Competitiveness, Employment*, Part C, 271. Post-Lisbon, it is important to note the operation of Articles 5 and 6 TFEU where the EU can exercise complementary competences to support Member States. Because the exercise of complementary competences is outside the scope of the ordinary legislative procedure, the provisions of Protocol 2 will not apply.

[9] See European Council Conclusions of Edinburgh, 12 December 1992, Part A, Annex 1, at 7.

[10] Inter-institutional Agreement on the Method of Application of the Principle of Subsidiarity in Article 5 EC, paragraph 2.

[11] The Edinburgh Council also addressed the question of the Danish electorate's rejection of the Maastricht Treaty in the 1992 referendum. One factor identified for this refusal was the view of the Danish people that European law was too intrusive. The Danes were also sceptical about economic and monetary union. By attempting to try and formulate a clear definition of the practice and procedure of subsidiarity, the Edinburgh Council was attempting to address some of the objections the Danes had towards the Maastricht Treaty and allow them to ratify the Treaty in a second referendum, which they did in 1993.

[12] SEC (92) 1990 final, 27 October 1992 (emphasis added).

> So that the Community can attain its objectives, certain obligations to act have been imposed upon it. These include, in particular, the creation of an area without internal frontiers, the strengthening of economic and social cohesion, and the establishment of economic and monetary union. (a) At the present stage in the Community's development, it is impossible, legally speaking, to determine whether all these objections to act entail exclusive powers for the Community and in particular whether they deprive Member States of the right to act.
>
> Historically, the concept of exclusive competence originally grew out of the obligation to establish the 'common market' which was spelled out in very firmly binding terms, including the fixing of a deadline under the Single European Act. In this sense it is possible to speak of a genuine obligation to act leading, in the course of time and through the rulings of the Court of Justice, *to the formation of a block of exclusive powers centred around the four fundamental freedoms and certain common policies essential to, or a corollary of, the establishment of an internal market.* What is involved here is:
>
> - the removal of barriers to the free movement of goods, persons, services and capital
> - the common commercial policy
> - the general rules on competition
> - the common organisation of agricultural markets
> - the conservation of fishing resources
> - the essential elements of transport policy
>
> (b) The demarcation lines of this block of exclusive powers will have to change as European integration progresses. They cannot remain frozen. For one thing the Maastricht Treaty provides for a single monetary and exchange rate policy which should ultimately lead to exclusive Community competence in the final stage of EMU. Furthermore, it is clearly not easy to draw a line between implementing the four freedoms and what some people refer to as the smooth operation of the single market. The dynamics of the four freedoms generate an impetus towards flanking policies which in turn call for the introduction of genuine policies (environment and cohesion for example) albeit ones that do not at present involve Community competence – that is the possibility of depriving Member States of the power to act.

The Commission's justification is based upon the presumption that, as European integration proceeds, this will inevitably lead to an exponential increase in EU legislative competence. Arguably, this interpretation suggests that the Commission only views subsidiarity as a principle that is primarily relevant during the integration process when the transition of competence from the Member States to the EU takes place. Some Member States will initially at least seek to maintain closer control over policies such as taxation and the environment,[13] but ultimately integration will create central control over these and other policies. Thus, far from being a principle that guarantees decision-making at the lowest level in the EU, from the Commission's submission it appears that, from the outset, the inclusion of subsidiarity in the Treaty is to make it politically acceptable for Member States to accept the gradual loss of competence within many important policy areas. It is this progressive transfer of competence to the EU, together with the accusation that this had occurred without appropriate mechanisms for democratic parliamentary control, that was the central issue in judicial challenges to the Treaty of Maastricht brought in the United Kingdom[14] and Germany.[15] For the Edinburgh European Council the aim was to exploit subsidiarity as a mechanism that created a balance between the exercise of EU and Member State competences. To achieve this, the Edinburgh Summit had to establish a clear and concise definition of subsidiarity that would meet the objective of European integration, but which simultaneously recognised the enduring legitimacy of national parliaments. Additionally, the practice of applying the subsidiarity principle within the legislative process would need to address the scepticism of electorates across the Member States where the Treaty of Maastricht was not greeted with overwhelming enthusiasm.[16] The Edinburgh Council concluded the following on the application of the subsidiarity principle which post-Lisbon still forms the basic criterion under which EU legislative action is justified by the Commission through the preparation of pre-legislative Impact Assessments:[17]

> For Community action to be justified, the Council must be satisfied that both aspects of the subsidiarity criterion are met: the objectives of the proposed action cannot be sufficiently achieved by Member States' action and they can therefore be better achieved by action on the part of the Community. The following guidelines should be used in examining whether the above mentioned condition is fulfilled:

---

[13] Post-Amsterdam, Article 6 EC required that environmental protection be added to the objectives of the common market contained in Articles 2 and 3 EC.

[14] *R* v *Secretary of State for Foreign and Commonwealth Affairs ex parte Rees Mogg* [1994] QB 552.

[15] *Brunner* v *Maastricht Treaty* [1994] CMLR 57.

[16] This can be seen by the Danish 'no' vote in the referendum held on 2 June 1992 in which 50.7 per cent of voters rejected the Treaty and the slender majority in the French referendum held on 20 September 1992 in which 51 per cent of voters approved the Treaty.

[17] EC Bulletin 12-1992, at 14.

- the issue under consideration has transnational aspects which cannot be satisfactorily regulated by action by the Member States; and/or
- actions by Member States alone or lack of Community action would conflict with the requirements of the Treaty (such as the need to correct distortion of competition or avoid disguised restrictions on trade or strengthen economic and social cohesion) or would otherwise significantly damage Member States' interest; and/or
- the Council must be satisfied that action at Community level would produce clear benefits by reason of its scale or its effects compared with action at the level of the Member States.
- The reasons for concluding that a Community objective cannot be sufficiently achieved by the Community must be substantiated by qualitative or, whenever possible, quantitative indicators.

This 'clarification' of subsidiarity within the Edinburgh Guidelines covers three distinct legal concepts and can be said to have its roots in the Treaties and case law of the Court.[18] First, the Edinburgh Guidelines confirm the principle of conferral that the EU shall act within the limits of the competences conferred upon it by the Member States in the Treaties. To this end, competences not conferred by the Treaties remain with the Member States and the EU can only act when it has been given the explicit power to do so. This implies, at the very least, that national powers are the norm and that the exercise of EU competence is the exception. However, post-Lisbon this issue must be considered within the context of complementary competences found within Articles 5 and 6 TFEU and that these may further restrict the legislative competences of national parliaments. Secondly, the Guidelines lay out a very strict interpretation of subsidiarity which requires that a clear benefit is derived from EU action and that this legislative action is necessary. This must be objectively justified and today this would take place within the Impact Assessment. Finally, EU legislative action must be proportionate and not go beyond what is necessary to achieve the objective. Thus Member States should retain some element of 'control' with regard to administrative implementation. It is a moot point whether the Edinburgh Guidelines could be realistically expected to act as an effective regulatory buffer against unnecessary or excessive EU legislative action. Moreover, such a response would be against both the spirit and aims of the Treaty of Maastricht which placed deeper integration at the core of the Treaty. However, the Danish 'no' vote in its referendum and the narrow French 'yes', together with the observations made by the Federal Constitutional

[18] Edinburgh European Council 'Presidency Conclusions', 11–12 December 1992, paragraphs 4 and 15.

Court (FCC) in *Brunner*, all provide evidence that deeper integration created a degree of unease within the Member States. As the FCC pointed out in *Brunner* and again in the *Lisbon Treaty judgment*, such integration would only be considered democratic and acceptable within the norms of the German Constitution if it occurred with the explicit consent of national parliaments. In particular, this requires improved monitoring of EU integration and the legislative process by national parliaments.

2.2 The Amsterdam Protocol on the Application of Subsidiarity and Proportionality

The contents of the Edinburgh Council Conclusions and the Inter-Institutional Agreement manifested themselves in the accompanying Protocol of the Treaty of Amsterdam on the Application of the Principles of Subsidiarity and Proportionality. The Guidelines for the application of subsidiarity by the EU institutions involved in the legislative process, which were laid down for the first time in the Council's Conclusions, were as a consequence of their inclusion in a Protocol codified in the primary law, which made the application of the subsidiarity principle and its supervision by national parliaments justiciable before the Court.

To protect national parliaments against the further erosion of their legislative powers the Treaty of Amsterdam containing the Protocol formalised the position of national parliaments within the EU polity. However, this Protocol, though legally binding, only offered limited assistance to national parliaments by making limited improvements to the conduct of their internal scrutiny procedures through improved transmission of documents and a minimum time in which national parliamentary scrutiny was to be completed. However, none of this amounted to direct influence over the EU legislative process. The primary achievement of the Protocol was to include formally the Edinburgh Guidelines on subsidiarity. The Amsterdam Protocol stated:

> 3. The principle of subsidiarity does not call into question the powers conferred on the European Community by the Treaty, as interpreted by the Court of Justice. The criteria referred to in the second paragraph of Article 5 EC of the Treaty shall relate to areas for which the Community does not have exclusive competence. The principle of subsidiarity provides a guide as to how those powers are to be exercised at the Community level. *Subsidiarity is a dynamic concept set out in the Treaty. It allows Community action within*

the limits of its powers to be expanded where circumstances so require, and conversely, to be restricted or discounted where it is no longer justified.[19]

By defining subsidiarity as a 'dynamic concept' the Amsterdam Protocol illustrates the conflict that continues to exist post-Lisbon with regard to the exercise of EU competences and is addressing the very point of what constitutes the outer reaches of justified EU legislative action. The expansion of EU powers 'where circumstances so require' indicates that policy areas which complement the core objectives of the Internal Market may become part of the EU regulatory framework. As seen in Chapter 2, this has included policy areas such as the environment and social policy where the absence of clear legal bases has not hindered EU legislative action. In the main, this expansion of EU competences into such policy areas has arisen because the Commission has dismissed arguments of subsidiarity and justified EU legislative action on grounds of necessity and the benefits of the scale of effects of EU action which have as the primary objective the improved functioning of the Internal Market. To this extent, it may be argued that the Amsterdam Protocol failed to operate as a mechanism through which EU action could be effectively benchmarked against subsidiarity by national parliaments, primarily because, though alluding to this function, the Protocol made no explicit reference to this task being undertaken by national parliaments, nor did it include any procedural mechanisms by which national parliaments could challenge, whether politically or judicially, the Commission's conclusion that a legislative proposal was subsidiarity compliant.

2.3 Subsidiarity in the Treaty of Lisbon: Article 5 TEU

The Convention entrusted with the development of a draft European Constitution dealt, in Working Group I, specifically with the subject of subsidiarity, in which an effective control of the principle of subsidiarity was the main issue under consideration. In the course of these deliberations, a new Protocol was drawn up, giving national parliaments rights of control, both preventive through the use of reasoned opinions, as well as *ex post* through the possibility of legal action before the European Court of Justice (ECJ). The content of the Treaty of Lisbon reflects, except for a few deviations, the formulations of the draft Constitutional Treaty which are relevant for the monitoring of subsidiarity. Under Article 5 (3) TEU, in policy areas which do not come within the scope of the exclusive EU competence, the Union shall act only if and 'insofar as

---

[19] Emphasis added.

the objectives of the proposed action cannot be achieved by the Member States ... but can rather by reason of scale or effects of the proposed action be better achieved at the EU level'.

This may, prima facie, suggest a presumption against EU action, but, since its inclusion in the Treaty of Maastricht, the precise meaning of subsidiarity for national parliaments has been subject to much debate.[20] In the United Kingdom, for example, reports produced by the EU affairs committees of both Houses of Parliament have consistently stated that subsidiarity starts with the premise that, in circumstances of concurrent competences, laws should be made domestically and EU action taken only when necessary and objectively justified.[21] The United Kingdom Parliament has therefore taken a very literal interpretation of Article 5 TEU, as illustrated by the arguments put forward by the United Kingdom in the *Working Time Directive* case.[22] By contrast, for Germany, subsidiarity is viewed as a constitutional device to guarantee democracy within the EU by defining the relationship between EU institutions and Member States, and in particular their national parliaments.[23] Moreover, at the level of the German *Länder* it is considered a principle through which they will ensure that competences granted under the German Constitution are not expropriated by the EU. In both the *Lisbon Treaty* and *Brunner* judgments, the FCC stated that democracy and accountability must be central to further EU integration, and in particular democracy as understood within the German constitutional model.

The role of the *Bundestag* and *Bundesrat*, according to the FCC in the *Lisbon Treaty* and *Brunner* judgments, is to participate in the decision-making process to ensure that fundamental rights protected by the German Constitution are upheld, and furthermore that the electorate is represented nationally and locally in the decision-making process. In effect, for Germany subsidiarity is a mechanism by which the EU may be held accountable domestically, whereas for the United Kingdom it is a

---

[20] See Cooper, I. (2006) 'The Watchdogs of Subsidiarity' at 281; Weatherill, S. (2005) 'Better Competence Monitoring' at 23; Gonzalez, J.P. (1995) 'The Principle of Subsidiarity' at 355; Estella, A. (2002) *The EU Principle of Subsidiarity and its Critique*; Davies, G. (2006) 'Subsidiarity' at 67–69.

[21] See for example HC 152 xxxiii-I (2001–2) *Democracy and Accountability in the EU and the Role of National Parliaments*. For an overview of how national parliaments view the application of the subsidiarity principle see Wyrzykowski, M. et al. (2010) 'General Report: The Role of National Parliaments in the European Union' Vol. 1.

[22] Case C-84/94 *United Kingdom* v *Council* [1996] ECR I-5755.

[23] See Judgment of 20 June 2009 *Bundesverfassungsgerich*t, BVerfG, 2 BvE 2/08 at paragraph 240.

device that seeks to retain legislative autonomy unless absolutely necessary to achieve a specific EU objective. This dichotomy of aims explains, at least in part, why there are limits to the operation of the early warning mechanism under Protocol 2. The ECJ has generally favoured a restricted interpretation which has been shared by the Commission and in whose view Article 5 TEU raises a presumption that the measure must satisfy a dual requirement of necessity and effectiveness for EU action to be justified.[24] It may be argued that this dual requirement is unnecessary[25] and that a justification for EU action could be determined by reference to a single question;[26] namely, 'can the objectives of the proposed action *only* be achieved by [EU-] wide action?' If the answer to this question is 'no', then action should be taken at the national level. On this interpretation the objective of subsidiarity monitoring should be to distinguish between those EU measures which *will* produce an EU-wide outcome and those which *must* produce an EU-wide outcome.[27] This distinction is very important for national parliaments because the single requirement determines a very specific task – that is, did the EU need to act to attain the objective? – and does not immediately require national parliaments to consider the related question of proportionality within Article 5 TEU, though it is often very difficult to separate the merits of EU action from the substance. Proportionality necessitates consideration of the scope and content of the proposal, which addresses the question of input legitimacy. By contrast, if subsidiarity monitoring should be concerned with promoting legislative competence, then this very narrow task of determining where legislative action should be taken need not necessarily be blurred or delayed by examining the effectiveness of the legislative proposal.[28] The focus of the interpretation outlined above is arguably more in tune with the allocation of input and output legitimacy post-Lisbon. Once national parliaments have employed Protocol 2 and concluded that EU legislative action is unnecessary, consideration of the effectiveness of any

---

[24] See COM (2008) 586 final *The Report of the European Commission on Subsidiarity and Proportionality 2007* at 2.

[25] See for example Wyatt, D. (2006) 'Could a Yellow Card for National Parliaments Strengthen Judicial as well as Political Policing of Subsidiarity?' at 5.

[26] Ibid. at 6. See also the written evidence of Professor Wyatt to the House of Lords Select Committee on the European Union. HL 101 (Session 2004–5) *Strengthening National Parliamentary Scrutiny of the EU* at 4–5.

[27] Ibid.

[28] See Chapter 6, where the findings of pilot Subsidiarity Monitoring Projects are discussed which suggest that national parliaments are regularly committing time to considering proportionality as well as subsidiarity.

legislation is unnecessary. Furthermore, even if national parliaments conclude that EU-wide action is required, this, at the very least, implies that the EU measure should only go as far as necessary to achieve the objective, questioning the need to formally consider proportionality.[29] But the problem that exists is that national parliaments do not necessarily begin their analysis of subsidiarity compliance from the same political perspective, even though the Commission's Impact Assessment is intended to provide such a definition. This is borne out by the fact that since its operation, the early warning mechanism under Protocol 2 has led to only one yellow card being raised.[30] The inclusion of the early warning mechanism in Protocol 2 is, no doubt, a radical procedural development for national parliaments through which they seek to ensure subsidiarity compliance.

As Chapter 6 explains, the purpose of Protocol 2 is to provide national parliaments with a pre-legislative constitutional intervention device, and if parliaments or chambers collectively reach the necessary threshold then the institution that introduced the proposal must, at the very least, review it. The early warning mechanism includes two different options – the 'yellow' and 'orange' card procedures – which provide for different thresholds to be attained before they may be applied, depending upon the legislative proposal. The objective of the early warning mechanism is to arrive at an assessment of whether a legislative proposal complies with the principle of subsidiarity following a review not just of the legislative proposal but also of the Commission's Impact Assessment. However, as will be seen in Chapter 6, the primary weakness with Protocol 2 is that it seeks to arrive at what can be defined as a 'collective' parliamentary response on the question of compliance of the legislative proposal with the principle of subsidiarity. However, this collective response is constituted by individual reasoned opinions that are the result of the individual scrutiny activities of national parliaments. On this interpretation Protocol 2 does not create a formal horizontal collective, nor does it amount to parliamentarisation, but rather it provides a framework through which national parliaments using their own scrutiny arrangements individually

---

[29] Under the Protocol the Commission is required to provide, inter alia, a financial and regulatory Impact Assessment of the proposed legislation. This more onerous assessment should benefit national parliaments by providing comprehensive and uniform documentation which enables the individual scrutiny committees to arrive at an informed and ideally consensual conclusion of whether the proposal complies with the principle of subsidiarity.

[30] See further the discussion in Chapter 6.

arrive at what *may* (whether by coincidence or design) subsequently be defined as a 'collective' decision on the question of subsidiarity.

3. APPLICATION OF THE SUBSIDIARITY PRINCIPLE

As a regulatory principle which determines the exercise of competence, the subsidiarity principle relates to the overall activities of the EU and, besides the law in the strict sense, it applies to implementation measures and the development of EU policies. The application of the subsidiarity principle consists of three steps:

- Responsibility criterion: Does the EU rely on a non-exclusive jurisdiction?
- Necessity requirement: Can the objectives of the intended action of the EU not be achieved sufficiently at the level of the Member States?
- Efficiency criterion: Does it result from scale or effects that the objectives of the measure are more efficiently secured at EU level?

Linguistically, Article 5 (3) TEU is now clearer compared with corresponding Article 5 EC under the Treaty of Amsterdam. It is now clear that the last two audit points have to be considered separately.[31] This is of particular importance for the justification by the Commission of a legislative proposal and also for subsidiarity control by the ECJ, which in the case of *ex parte British American Tobacco*[32] was solely based on the criterion, whether the object of the proposed action at Union level could be reached better.[33] The assessment of subsidiarity is difficult because both the second and third criterion operate with indefinite terms – 'sufficient' and 'better' – which makes legal control challenging. This is a flaw which was not addressed by the Treaty of Lisbon. On the contrary, the minutes of the meetings of Working Group I of the Convention give

---

[31] The linguistic link between the two elements is made by the word 'but' in Article 5 (3) TEU. By contrast, the phrase 'and therefore' in Article 5 (2) EC was confusing, as by this wording it was suggested that there must be only one item to be checked.

[32] Case C-49/01 *R* v *Secretary of State for Health ex parte British American Tobacco and Imperial Tobacco* [2002] ECR I-11453. This judgment bears out the analysis put forward by Estella, A. (2002) *The EU Principle of Subsidiarity and its Critique*.

[33] Case C-49/01 *R* v *Secretary of State for Health ex parte British American Tobacco and Imperial Tobacco* [2002] ECR I-11453 at paragraph 183.

the impression that the question of substantive criteria in subsidiarity control was neglected, or that clarifying modifications and additions were not possible due to lack of consensus about the interpretation of the content of the subsidiarity principle.[34]

3.1 Jurisdictional Criterion

In the framework of the subsidiarity check, the preliminary question of competences is limited to the type of competence being exercised according to the wording of Article 5 (3) TEU. By comparison to the pre-Lisbon position, there is no change with regard to the exercise of competences (see ex-Article 5 (2) EC). Thus, it continues to be necessary to determine whether the underlying competence of the legislative act is of an exclusive nature, because in such circumstances of sole legislative competence, a test of subsidiarity is naturally eliminated.[35] The Member States cannot act independently other than for the purposes of implementing legislation. The areas of exclusive competence are listed in Article 3 TFEU and include the regulation of competition rules necessary for the functioning of the Internal Market.[36] The application of subsidiarity as a regulatory principle against the exercise of EU competence is therefore only considered in fields of competence lying outside Article 3 TFEU. The systematic division of exclusive, shared or complementary competences was for the first time introduced by the Treaty of Lisbon and makes it possible to determine that subsidiarity has to be verified by the EU with regard to the utilisation of both shared competences[37] as well as competences for support, co-ordination or to supplement national legislation.[38] However, if the EU determines that legislative harmonisation is required within the framework of shared competences, the Member States are blocked from introducing independent legislation. With regard to the operation of complementary competences, the EU shall promote the Member State's policies with legally specified objectives. These include, within Article 6 TFEU, health and social policies, industry, culture and tourism. European and national measures shall complement each others' effectiveness, without competition of competences in the policies concerned, but the early warning mechanism of

[34] See CONV 286/02 Conclusions of Working Group I on the Principle of Subsidiarity.

[35] See Article 2 (1) TFEU.

[36] See Article 3 (1) (b) TFEU.

[37] See Article 2 (2) in conjunction with Article 4 TFEU.

[38] See Article 2 (5) in conjunction with Article 6 TFEU.

Protocol 2 does not extend to the application of complementary competences. The restriction of independent objectives in the framework of supporting policies is permitted under Article 6 TFEU, in so far as this is factually linked to the policy actions of the Member States. In the operation of Article 6 TFEU, the EU, and specifically the Commission, assumes a political function which, regardless of national competences, enables the Commission to undertake a co-ordinating function between Member States. In such circumstances, examining the application of the subsidiarity principle is difficult – but it is the precise examination of the respective competence standard which is more important. That is to say, the EU must confine itself to complement, support and promote within the limits set through the design of the competence Member States' policies which can be very detailed. Any explicit harmonisation of Member States' legislation is not possible, because this would intrude upon national competences.[39] The limits of EU action are therefore already defined by the close wording of Article 6 TFEU and to that end any co-ordination of policy areas specifically mentioned within Article 6 TFEU must be 'of necessity'. This reinforces the subsidiary nature of EU action and makes it clear that the responsibility for policy-making remains with the Member States. EU involvement must be interpreted in a more restricted manner than in other policies where the Treaty provides for legislative harmonisation. This can be seen in those policy areas outlined in Article 6 TFEU, for example culture and health, where the term 'necessary' appears explicitly in the Treaty provisions regulating the exercise of EU competence in those policy areas.[40] What is unclear from the Treaty is how the basis for EU competence for legislative action is to be examined by a test that is limited solely to the principle of subsidiarity. This question arises directly from the operation of the subsidiarity early warning mechanism within the national parliaments and the Committee of the Regions which by its nature is very limited in scope. Moreover, the limited opportunity for judicial control of subsidiarity, as laid down in Article 8 of Protocol 2 and Article 5 (3) TEU, results from the unassailable principle of the conferral of powers under the Treaty, together with the political limits of subsidiarity monitoring itself and the reasonableness justification within Article 5 TEU. The FCC took up this

---

[39] See Article 2 (5) (2) TFEU.

[40] See Article 167 (2) TFEU (culture) and Article 168 (2) TFEU (public health) respectively.

issue in the *Lisbon Treaty judgment* by questioning the effectiveness of the early warning mechanism as a means of both political and legal control:[41]

> The effectiveness of this mechanism depends on the extent to which the national parliaments will be able to make organisational arrangements that place them in a position to make appropriate use of the mechanism within the short period of eight weeks. It will also be decisive whether the standing of the national parliaments and of the Committee of the Regions to bring an action will be extended to the question, which precedes the monitoring of the principle of subsidiarity, of whether the European Union has competence for the specific lawmaking project.

To regard the competence basis specified in a legislative act as given and to investigate on this basis whether the subsidiarity principle has been complied with are quite possible. It must, however, in proceedings under Article 8 of Protocol 2 be possible for the plaintiffs to point out an obvious violation of authority limits, as it must then be permitted for the judges to put on the brakes. Otherwise, the ECJ could fall into the awkward situation of having to say 'yes' to subsidiarity, although the Union is not entitled to any competence to legislate. So if there are clear indications that the conditions of the selected basis of competence are not met, it must be possible for the ECJ to discuss jurisdictional boundaries in advance of the actual test of subsidiarity. Otherwise, the political exercise of subsidiarity review is very limited.[42]

3.2 The Requirement of Necessity

The overriding presumption within Article 5 TEU is that the EU cannot act if the objectives of the proposed action can be achieved sufficiently by the Member States. In addition, a new development within Article 5 (3) TEU requires that this assessment of 'necessity' also includes consideration of regional and local levels of governance and whether they are better placed to legislate than the EU. Such a provision is particularly important given the internal constitutional changes that have occurred in many Member States since the Treaty of Maastricht, with a greater emphasis upon decentralisation. The fundamental question which is

---

[41] Judgment of 20 June 2009 *Bundesverfassungsgericht*, BVerfG, 2 BvE 2/08 at paragraph 305.

[42] See Craig, P. (2012) 'Subsidiarity' at 75–77; Estella, A. (2002) *The EU Principle of Subsidiarity and its Critique* at 120–125; Davies, G. (2006) 'Subsidiarity' at 78.

asked is whether it is necessary to operate and regulate at a higher level if the Member States themselves are not capable of implementing the pursued objectives closer to the citizens. In most instances, the answer will inevitably be 'yes' because that is the fundamental requirement of legislative harmonisation. However, the harmonisation of different rules in the Member States with a legislative act cannot be identified, and nor should it be presumed as an objective of Article 5 (3) TEU. If this were to be the case the test of whether the Member States would not be capable of acting independently would be de facto undermined. Furthermore, it would not be recognised that even with the operation of the principle of mutual recognition, barriers in the Internal Market caused by different rules in the Member States can still be overcome.

This is certainly the case with regard to the proposed Directive for a European Sales Law which was discussed in Chapter 2. In this example, it is difficult to accept an argument of necessity for a single EU sales law where the Internal Market already functions in this regard and where there already exists significant cross-border activity. To determine whether there is a 'necessity' for EU legislation it is crucial to consider the material scope of the legislative measure, the Treaty base and the objective of achieving desired regulatory outcomes, for example the introduction of certain product standards. As has been seen in Chapter 2, integration clauses may, for example, affect the target definition of the legislative proposal and though the measure may be classified as an Internal Market measure which seeks to harmonise certain product standards, the exercise of EU competence and the centre of gravity of the legislative proposal may lie elsewhere. For example, as seen in the *Tobacco Advertising Directive Case*[43] the Court held that the primary objective of the measure was the protection of public health through restricting the advertising of all forms of tobacco products rather than securing the integrity of the Internal Market.[44] Thus ancillary objectives such as the promotion of public health, the environment or consumer protection, which reflect certain Treaty values and objectives, must also be considered by the EU legislators when enacting harmonising legislation. However, in those circumstances, where the centre of gravity of the legislation moves beyond the purpose of legislative harmonisation and the improved functioning of the Internal Market, and encompasses broader policies for which the EU does not have explicit permission to

---

[43] Case C-376/98 *Germany* v *European Parliament and Council* [2000] ECR I-8419.

[44] Ibid. at paragraph 54.

harmonise, national parliaments must remain vigilant and benchmark such proposals against subsidiarity.[45] The area of environmental policy illustrates the difficulty of determining where the precise scope of EU action should lie, particularly because in the case of environmental effects, for example with water pollution, the negative effects will not necessarily be confined to one Member State. Thus EU action may be considered as appropriate and indeed necessary to provide a comprehensive regulatory regime, but linking the target of a proposed legislative act to the justification in Article 5 (3) TEU is questionable because the objective is determined by the Commission, to which the principle of subsidiarity is addressed.

It is obvious that with the formulation of the legislative objective by the Commission, the outcome of the necessity test can be significantly influenced. This leads to the crucial question with regard to the operation of the principle of subsidiarity; namely, whether the Member States cannot sufficiently realise the objectives themselves. On this point Article 5 (3) TEU may be interpreted in two ways. First, it would depend on the actual *performance* of the Member States to regulate a matter to achieve the desired policy objective. Secondly, what *motivation* would the Member States have regarding whether to regulate or not? In the latter case a Member State stating that it 'cannot' legislate is equivalent to it announcing that it 'does not want' to legislate. In such circumstances the application of Article 5 (3) TEU would be inappropriate without first considering whether there is a *genuine* cross-border regulatory issue or whether the matter is purely a national affair and that, as such, it may be regulated by the Member States themselves – whether centrally, regionally or locally. The necessity requirement would, in such circumstances, be a subjective judgment of the Commission and would be unlikely to be successfully challenged by way of judicial review. In the *Lisbon Treaty judgment*, the FCC pointed out that the exercise of the competences shifted to the EU 'in the interests of European peace and unification and especially where it is concerned with the coordination of cross-border issues and ensuring a common economic and legal area, where Union citizens can develop freely (Article 3 (2) TEU)'.[46] However, though the FCC therefore concludes that if a specific cross-border element exists EU legislation is acceptable, it rejects the argument that the existence of a cross-border dimension leads to an irrefutable presumption in favour of

---

45 This was certainly the case in both the *Bundesrat* and *Bundestag* in their scrutiny of the Tobacco Advertising Directive.

46 Judgment of 20 June 2009 *Bundesverfassungsgericht*, BVerfG, 2 BvE 2/08 at paragraph 248.

EU action, especially in circumstances where flanking policies such as the environment may be at issue. According to the FCC the EU must not determine a necessity requirement in circumstances where the Member States *would* be able to meet the policy objectives independently, because Article 5 TEU should not be construed as reading that co-ordinated action by the Member States for the goals 'to be sufficiently achieved' is required, even if these may be achieved by other means. Thus the requirement of necessity under Article 5 TEU should encompass not only an evaluation of the policy aims, but should also include an objective assessment of the capacity of Member States to legislate independently. Article 5 of the Amsterdam Protocol on Subsidiarity included a mandatory criterion test to determine whether there is a transnational or cross-border element to the legislative proposal, which essentially required the removal of domestic barriers that restricted integration within the Internal Market or prevented competition. However, Protocol 2 does not include such a provision for a substantive subsidiarity test.

This is very unfortunate, not least because an opportunity was missed to set out clear guidelines, within the Treaty, for the interpretation of the vague legal terms found in Article 5 (3) TEU and to steer the Court accordingly when testing the provisions. Despite this omission, the question of the cross-border dimension remains essential and the EU Scrutiny Committee in the House of Commons has argued that, notwithstanding the formal absence within the Treaty, the Amsterdam Protocol criterion remains valid.[47] In particular this is essential for national parliaments to judge that the necessity criterion can be answered affirmatively. Because of the very flexible wording of policy objectives, examining the underlying facts surrounding the policy and the legislative proposal is crucial; that is, on a factual analysis are the Member States capable of realising the objectives of the EU independently, in circumstances where a problem has cross-border character and therefore can only be solved across borders? With the distinction between product and production standards for goods and services it becomes clear at what point there is a need for harmonisation of diverging national rules at the European level. Product standards regulate quality or safety of the products, including potential liability issues. Production standards concern rules which regulate the production of the goods themselves, for example matters regarding working hours, social standards and safety

---

47 House of Commons Reasoned Opinion of 22 May 2012 at paragraph 12 on a COM (2011) 635 final *Proposal for a Regulation of the European Parliament and of the Council on a Common European Sales Law.*

regulations, and not the properties of the product itself. Nationally divergent product standards are clearly barriers in the Internal Market because the companies concerned must take into account different legal systems in cross-border sales, which may deter them from being active across borders. Mutual recognition of product requirements of a Member State through the national laws of other States is not feasible and EU-wide harmonisation is therefore most suitable. It is different, however, for different national production standards. These do not, in general, lead to regulatory barriers to cross-border trade despite the contrary claims of stakeholders, but only change the relative competitiveness of enterprises, in a similar manner to the way in which differing wage levels may affect competitiveness. With production standards, a cross-border reference is therefore absent and any attempt at legislative harmonisation would, prima facie, infringe the subsidiarity principle. Moreover, in addition to identifying a specific cross-border problem element, any appraisal of subsidiarity should also question whether independent legislative measures of the Member States would violate contractual requirements or whether the interests of other Member States would be impaired significantly. In paragraph 5 of the guidelines on the Amsterdam Protocol on Subsidiarity, the correction of distortions of competition, the avoidance of trade restrictions and the strengthening of economic and social cohesion were mentioned as examples which may justify EU action. This is an appropriate review of primary law which is still valid post-Lisbon. The Commission also seems to follow the idea that the criteria of the guidelines, which live on in the Edinburgh Council Conclusions of 1992, have to be observed. For example, in the Impact Assessment for the Urban Mobility Action Plan,[48] the Commission continually refers to these criteria for the necessity test under the post-Lisbon subsidiarity provisions.[49] Thus the primary objective remains: 'necessity' of EU action is justified to bring down barriers within the Internal Market, whether technical, fiscal or substantive, which independent legislation by the Member States could not achieve. Necessity does not therefore mean EU legislation for the purposes of deeper integration without consideration of the circumstances of the need for EU legislation.

[48] COM (2009) 490 final *Action Plan on Urban Mobility*.

[49] Ibid. See also SEC (2009) 1211, *Commission Staff Working Document on Urban Mobility* at 73 (Annex IV: The EU's right to act).

3.3 The Efficiency Criterion: Added Value through Regulation at the EU Level

It must be possible to establish that the objectives of the proposed actions are better achieved at the EU level because of their scope or their effects. For that, qualitative and, where possible, quantitative criteria should be given as set out in Article 5 of Protocol 2. It is necessary to ensure that action at the Union level actually has a significant added value which can be measured. This further condition, in addition to the necessity requirement, is important because similar or other difficulties might turn up for the EU which prevent a preferable solution to the problems by comparison to that which could be achieved at the level of Member States. Legal control of this criterion is difficult because of the lack of a substantive scale by which to measure this efficiency. Compared with the necessity requirement, the test of efficiency is more subjectively coloured, as an evaluative assessment of the effectiveness of each measure is required in every specific case. This inevitably entails the exercise of a political discretion in arriving at the judgment and some objective measurement of this efficiency should be demonstrated, which may then be subject to judicial review.[50]

The exercise of political discretion can be seen as a barrier to effective judicial review. There are concerns that in the context of solely basing efficiency upon the exercise of a political discretion, the Court may be reluctant to challenge the Commission's position.[51] The parameters to be determined are, according to Article 5 (3) TEU, the scale *or* effects of the objectives strived for with a measure, to determine the added value of EU legislation, which include qualitative and, wherever possible, quantitative criteria. Legal control is therefore directed to the justification of the compatibility of draft laws with subsidiarity and proportionality, which has to be provided mandatorily by the Commission.[52] If there exists, in addition, a subsidiarity statement accompanying the legislative proposal[53]

---

[50] See CONV 286/02, *Conclusions of Working Group I on the Principle of Subsidiarity* at 2.

[51] See Case C-49/01 *R* v *Secretary of State for Health ex parte British American Tobacco and Imperial Tobacco* [2002] ECR I-11453. See for example Case 5/71 *Zuckerfabrik Schöppenstedt* v *Council* [1971] ECR 975. Moreover, Lasok, D. and Bridge, J.W. (1994) *Law and Institutions of the European Union* at 386 state that it is 'unthinkable that every damage should be made good and every misconduct could lead to compensation'.

[52] See CONV 188/02 Summary of the meeting on 10 July 2002 at 5.

[53] As required by Article 5 of Protocol 2.

or a reasoned decision of the Commission resulting from parliamentary subsidiarity objections as part of the 'early warning system', then this information should also be considered within the overall quantitative and qualitative analysis. General statements such as that of 'improving the functioning of the Internal Market', or abstract legal considerations on the part of the Commission are, of themselves, insufficient to provide the necessary justification for EU legislation on grounds of efficiency. The Commission must be clearer with its explanation of why EU action is more efficient and of value added by comparison with Member States' legislation. This is because it is precisely this justification control which has to compensate for the use of too vague and indeterminate terms by the Commission and for the absence of detailed independent quantitative evidence. Thus in order to determine the necessary added value for a legislative draft, which will only be relevant at some future point, the Commission must be able to provide some 'prognosis decisions' of how and why EU legislation will be better.[54] This should, as a matter of course, include financial and administrative benefits that are to be gained as a consequence of EU action. It is important to note that if a cost–benefit consideration would be in support of EU legislation, it should also include examining the effects of the EU's deciding that harmonising legislation is not required, and this conclusion should itself also stand up to scrutiny by judicial review.

4. JUSTICIABILITY OF THE SUBSIDIARITY PRINCIPLE

Since it was first included in the Treaty of Maastricht, the principle of subsidiarity has been the subject of much debate with regard to whether it is a legally binding and judicially verifiable principle, or if it only operates as a political maxim which is part of the legislative process. The latter would mean that non-binding guidelines have to be taken into account when the EU institutions are exercising their powers, but if they are disregarded this would not lead to an act being declared void by the ECJ. The specific nature of subsidiarity as a regulatory principle when the EU is exercising powers is that the principle of conferral, under which legislative competence is attributed to the EU, remains untouched. The question that arises with regard to the application of subsidiarity is

[54] This will also include a regulatory analysis which encompasses economic considerations and what, if any, economic benefits arise from EU legislative action.

whether in circumstances of shared competences, subsidiarity formally places limits upon the EU institutions and that their actions are subject to judicial review on grounds of procedural propriety as well as in accordance with the principle of proportionality. The relationship between the principle of subsidiarity and the principles of conferral and proportionality cannot be ignored, as the judgment of the *Tobacco Advertising Directive case* demonstrates, and where the purpose and rationale for the inclusion of the principle of subsidiarity in the EU Treaties undoubtedly influences the Court's reasoning. Taken together, these three regulatory principles have been shaped into binding guidelines for EU legislative action, and are therefore, in the reformulated version of Article 5 TEU, undoubtedly justiciable. Though there may be an absence of a single precise definition of these principles, and especially the principle of subsidiarity, this does not prevent indefinite terms and definitions, which are open to various interpretations, from being subject to judicial review.

In the Preamble to the TEU the Member States have formulated a political statement which provides that 'an ever closer Union' should be created by 'decisions being taken as close as possible to the citizen'. There is an obvious contradiction in this statement as 'an ever closer Union' necessitates integration achieved, in large part, through harmonisation and centralised decision-making and policy co-ordination. This, however, should not stop the Court from applying the principle of subsidiarity and recognising that the application of this principle should not be restricted to the interpretation in the Preamble. Subsidiarity is also about good governance, procedural propriety and accountability, and as such the Court has an obligation to ensure that EU legislative acts conform with these objectives, as well as ensuring that the decisions are taken as closely as possible to the citizen. The ECJ has experienced difficulties with reviewing the application of the subsidiarity principle, but finally expressed that it considered the principle of subsidiarity to be justiciable.[55] Of primary importance was the judgment of the ECJ in *ex parte British American Tobacco*.[56] To date, the judges have not held any legal act to be void for violation of the principle of subsidiarity; either the

---

[55] See Joined Cases C-154/04 and C-155/04 *Alliance for Natural Health* [2005] ECR I-6451.This was confirmed in Case C-58/08 *Vodafone Ltd and others* v *Secretary of State for Business Enterprise and Regulatory Reform* [2010] ECR I-4999.

[56] See Weatherill, S. (2011) 'The Limits of Legislative Harmonisation Ten Years after *Tobacco Advertising*' at 827; Horsley, T. (2011) 'Subsidiarity and the European Court of Justice'; Davies, G. (2006) 'Subsidiarity'.

Court has altogether avoided a review of the application of the principle,[57] has only considered the effect of a failure of the formal duty to give reason for compliance with subsidiarity,[58] or has carried out its review unsystematically, largely because of the vagueness of the actual provisions within what was then Article 5 EC.[59] Moreover, this vagueness has not been adequately addressed by the changes made in Article 5 TEU or Protocol 2 with regard to the precise scope and application of the principle or to provide a clear definition which sets out precisely what the regulatory purpose of the principle is. Protocol 2 offers few clues for any content-related review by the Court which formally tests whether legislative action is better achieved at the EU level.

On the contrary, Protocol 2 has primarily taken the form of a procedural instrument, which provides mechanisms for the political 'control' of subsidiarity by national parliaments, thereby reinforcing political rather than judicial control. The current Protocol 2 is therefore, by contrast to the Amsterdam Protocol, more limited because the latter at least included some binding guidelines through which to benchmark whether the principle of subsidiarity had been respected in the legislative process, such as the presence of the requirement of a cross-border dimension in the proposed legislation. However, these guidelines were never explicitly addressed by the ECJ in its case law. Finally, under Protocol 2, national parliaments and the Committee of the Regions, in addition to the Member States, have been given the possibility of appeal in accordance with Article 8 of Protocol 2. This allows for judicial review under Article 263 TFEU to seek an annulment of a legislative act for its infringement of the subsidiarity principle. The Treaty therefore expressly recognises judicial control, albeit in limited circumstances, in case of a violation of the principle of subsidiarity, which given the location of the Procedure within Protocol 2, implies at the very least that this judicial review arises following the early warning mechanism and that the EU institutions had failed to respect the showing of a yellow card. But such a circumstance will be rare as any yellow card raises a presumption that the EU institutions will decide not to proceed with the legislative proposal in that form. However, notwithstanding the limited opportunities, especially for national parliaments to utilise Article 8 of Protocol 2,

---

[57] See Case C-84/94 *United Kingdom* v *Council* at 21.

[58] See Case C-49/01 *R* v *Secretary of State for Health ex parte British American Tobacco and Imperial Tobacco* [2002] ECR I-11453.

[59] See Case C-233/94 *Germany* v *European Parliament and Council* (*Deposit Guarantees*) [1997] ECR I-2405.

the inclusion of this provision formally recognises the existence of judicial control and therefore the justiciability of the subsidiarity principle.

4.1 Subsidiarity: A Political or Legal Principle?

What is clear from the discussion within this chapter is that subsidiarity is a regulatory principle which operates to determine that, in circumstances of concurrent competences, legislative action is most appropriate at the level of the Member State. Ultimately this is a political judgment decided by political actors and institutions and based upon the application of the criteria of necessity and efficiency. But the evidence overwhelmingly illustrates that the Commission almost always succeeds in establishing the presence of these criteria, even if there is evidence of statistical or empirical doubt.[60] To that extent the political nature of the principle, whose application involves political choices on the part of the Commission and which are monitored by national parliaments, cannot be disputed. Yet the application of the principle also raises questions with regard to the scope of the principle and precisely how the criteria of necessity and efficiency are determined and by reference to what evidence.

To this extent the use of these criteria forms a key part of the Commission's Impact Assessment, which was discussed in Chapter 2, and it is the determination of these criteria and the process by which they are applied that can be subjected to judicial review. In short, judicial review can, at least theoretically, offer the opportunity to substantively challenge the justification for EU action as well as the process by which the Commission arrived at that decision. Ever since the Inter-Institutional Agreement[61] on subsidiarity was entered into by the Council, Commission and European Parliament, the Commission has been required to provide a justification under the principle of subsidiarity, which under the Better Regulation Agenda means within the Impact Assessment. In addition, both the Council and European Parliament are required to provide a subsidiarity justification for each legislative proposal and the Commission produces an annual report in which it outlines how the principle has been applied. Thus since its inception there has been the

---

60 This issue certainly arose following the proposal for a draft Regulation for a Common European Sales Law. House of Commons Reasoned Opinion of 22 May 2012 at paragraph 12.

61 European Parliament, Council and Commission, Inter-Institutional Agreement on Better Law Making, OJ C 321, 31.12.2003, at 1.

existence of a formal mechanism through which the principle of subsidiarity is taken into account within the legislative process, and this has been reinforced by the Amsterdam Protocol on Subsidiarity and Proportionality[62] and post-Lisbon by Protocol 2. The question which remains just as relevant and opaque post-Lisbon is whether, and under what circumstances, the adoption of legislation under these procedures can be challenged before the ECJ. Essentially, the primary issue before the Court is how to interpret that there is a 'necessity' for EU action. It perhaps may be more accurate to phrase the subject matter of the question as one of 'political necessity' because the Commission's position arises from a de facto presumption that legislative action at the EU level and using the ordinary legislative procedure is the only method by which the policy objective can be secured.[63] This implies that independent legislation across the Member States would fail to deliver the required degree of harmonisation that is necessary to secure the policy objective. There are undoubtedly cases where this will be correct, and environmental protection is a good example. But there will also be more marginal policy areas, such as the proposed Directive for a European Sales Law, where the political and legislative justifications are less convincing and the argument of necessity may be rebutted.[64] Determining whether the legislative institutions have made a correct political judgment is an issue which the Court has only had to consider on a few occasions. For example, in the application of Article 352 TFEU,[65] which in its present and previous guises includes a general power for the EU to legislate in the absence of a specific Treaty base where it is necessary to achieve one of the objectives of the Treaties, the Court has been required to review a political determination of the related concept of the 'necessity

---

[62] In particular Article 9 of this Protocol laid down very specific obligations upon the Commission when proposing legislation. In part, Article 9 replicated the Inter-Institutional Agreement of 1993 but it also required wider consultation before proposing the legislation from which the present scheme of Impact Assessments can be said to have arisen. This included the Commission outlining the financial and administrative burdens of a legislative proposal falling upon the Community, national governments, local authorities, economic operators and citizens, and that these should be kept to a minimum and proportionate.

[63] See Craig, P. (2012) 'Subsidiarity' at 83–85.

[64] See further COM (2011) 635 final *Proposal for a Regulation of the European Parliament and of the Council on a Common European Sales Law.*

[65] Formerly Article 308 EC and Article 235 EC where the justification read as 'one of the objectives of the common market' and which was narrower than that found in Article 352 TFEU.

for EU action' and whether the use of this general Treaty base is legitimate.[66]

The Court has held that in reviewing the exercise of political decision-making to use the general Treaty base the Court is required to review the actions of the Council, an inherently political institution. In that context, the Court's review is confined to considering whether the Council had acted beyond the limits of its discretion; a difficult task made all the more so because the limits of this discretion are not clearly defined.[67] This would appear to indicate, and as the case law on subsidiarity confirms, that the Court is prepared to show both deference and a significant margin of appreciation to the institutions when exercising a political discretion with regard to legislative acts. The limited judicial review by the Court of the exercise of political discretion is not confined exclusively to the Council, but also extends to acts of the Commission. This is evident in the context of the institutional liability line of case law under Article 340 TFEU, and especially where the legislative act involves the exercise of economic choices by the Commission or other institutions. Under Article 340 TFEU, which is based on a principle of non-contractual liability, individuals may apply to the Court for compensation against an EU institution for damage which has been suffered as a direct consequence of the acts of that institution. Article 340 TFEU can therefore be seen within the context of the administrative and legislative activities of the institutions and falls within a general principle of governance and sound and efficient administration. Under Article 340 TFEU it is therefore necessary to consider the damage arising out of the conduct complained of and, according to Lasok and Bridge, it is 'unthinkable that every damage should be made good and every misconduct could lead to compensation'.[68] For example, in *Zuckerfabrik Schöppenstedt*[69] the Court restricted the application of Article 340 TFEU when the nature of the EU's liability in damages is in respect of 'legislative action involving measures of economic policy'. According to the Court, such legislation involves 'choices of economic policy', leaving a large degree of discretion in the hands of the institution which presumably should seek to act in the public interest. This case law, in which the Court

66 See for example Case 8/73 *HZA Bremerhaven* v *Massey-Ferguson* [1973] ECR 897 and Case 203/80 *Casati* [1981] ECR 2595.

67 Joined Cases C-402/05 P and C-415/05 P *Kadi and Al Barakaat International Foundation* v *Council and Commission* [2008] ECR I-6351.

68 See Lasok, D. and Bridge, J.W. (1994) *Law and Institutions of the European Union.*

69 See Case 5/71 *Zuckerfabrik Schöppenstedt* v *Council* [1971] ECR 975.

has been asked to review the operation and impact of the political process, indicates that the Court is unlikely to substitute a political decision, arising from the detailed operation of the policy process, with a judicial interpretation that is based upon an *ex post* review. This appears to extend to an *ex post* application of the subsidiarity principle. Accordingly, the bar for a successful challenge of this political discretion has been set very high by the Court, and in the context of reviewing the operation of the subsidiarity principle there is, at present, no reason to suggest that, post-Lisbon, the Court will behave any differently and that judicial review of decision-making on grounds that a legislative proposal breaches the subsidiarity principle will remain an uphill struggle.

4.2 Subsidiarity before the ECJ

The primary obligation of the Court under Article 19 TEU is to ensure that 'in the interpretation and application of the Treaties the law is observed'. This includes the application of the subsidiarity principle, which is a fundamental principle of EU law.[70] However, the case law illustrates that the Court is extremely reluctant to strike down a legislative proposal because it infringes the principle of subsidiarity. This is the case especially where a substantive infringement has been alleged,[71] though the Court has shown some willingness to overturn a legislative act on procedural grounds, though not necessarily where this involves a direct breach of the principle of subsidiarity.[72] Formal consideration by the Court of the principle of subsidiarity has been sporadic and a subsidiarity argument has been used in a relatively low number of instances by Member States to challenge either a legislative act or as a defence against a judicial action by the Commission. For example, in the 1995 case of *Bosman*[73] the Court rejected the German government's submission that, based on the principle of subsidiarity, provisions such as Article 45 TFEU (ex Article 39 EC) should not bind private organisations. In essence the Court allowed horizontal application of Article 45 TFEU (ex

---

[70] See Craig, P. and de Búrca, G. (2011) *EU Law* at 94–100.

[71] See for example the *Working Time Directive* and *Deposit Guarantee judgments*.

[72] See the *Tobacco Advertising judgment*.

[73] Case C-415/93 *Union Royale Belge des Sociétés de Football Association* v *Bosman* [1995] ECR I-4921.

Article 39 EC),[74] which the Court justified on the ground that when considering fundamental rights such as those contained within Article 45 TFEU (ex Article 39 EC) subsidiarity would not be a primary consideration. These Treaty rights are absolute and the Court's primary purpose when protecting them is to prevent Member States from introducing barriers that prevent the exercise of the Treaty right. On this analysis, it is doubtful that the Court ever really considered subsidiarity in *Bosman* because Article 45 TFEU (ex Article 39 EC) is fundamental to the functioning of the Internal Market. The fact that the European Football Association, UEFA, is the pan-European governing body of football inevitably led the Court to conclude that a significant cross-border element would be present in the football transfer market that enables an individual to claim rights under the Treaty which the Court is under a duty to protect.[75] In *Germany* v *Parliament and Council*[76] the German government challenged a directive which required all credit institutions to participate in a compulsory guarantee scheme which provided protection to all depositors.

The German government argued that a voluntary scheme was already in existence in Germany that provided a similar level of protection, and that from a subsidiarity perspective, the measure did not take into account existing national practices. The Court held that as the measure was intended to harmonise practices within the Community and provide minimum enforceable standards, voluntary schemes as in the German case could not be permitted to continue to operate. As far as the subsidiarity issue was concerned, the Court stated that Article 296 TFEU (ex Article 253 EC), under which this directive was introduced, did not require the Community measures to contain an express reference to the subsidiarity principle. All that was required was a clear statement in the recitals to the measure that the Community believed that the aims of the measure could be best achieved by Community action. Harmonisation of Community policy is clearly central to this judgment. Yet this is done without reference to the existing regulating framework within Germany, other than to say that as harmonisation is the priority of the Community, subsidiarity arguments cannot be used to undermine this. The Court was asked to adjudicate on the question of competences and in effect

---

74 Compare this with Case 152/84 *Marshall* v *South West Hampshire Area Health Authority (Teaching)* [1986] ECR 723 and the Court's approach to the horizontal application of Community law.

75 See Weatherill, S. (1996) 'After *Keck*' at 885; Cygan, A. (2001) *National Parliaments in an Integrated Europe* at 26–32.

76 Case C-233/94 [1997] ECR I-2405.

side-stepped the question by justifying the Community action on the basis of harmonisation and integration. However, in doing this the Court failed to address the substantive issue of when and under what circumstances the Court *will* be prepared to challenge a measure and strike it down as being incompatible with the principle of subsidiarity. This case, and the one discussed below, illustrate the lack of any activist or interventionist manner on the part of the Court when a Member State challenges decisions of the EU institutions on grounds of infringement of the subsidiarity principle. The Court discussed the operation of the subsidiarity principle comprehensively in the *Working Time Directive judgment*.[77] In this case the United Kingdom challenged a directive on maximum weekly working times and minimum rest periods on the basis that it was introduced under the incorrect Treaty base. The measure was introduced under Article 153 TFEU (ex Article 137 EC) as a health and safety measure. However, the United Kingdom argued it should have been introduced under Article 115 TFEU (ex Article 94 EC) or Article 352 TFEU (ex Article 308 EC), both of which required unanimity and thus less scope for agreement in the Council, with the possibility of the veto being exercised. The United Kingdom did not consider the proposed directive to be a health and safety measure and furthermore argued that it was disproportionate in its application. Either way, the United Kingdom believed that the directive addressed laws that should be a matter for individual Member States. In its judgment the Court stated:

> Para. 47: it is the responsibility of the Council, under Article 137 EC, to adopt minimum requirements so as to contribute, through harmonisation to achieving the objective of raising health and safety protection for workers which in the terms of Article 137 EC is primarily the responsibility of Member States. Once the Council has found it necessary to improve the existing level of protection as regards health and safety of workers and to harmonise the conditions in this area while maintaining the improvements made, achievement of that objective through the imposition of minimum requirements necessarily presupposes Community-wide action, which otherwise, as in this case, leaves enactment of the detailed implementing provisions required largely to the Member States.

The Court continued:

> Para. 55: The argument for non-compliance with the principle of subsidiarity can be rejected at the outset. It is said that the Community legislature has not established that the aims of the directive would be better served at the

[77] Case C-84/94 *United Kingdom* v *Council* [1996] ECR I-5755.

> Community level than at the national level. But that argument as so formulated, really concerns the need for community action, which has already been examined in paragraph 47 of this judgment.

Essentially the Court acknowledges the existence of subsidiarity as a regulatory principle but is not prepared to challenge the political decision of the Council. This clearly raises the question of whether there are any circumstances when the Court is prepared to strike down a legislative act for infringing subsidiarity.[78] One observation that arises from the *Bosman*, *Germany* v *Parliament and Council* and *Working Time Directive* judgments, which were delivered soon after the principle of subsidiarity became a general principle of EU law, is that in circumstances where disputes concerned the enforcement of fundamental rights within the Treaty, the Court would be very reluctant to challenge the decision-making discretion of the EU institutions. Thus in *ex parte British American Tobacco*[79] the Court held that once the EU concludes that it is 'necessary to adopt common rules to regulate the Internal Market', which could only be achieved through harmonising legislation, then such legislative action must inevitably comply with subsidiarity.

Perhaps the high-water mark for subsidiarity before the Court came in the judgment of *Germany* v *Parliament and Council (Tobacco Advertising Directive)*,[80] even though subsidiarity was not the core issue in this dispute. In this case the Court acknowledged the boundaries of EC competence and rejected the argument that economic integration per se is a justification for legislative action. The dispute arose because a directive had been agreed, using the Community method, which banned all forms of tobacco advertising, including the use of static advertising, with the exception for minimal promotion of tobacco products at the point of sale. The Commission used Article 53 (2) (ex Article 47 (2)), Article 62 TFEU (ex Article 55 EC) and Article 114 TFEU (ex Article 95 EC) as the legal base, and argued this was a 'necessary' Internal Market measure which sought to create a uniform market in tobacco products by restricting the use of advertising, which varied significantly across the Member States. The Court agreed with the submissions of the German government that the measure went beyond the scope of the Treaty base. The measure,

---

[78] See HL 80 (Session 1990–91) *Political Union*.

[79] Case C-49/01 *R* v *Secretary of State for Health ex parte British American Tobacco and Imperial Tobacco* [2002] ECR I-11453, in particular paragraphs 177 and 185.

[80] Case C-376/98 *Germany* v *Parliament and Council (Tobacco Advertising Directive)* [2000] ECR I-8419.

banning all forms of tobacco advertising, had broader impact than the Internal Market and in particular had a public health objective which was beyond the scope of Article 168 TFEU (ex Article 152 EC), and this included the use of the general Treaty base under Article 352 TFEU (ex Article 308 EC).

Though the *Tobacco Advertising case* raised issues primarily of use of the correct Treaty base and whether EU competence had been confirmed, the Court did examine these issues, at least in part, through the prism of subsidiarity and the purpose for which this principle exists in EU law.[81] In areas of shared competence, which includes the regulation of the Internal Market, the exercise of competence by, in this case the EU, is precisely within the scope of the subsidiarity principle. The Court refers to the exercise of competence and the power of conferral within Article 5 TEU (ex Article 5 EC) in its reasoning, and draws upon the justification for and purpose of subsidiarity in its reasoning.[82] Thus with regard to the prohibition of static advertising, this could, in the Court's view, be distinguished from magazines and television, where the images would potentially cross a border. In the case of static advertising, this should in the Court's view be a matter for the Member States to determine under their own laws. In the view of the Court, such national measures did not form obstacles to free movement or infringe competition which necessitated harmonising legislation under Article 95 EC, but were to be viewed merely as disparities between national laws.[83] However, whether this is strictly concerned with the application of the subsidiarity principle is open to debate, and the reasoning could be explained by analogy with the product characteristics/selling arrangements distinction that had arisen from the *Keck*[84] line of cases. Here it will be recalled that selling arrangements, which would include advertising, may be regulated by Member States where the legislation was proportionate and did not impede the functioning of the Internal Market. Thus the non-prohibition by a Member State of the use of static tobacco advertising would fit within this rubric. In the *ex parte British American Tobacco judgment* the Court refined the reasoning used in the *Tobacco Advertising Directive judgment*. It provides what Weatherill has described as a 'drafting guide' for the proper scope of legislative harmonisation and, by implication, for

---

[81] See Horsley, T. (2011) 'Subsidiarity and the European Court of Justice' at 4–5 and Cygan, A. (2001) *National Parliaments in an Integrated Europe*.

[82] Horsley, T. (2011) 'Subsidiarity and the European Court of Justice' at 4–5.

[83] *Tobacco Advertising Directive judgment* at paragraph 95.

[84] Cases 267 and 268/91 *Keck* [1993] ECR I-6097.

the proper application of the subsidiarity principle.[85] The Court's judgment in *ex parte British American Tobacco* seeks to define the outer limits of EU competence to regulate the Internal Market. The Court stated that the EU does not by virtue of Article 5 (3) TEU and the principle of subsidiarity therein enjoy an exclusive competence to regulate *all* economic activity in the Internal Market.[86] As such, EU competences are limited to the elimination of trade and other barriers and to preventing the distortion of competition. Thus it may be concluded that EU action should only be permitted where it seeks to prevent the negative effects of domestic legislation and as was recognised within Article 5 of the Amsterdam Protocol on Subsidiarity, but not within the current Protocol 2. Most recently, this approach has been confirmed by the Court in the *Vodafone judgment*.[87] In this case the Court was asked, inter alia, to consider whether an EU Regulation[88] which set standard roaming charges for mobile phone users across the EU infringed the principle of proportionality. The hub of the issue was how it could be determined that the measure was necessary to the efficient functioning of the Internal Market and that differential prices across the Member States were not just a question of disparities between national rules regulating mobile phone operators, but that there was a genuine cross-border element in existence. The Court held that the measure was proportionate to protect consumers from high roaming charges. On subsidiarity grounds the Court justified EU legislative action on the basis that there was a genuine Internal Market in roaming services which could only be regulated through harmonising legislation. In its Impact Assessment the Commission concluded that individual legislation by the Member States would inevitably be heterogeneous in both substance and form. In particular, the Impact Assessment recognised that EU legislation was required to regulate a market that consisted of both a wholesale and a direct consumer market, both of which were subject to significant cross-border

[85] Weatherill, S. (2011) 'The Limits of Legislative Harmonisation Ten Years after *Tobacco Advertising*'.

[86] Ibid at 836.

[87] See Case C-58/08 *Vodafone Ltd and others* v *Secretary of State for Business Enterprise and Regulatory Reform* [2010] ECR I-4999 at paragraphs 72–73.

[88] Regulation No. 717/2007/EC on Roaming on Public Mobile Networks in the Community and Amending Directive 2002/21/EC.

activity[89] and interdependent upon each other. This, the Court concluded, necessitated a common approach and comprehensive legislation which would guarantee the smooth functioning of the Internal Market. The above examination of the Court's case law illustrates that subsidiarity, as is common with all regulatory principles, must be subject to judicial review. Judgments such as *Vodafone* illustrate that in the context of the ordinary legislative procedure the principle of subsidiarity creates regulatory expectations amongst both Member States and non-State actors with regard to which level of governance will be legislated and how. The judgment in *Vodafone* primarily confirms what has been accepted for many years; namely that a Commission justification within an Impact Assessment that harmonising legislation is required is very difficult to rebut at the conclusion of a legislative process through the use of *ex post* judicial adjudication. Recognition of economic imperatives by the Commission within the Impact Assessment and the discretion that it exercises undoubtedly influenced the Court in *Vodafone* and other cases when faced with adjudicating on the application of subsidiarity. This would appear to reinforce the view that the application of the subsidiarity principle is most beneficial at the stage of law-making through effective political scrutiny and at a stage when some direct influence can be exerted on the EU institutions, rather than *ex post* before the Court.

5. CONCLUDING REMARKS

Subsidiarity is one of the fundamental principles of EU law. The inclusion of the principle within Article 5 TEU, and within previous versions of the Treaties, underscores that EU legislation should be made as closely as possible to the citizen. This is essential if EU legislation, and the integration process more generally, are to have the necessary legitimacy amongst EU citizens. But it is without question that the appropriate level of governance to legislate will, in the overwhelming majority of cases, be the EU, and so the question becomes one of how the EU justifies this centralised legislative action to citizens and especially why the same objective cannot be achieved by Member States acting independently. In many cases the justification has been to ensure the integrity of the Internal Market and safeguard against the creation of barriers by the Member States. For this reason, in an EU of twenty-eight

[89] See Weatherill, S. (2011) 'The Limits of Legislative Harmonisation Ten Years after *Tobacco Advertising*' at 832–834; Horsley, T. (2011) 'Subsidiarity and the European Court of Justice' at 12–14.

Member States, independent legislation will not be a realistic option. Yet, despite the economic imperatives of centralised action, EU legislative action should not be automatically presumed. As seen in Chapter 2, together with the discussion within this chapter, Impact Assessments, in which the primary justifications are made, should not be viewed by the Commission as merely procedural mechanisms through which the need for regulatory assessments are reduced to a 'tick-box' exercise. Impact Assessment exists for substantive reasons and as such the Commission must put a robust and fully evidenced argument against the application of the subsidiarity principle at the core of its evaluations. The need for a clear subsidiarity justification accompanying all legislative proposals brings the discussion back to the question of whether it is most appropriate to consider subsidiarity as a legal or political principle. There is no doubt that, as the discussion on its application by the Court illustrates, subsidiarity raises specific legal standards which must be met within the legislative process. But the Court's lukewarm response to the subsidiarity challenges it has reviewed, and in particular its reluctance to use it as a regulatory buffer through which to challenge Commission justifications within Impact Assessments, redirect the debate away from the legal discussion and back to the political aspects of the principle and how its application can be controlled within the decision-making process. In practice, post-Lisbon, this means national parliaments raising questions of subsidiarity directly to the EU institutions, and in particular challenging Commission arguments of necessity and value added through the operation of the early warning mechanism within Protocol 2. It is these new opportunities to monitor the application of subsidiarity which will now be considered in more detail in Chapter 6.

6. Subsidiarity control after Lisbon

1. INTRODUCTION

The allocation of subsidiarity monitoring in Article 12 TEU to national parliaments together with the requirements within Protocol 2 is the single most important development for national parliaments since their contribution was first recognised in Declaration 13 of the Treaty of Maastricht. There are three reasons for this. First, as seen in Chapter 5, the principle of subsidiarity raises the presumption that legislation will be made at the appropriate level of governance and the monitoring provisions within Protocol 2 are the first formal Treaty provisions which provide for this. Secondly, under Protocol 2 national parliaments are expected to co-ordinate their domestic scrutiny activities, principally through the Conference of European Affairs Committees of national parliaments (COSAC),[1] to arrive at a single conclusion of whether a legislative proposal complies with the subsidiarity principle. But in relation to this task there remain difficulties, not least because, as seen in the previous chapter, the Treaty of Lisbon does not provide a clear and unambiguous explanation of what constitutes subsidiarity. Finally, the recognition of national parliaments as guardians, or gatekeepers, of the exercise of EU competence can be considered as a more general acknowledgement of the continued presence and importance of the entity of the nation State within the process of EU integration. National parliaments, above all other institutions, provide a tangible expression of this entity and it is they that have dutifully ratified each new Treaty that has enabled deeper EU integration. Protocol 2 includes what has become known as an 'early warning mechanism' for subsidiarity monitoring.

This provides national parliaments with a pre-legislative constitutional intervention device, and if parliaments or chambers collectively reach the

[1] The Conference of European Affairs Committees of national parliaments, founded in 1989, is known by the acronym COSAC from its French title (*Conférence des organes spécialisés dans les affaires communautaires*). COSAC meets biannually in the Member State holding the Presidency of the Council and six members represent each parliament.

necessary threshold then the institution that introduced the proposal must, at the very least, review it. The early warning mechanism includes two different options – the 'yellow' and 'orange' card procedures – which provide for different thresholds to be attained before they may be applied, depending upon the legislative proposal. The objective of both mechanisms is for national parliaments to arrive at a *political* assessment of whether a legislative proposal complies with subsidiarity.[2] The uniqueness of the early warning mechanism is that, for the first time, it seeks to create a European understanding of how subsidiarity is to be determined, but this is hampered by the absence of a clear definition of what constitutes subsidiarity. Moreover, this 'Europeanised' understanding of subsidiarity and how it applies to a legislative proposal arises from the individual scrutiny activities of national parliaments,[3] which execute this task using different parliamentary scrutiny procedures. This heterogeneity of procedure has scope to produce significantly different outcomes with regard to how national parliaments view the compatibility of the document with the principle of subsidiarity. On this interpretation Protocol 2 does not create, as some authors have suggested, a horizontal collective bloc of national parliaments which can be considered as some new form of 'EU organ'.[4] After the entry into force of the Treaty of Lisbon national parliaments or the respective chambers of those parliaments – for example the House of Commons, *Folketing*, *Bundestag* or *Sènat* – have the possibility to complain about a breach of subsidiarity, as soon as the draft of a legislative act is submitted. This constitutes a possibility of a preventive control at the start of the legislative procedure, but does not amount to direct involvement in the mechanics of the ordinary legislative process, which remains with the Council and European Parliament. The parliaments or chambers direct their 'reasoned opinions' on the application of subsidiarity with regard to the legislative proposal within eight weeks after transmission to the presidents of the European Parliament, Council and Commission.[5] If the required thresholds are met that a

2 See Weatherill, S. (2005) 'Better Competence Monitoring' at 26.

3 For example, in her case study of the Danish scrutiny system, Møller Sousa shows how the incentive of improved opportunity for subsidiarity monitoring works against more active involvement in European affairs, with the MPs feeling that neither the media nor the voters are interested in EU matters. See Møller Sousa, M. (2008) 'Learning in Denmark?' at 441.

4 See, for example, Passos, R. (2008) 'Recent Developments Concerning the Role of National Parliaments in the European Union' 35 and Kiiver, P. (2011) 'The Early Warning System for the Principle of Subsidiarity' at 98.

5 See Article 6 of Protocol 2.

certain number of parliaments or chambers object that the legislative proposal infringes the principle of subsidiarity then the Commission may be required to review the proposal.

2. THE NEED FOR SUBSIDIARITY MONITORING

The Constitutional Convention recommended that national parliaments should assume responsibility for monitoring the application of the subsidiarity principle within the legislative process.[6] The conclusions of Working Group I[7] suggested a shift with regard to not only the technical task of subsidiarity monitoring, but that with the allocation of this task to national parliaments the pendulum of direct political influence would swing in their favour.[8] Working Group IV considered the wider role of national parliaments in EU affairs, including their participation in subsidiarity monitoring. Working Group IV sought to address the most commonly cited limitation of effective involvement by national parliaments in EU affairs;[9] namely that national parliaments through their participation in EU affairs could be categorised as either 'strong' or 'weak' actors.[10] Moreover, it was this heterogeneous participation through which different internal parliamentary procedures allowed for varied levels of scrutiny of EU affairs which directly impacted upon the influence exerted over the minister.

---

[6] CONV 71/02 Mandate of the Working Group on the Principle of Subsidiarity at paragraph 21.

[7] CONV 286/02 Conclusions of Working Group I on the Principle of Subsidiarity.

[8] See further Besselink, L.M. (2006), 'National Parliaments in the EU's Composite Constitution' at 119; Kiiver, P. (2012) *The Early Warning System for the Principle of Subsidiarity* Chapter 5.

[9] See CONV 353/02 Final Report of Working Group IV on the Role of National Parliaments at paragraph 20 and CONV 204/02 Is there a Role for National Parliaments in Subsidiarity Monitoring?

[10] See Goetz, K. and Meyer-Sahling, H. (2008) 'The Europeanisation of National Political Systems: Parliaments and Executives' **3:2** *Living Rev Euro Gov*, available at http://www.livingreviews.org/lreg-2008-2 (accessed 12 April 2010).

2.1 The Democratic Justification

There is no question that national parliamentary participation in EU affairs has varied significantly across the EU Member States.[11] Indeed, it may be argued that, notwithstanding subsidiarity monitoring, national parliaments are still peripheral within the EU polity and EU governance.[12] Working Group IV of the Convention[13] acknowledged the criticism of differentiated participation in EU affairs within national parliaments to the extent that this decreased both political accountability and legislative legitimacy within the EU. Thus it may be implied from this conclusion that national parliaments, through subsidiarity monitoring, have some capacity to improve legislative legitimacy, but this assumption is questionable for several reasons. First, subsidiarity monitoring is a procedural device and by itself does not address broader questions of institutional legitimacy or legislative transparency, for example such as that raised by the use of Trilogues. Secondly, no evidence was presented to Working Group IV that national parliaments view themselves as a bridge between the EU and citizens and as such they are interested in providing output legitimacy.[14] Indeed, the reverse could be argued; national parliaments use subsidiarity monitoring not to legitimise EU action, but to ensure that EU legislative powers are not exceeded at their expense.[15] The Treaty of Lisbon assigns to national parliaments the task of subsidiarity monitoring for two identifiable reasons.[16] First, to address the disparity of 'weak' and 'strong' parliaments Protocol 2 introduces a harmonised minimum standard for EU scrutiny activities and which presumes that effective subsidiarity monitoring can only be achieved through co-ordinated parliamentary

---

[11] See Kiiver, P. (2006) *The National Parliaments in the European Union* at 41–42.

[12] See Raunio, T. (2010) 'Destined for Irrelevance? Subsidiarity Control by National Parliaments' Working Paper 36/2010. 19/11/2010 Elcano Royal Institute Madrid – Spain, available at http://www.realinstitutoelcano.org/wps/portal/rielcano_eng (accessed 24 January 2011).

[13] See CONV 353/02 Final Report of Working Group IV on the Role of National Parliaments at paragraphs 4–8.

[14] See Raunio, T. (2010)'Destined for Irrelevance? Subsidiarity Control by National Parliaments' Working Paper 36/2010. 19/11/2010 Elcano Royal Institute Madrid – Spain, available at http://www.realinstitutoelcano.org/wps/portal/rielcano_eng (accessed 24 January 2011).

[15] See Weatherill, S. (2005) 'Better Competence Monitoring' at 25.

[16] For a comparison of the provisions in the Constitutional Treaty and Treaty of Lisbon see Barrett, G. (2008) '"The King is Dead, Long Live the King"' at 66.

co-operation within an organised horizontal collective. This creates an environment for political dialogue between national parliaments. Secondly, and in marked development from the Amsterdam Treaty, subsidiarity monitoring by national parliaments is intended to provide some degree of output legitimacy to EU legislative acts.[17] By assigning subsidiarity monitoring to national parliaments the Treaty of Lisbon decouples the dual requirements of input and output legitimacy which Maurer has identified as arising from the legislative function of the European Parliament.[18] The allocation of subsidiarity monitoring to national parliaments indicates that the Treaty of Lisbon presumes, perhaps incorrectly, that citizens are more likely to accept EU legislation if national parliaments confirm that it is compliant with EU competences.

The Treaty of Lisbon, through the operation of the early warning mechanism in Protocol 2, includes a procedure of quasi-compulsory political dialogue between national parliaments. This dialogue takes place as part of the legislative process, but after the process of policy formulation. Moreover, as highlighted in Chapter 4, with the use of Trilogues and greater agreement between the European Parliament and Council at first reading, the opportunity for national parliaments to exert direct influence over the legislative process is becoming increasingly limited. The inclusion of Protocol 2 has led some commentators to conclude, perhaps prematurely, that, post-Lisbon, national parliaments have acquired a form of 'institutional' status under the Treaties, primarily as a result of their subsidiarity monitoring activities, but also because of the new arrangements for the review of *Passerelle* clauses outlined in Chapter 3. For example, Passos asserts that national parliaments became a 'new actor in the European Union legislative process to be added to the existing European Parliament–Council–Commission triangle'.[19] While there is no doubt that improved recognition within the Treaty of EU

---

[17] In evidence to the House of Commons European Scrutiny Committee on 14 May 2008 Professor Alan Dashwood stated: 'It is my view that the European Union is a unique polity. It is what I call a constitutional order of sovereign states. … We have to have a system of dual legitimation through the European Parliament, which is directly elected, but also through the responsibility of ministers meeting within the Council to their national parliaments and electorates. I see the new Subsidiarity mechanism as reinforcing that second aspect of the dual legitimation which the EU system requires.' See HC 563 (2007–8) *Subsidiarity, National Parliaments and the Lisbon Treaty*, at 39, Q. 33.

[18] See Maurer, A. (2001) 'National Parliaments in the European Union Architecture'.

[19] See Passos, R. 'Recent Developments Concerning the Role of National Parliaments in the European Union' and Jancic, D. (2008) 'A New Organ of the

scrutiny activities and subsidiarity monitoring offers new opportunities for national parliaments, these developments must be placed in the context of a massive expansion of EU competences since the Treaty of Maastricht, the greater use of the ordinary legislative process and the judicial reluctance to annul legislative acts because they infringe the principle of subsidiarity. Taken together, these factors illustrate that far from being a cognate group of influential institutions, national parliaments remain peripheral to both the substance and direction of integration. In this context the practice of subsidiarity monitoring, which to date can be summed up as insipid with only mixed results, constitutes what can be best categorised as a procedural device which seeks to exert control over a particular element of the policy and legislative process. This analysis is subject to change over time, and there will undoubtedly be cases where subsidiarity monitoring will produce the desired effect,[20] but for the main part subsidiarity monitoring that concludes in the application of a legislative brake is likely to be a sporadic occurrence. In February 2005 the Commission adopted a ten-point plan which aimed to involve all relevant parties, particularly national parliaments, in European integration. This was developed in 2006 as part of 'Plan D' for democracy, dialogue and debate,[21] as a result of which Commissioners attended over a hundred meetings with national parliaments and also participated in inter-parliamentary meetings between the European Parliament and national parliaments. In its Communication, *A Citizens' Agenda: Delivering Results for Europe*[22] the Commission stated that it would 'transmit directly all new proposals and consultation papers to national parliaments, inviting them to react so as to improve the process of policy formulation'. This commitment, which is now more commonly referred to as the Barosso Initiative, was described as potentially 'revolutionary'[23] and was welcomed by the European Council in June 2006:[24]

European Union': "National Parliaments Jointly"' Federal Trust Policy Commentary, available at http://www.fedtrust.co.uk/uploads/Parliaments_Jointly.pdf (accessed 10 January 2010).

[20] See the discussion below concerning the yellow card shown following the proposed Regulation for collective action at p. 165ff.

[21] COM (2005) 494 final *The Commission's Contribution to the Period of Reflection and Beyond.*
13 October 2005.

[22] COM (2006) 211, *A Citizen's Agenda* 10 May 2006.

[23] This was the view expressed by 'eurosceptic' Danish MEP, Jens-Peter Bonde. See EU Observer 16 June 2006.

[24] European Council Presidency Conclusions, 16 June 2006, paragraph 37.

> The European Council notes the inter-dependence of the European and national legislative processes. It therefore welcomes the Commission's commitment to make all new proposals and consultation papers directly available to national parliaments, inviting them to react so as to improve the process of policy formulation. The Commission is asked to duly consider comments by national parliaments – in particular with regard to the subsidiarity and proportionality principles. National parliaments are encouraged to strengthen cooperation within the framework of the Conference of European Affairs Committees (COSAC) when monitoring subsidiarity.

The Commission began to provide national parliaments directly with non-legislative and consultative documents and its new legislative proposals (except classified documents) in September 2006. The Commission also introduced a new internal procedure for taking action to respond to feedback from national parliaments under the new arrangement.[25] Though not part of the early warning mechanism, there is no doubt that an improved range of documents at an earlier stage of the policy cycle would assist national parliaments in making subsidiarity decisions.

2.2 The Institutional Justification

Working Group I made three significant proposals with regard to the institutional arrangements for subsidiarity monitoring. In particular, these were influenced by ensuring that those levels of governance which are most affected by transfer of legislative competence should have the task of monitoring how this competence is exercised. Obviously this included national parliaments, but in recognition of the internal constitutional changes within many Member States since the Treaty of Maastricht, which have favoured greater decentralisation, Working Group I acknowledged that regional institutions were also stakeholders in this process. To that extent the Conclusion of Working Group I identifies that the Committee of the Regions (CoR) should have improved standing with

[25] According to the Commission's annual report on relations with national parliaments, during the first eight months of implementation (up to April 2007), eighty-three opinions were expressed by twenty-two parliaments on forty-four Commission proposals. Fifty-five of these were from second chambers or both chambers together. During this period the French Senate, which alone accounted for thirty requests, asked for additional information regarding the Commission's replies on four proposals. *Memo to Inter-Institutional Relations Group*, SP (2007) 2202/4, 8 May 2007.

regard to subsidiarity monitoring. The three key proposals of Working Group I were:[26]

- reinforcing the application of the principle during the legislative process;
- establishing an early warning system for national parliaments and the CoR to reinforce monitoring compliance;
- broadening the right of referral to the European Court of Justice to national parliaments and the CoR in circumstances of a breach of the subsidiarity principle.

Working Group I concluded that monitoring subsidiarity was a shared responsibility between the Commission, European Parliament and national parliaments.[27] However, the Report went further and singled out that national parliaments would have 'an essential role to play',[28] an objective which manifested itself in Article 12 TEU. Crucially, such a statement signalled that there was no intention to establish specific committees at the EU level to monitor application of subsidiarity. The question which this raises is why are national parliaments placed at the centre of monitoring application of the subsidiarity principle? There are three identifiable reasons for this conclusion. First, EU institutions are not in practice keen on applying the subsidiarity principle. After all, the principle defines vertical power sharing and is used to determine how competences should be divided between different levels of governance. The discussion in Chapter 5 illustrates that the Commission, in particular, does not view subsidiarity as a regulatory principle which should stand as a barrier to further integration. As conventionally understood, subsidiarity requires that decisions should be taken at the lowest level consistent with effective action. For an integrationist Commission or European Parliament, a principle which acknowledges that national action may be preferable to EU regulation could be perceived as inconsistent with integration, and accordingly considered to have limited application within the decision-making process. Secondly, national parliaments do not have an inherent institutional interest in transferring powers to the EU level and much of the debate in the Constitutional Convention focussed on what further legislative competence the EU needs.

---

[26] CONV 286/02 Conclusions of Working Group I on the Principle of Subsidiarity at 3.

[27] Ibid. at 5–6.

[28] Ibid.

This is very much a 'live' issue in the operation of Articles 5 and 6 TFEU and complementary competences. Thirdly, because they are generally considered closer to the citizen than EU institutions, national parliaments are more likely to reflect the views of the citizen on such matters.[29] Taken together, these latter two points go to the heart of the concerns raised in the Commission's White Paper and Laeken Declaration that there is a feeling of disconnection in the relationship between citizens and the EU. If national parliaments are to be placed in this pivotal position vis-à-vis monitoring subsidiarity, would this lead to a greater acceptance of EU action by citizens? After all, if through completion of subsidiarity monitoring national parliaments have accepted the legislation as being non-intrusive and not prescriptive, would it not follow that the citizens which they represent will adopt the same attitude? This is a big assumption to make and one which the conclusions of the Convention or the Treaty of Lisbon do not necessarily justify. Such an assumption fails to recognise that citizens' feelings of disconnection and mistrust of decision-making institutions also exist at the national level within the political systems of several Member States.[30] Subsidiarity monitoring, which constitutes a broadly mechanical and procedural exercise, cannot provide a comprehensive answer to the much deeper issues of accountability of decision-makers and more direct participation by citizens in EU decision-making. Working Group I recommended several amendments to the Amsterdam Protocol that are designed to address the lack of national parliamentary involvement. The most significant proposal was for the creation of the 'early warning system' that would allow national parliaments to issue a reasoned opinion regarding the compliance of each proposal with subsidiarity. Such reasoned opinions would be sent to the Presidents of the European Parliament, Council and Commission. In its final report, Working Group I concluded that if negative opinions from one-third of national parliaments are delivered, the Commission would be requested to re-examine the proposal, with the options of maintaining, amending or withdrawing it completely. The Commission would retain an ultimate discretion to override national parliamentary opinion by re-submitting the proposal. On this interpretation, the use of the early warning mechanism, at least theoretically,

---

[29] Ibid., paragraph 24.

[30] This is an issue that has been brought into focus and perhaps exaggerated since the 2008 financial crisis with the establishment of technocratic governments in Italy and Greece. These governments existed almost exclusively for the purpose of meeting the requirements of EU financial discipline, which has generally proved to be very unpopular.

offers improved opportunities to national parliaments for greater involvement in the European legislative process without lengthening the process itself. This is because they are obliged to provide any opinions within an eight week period between proposal and inclusion on the Council's agenda. This at least addresses an oft-cited justification for not bringing national parliaments into the decision-making loop, in particular that any formal role for them would further delay an already lengthy decision-making process. But does this Protocol go far enough? The next section examines the Treaty of Lisbon provisions for subsidiarity monitoring and whether they provide a new paradigm for collective participation in decision-making and if this can help to secure improved output legitimacy of EU legislation.

3. THE EARLY WARNING MECHANISM

Attached to the Treaty of Lisbon was an enhanced Protocol 2 on the Application of the Principle of Subsidiarity and Proportionality, which set out what have become known as the 'yellow card' and 'orange card' procedures for subsidiarity monitoring. The key feature of this early warning mechanism is that it provides national parliaments with an opportunity to object to legislative proposals with a view to having them amended or withdrawn. National parliaments may submit a 'reasoned opinion' within an eight week period[31] to the institution proposing the draft legislative act (usually the Commission), outlining why the proposal does not comply with the principle of subsidiarity. If one-third or more of EU national parliaments submit reasoned opinions,[32] the originating institution is usually bound to review its proposal with a view to maintaining, amending or withdrawing it. If more than half the Member States submit reasoned opinions and the institution decides to maintain the proposal, then this institution must submit its own reasoned opinion in support of this decision to the Council and European Parliament, each of which can strike down the proposal. Under Protocol 2 national

---

[31] Compared with the Constitutional Treaty, the deadline for filing a subsidiarity complaint has been extended by two weeks from six to eight weeks. In parallel, it is regulated in Protocol 1 On the Role of National Parliaments in the European Union that a bill can only be put on the provisional agenda of the Council eight weeks after transmission to the national parliaments, unless there is a justified case of particular urgency (see Article 4 of Protocol 1).

[32] The threshold drops to a quarter for legislation in the field of co-operation in criminal matters under Article 82 TFEU.

parliaments can apply to the European Court of Justice for judicial review of EU legislation on the grounds that this legislation infringes the subsidiarity principle. In most cases this will be through a proxy application made by the government and not directly by a national parliament as there is no specific *locus standi* for national parliaments under Article 263 TFEU. The innovative feature of the early warning system is that it allows the national parliaments to draw attention to their concerns at an earlier stage of the legislative cycle. While this is helpful, it must be borne in mind that this intervention occurs well into the overall decision-making process. In addition, as already noted in Chapter 4, a subsidiarity review at the beginning of the formal legislative process is a double-edged sword; yes, national parliaments are involved earlier, but the subsidiarity analysis and parliamentary scrutiny more generally occur before the Trilogues, or after the Council and European Parliament have agreed a compromise legislative act at first reading.[33] In either case, there is significant scope for the impact of this subsidiarity review to be reduced. Finally, the requirements of Protocol 2 are precise: under Article 7 (1) the Commission is only required to take note of 'reasoned opinions' for the specific vote quorum to be reached. Otherwise, an observation or complaint by a national parliament which is communicated to the Commission is merely viewed as a non-binding plea, which has to be 'considered', and will not be counted for the purposes of being a reasoned opinion under Protocol 2. Thus national parliaments must be very precise with regard to their communication to the Commission and must formally state that they are submitting a reasoned opinion.

3.1 The Yellow and Orange Card Procedures in Practice

The yellow and orange cards create a new dynamic for national parliaments by giving them the right to express concerns on subsidiarity directly to the institution which initiated the proposal. In reviewing the original provisions within the Constitutional Treaty, the House of Lords EU Committee Report stated that 'the raising of a yellow card would

---

[33] In the Convention and the subsequent debates many have voiced concerns about national parliaments becoming involved only in the initial stages of the legislative process, as the amendments by Council and the European Parliament may significantly alter the content of the proposal, and hence also at least theoretically make it problematic in terms of subsidiarity, even if the original draft act did not violate the subsidiarity principle. See further Maurer, A. (2008), 'National Parliaments in the Architecture of Europe after the Constitutional Treaty' at 58.

have a significant effect on the EU Institutions … if national parliaments operate the mechanism *effectively* it would be hard for the Commission and the Council to resist such sustained political pressure'.[34] 'Effectively' implies the need for substantial agreement between national parliaments that is achieved through a proactive horizontal political dialogue. Under Protocol 2 each national parliament is allocated two votes.[35] If a parliament is divided into two chambers, each chamber has an own voice and a right of forming an independent conclusion on the question of subsidiarity compliance. The threshold is set at one-third of the total number of votes for the operation of a yellow card. It is lowered to a quarter in case of measures of judicial co-operation in criminal matters,[36] police co-operation[37] and administrative co-operation under Article 74 TFEU.[38] These cases of the need for a reduced quorum reflect the sensitivity of justice and home affairs policy, which has only reluctantly been opened to a transfer of powers to the Union and the use of qualified majority voting (QMV). To reinforce this proposition, Article 69 TFEU explicitly points out the role of national parliaments in the observance of the subsidiarity in these policy areas which clearly corresponds to the highlighted significance of the subsidiarity control by a reduced quorum. If the quorum for subsidiarity objection is met the Commission has to decide whether to persevere with the legislative proposal in its original form, amend the proposal or withdraw it.[39] In addition any decision, and especially a retention of the original draft, must be fully justified. This offers national parliaments an opportunity, but perhaps more accurately the opportunity will be pursued by the Council, to examine the justification and whether the Commission's decision is justified on both legislative and legitimacy grounds. The requirements when considering subsidiarity compliance under the ordinary legislative procedure are even more prescriptive; namely, if a simple majority of the votes allocated to the national parliaments is reached with the number of reasoned

---

[34] Emphasis added. In evidence to the House of Lords Select Committee on the European Union, Sir David Edward stated that if national parliaments did not raise subsidiarity objections at the yellow card stage then it may be harder for any party to run subsidiarity arguments later. See HL 62-I (Session 2007–8) *The Treaty of Lisbon* at paragraph 11.40.

[35] Article 7 (1) (2) Protocol 2.

[36] Article 82 TFEU.

[37] Article 87 TFEU.

[38] Article 7 (2) Protocol 2 in conjunction with Article 76 TFEU.

[39] Article 7 (2) Protocol 2.

opinions,[40] then the Commission's decision to maintain the legislative proposal has to be presented to the European Parliament and the Council as the Union legislators. In the circumstances of an orange card the European Parliament and Council must, before the conclusion of the first reading, benchmark the proposal against the subsidiarity criteria, taking into account the views of the national parliaments and the Commission. If the Council, acting by a majority of 55 per cent, or the European Parliament by a majority of the votes cast, find against the proposal, then it will fall.[41] A veto instrument is not available to the national parliaments within the early warning system and they do not have the power to formally apply a brake to the legislative process, not even in circumstances when they fulfil a required quorum. Hence national parliaments cannot show a 'red card'. The absence of a 'red card' has been identified as a significant omission from the Treaty of Lisbon.[42] The idea that national parliaments can exert a brake over the legislative process is, from a parliamentary perspective, an attractive one,[43] but Working Group IV of the Convention rejected the idea of national parliaments being able to curb the legislative process.[44] They do not have any formal legislative function alongside the Council and European Parliament, making a 'red card' unnecessary. Under the ordinary legislative procedure it is the European Parliament, through discharging its task of providing input legitimacy, which can reject a legislative proposal or propose amendments to it.

---

40 Article 7 (3) Protocol 2.

41 See Barrett, G. (2008) "'The King is Dead, Long Live the King'". As Barrett points out, this may give the Commission an advantage as it can respond to the complaints of national parliaments and defend its case by putting forward contrary arguments or explanations. It should also be noted that the European Parliament and Council only become involved if the Commission chooses to maintain the original proposal. If the Commission withdraws or amends it, then the procedure is completed.

42 See HC 563 (2007–8) *Subsidiarity, National Parliaments and the Lisbon Treaty* at 11.

43 There is one exception where the equivalent of a 'red card' may be applied by a single national parliament. This may arise with decisions taken under Article 81 (3) TFEU which determine those aspects of family law with cross-border implications which may be the subject of acts adopted under the ordinary legislative procedure. Any proposal under Article 81 (3) TFEU must be notified to national parliaments and any one may block it by indicating its opposition within six months.

44 See CONV 353/02 Final Report of Working Group IV on the Role of National Parliaments at paragraph 27.

3.2 Judicial Review of Subsidiarity

Chapter 5 discussed judicial interpretation and application of the subsidiarity principle as a substantive reason by which to challenge an EU legislative act. This *ex post* action for judicial review has been mostly brought by Member States which seek to annul the legislative act. However, it would be incorrect to assume that such proceedings were not, in large part, influenced by the stance of the national parliament with regard to the legislative proposal.[45] It is beyond question that the political position of the legislature will have significant bearing upon whether a Member State seeks to commence proceedings before the Court. Article 8 of Protocol 2 formalises this opportunity for judicial review and grants Member States the power to bring an action for judicial review on behalf of their national parliament of legal acts adopted by a normal or special legislative procedure.[46] In addition, the CoR may also bring an action for judicial review directly before the Court against legislative acts about which the TFEU provides they should have been consulted. An action for the infringement of the subsidiarity principle can be levied not only by a Member State or by a Member State on behalf of the national parliament, but also by one of the chambers of parliament, if national law so provides. Since Article 8 of Protocol 2 explicitly refers to Article 263 TFEU, it is a special form of an action for annulment, but Article 263 TFEU does not refer explicitly to national parliaments as having any form of *locus standi*. Though national parliaments have the opportunity to seek judicial review this will inevitably be in the form of a proxy action brought on their behalf by the Member State. The Member State's legal action on behalf of the national parliament or a chamber is not dependent on the use of the 'early warning system' and the filing of a subsidiarity complaint. Protocol 2 clearly distinguishes between political control before and judicial control after the adoption of a legislative act. Thus the right to pursue a legal action for infringement of the subsidiarity principle is not eliminated by virtue of a Member State having cast a vote in favour of the legislative act in the Council, because Article 8 of Protocol 2 provides for the exercise of independent procedural rights by

---

[45] Proxy actions brought by Member States on behalf of national parliaments are not a new development introduced by the Treaty of Lisbon. For example, in the *Tobacco Advertising* dispute, which was a case concerning EU legislative competence rather than subsidiarity, the German government commenced an action before the Court following objections to the legislation raised within the *Bundestag*. See Chapter 5.

[46] Article 289 (3) TFEU.

national parliaments. The formal revaluation of national parliaments by assigning to them the dual control instruments of subsidiarity monitoring and judicial review represents a logical step, since they are the primary institutions which have been affected by the process of progressive integration and the associated loss of legislative power. The Federal Constitutional Court (FCC) pointed out in the *Lisbon Treaty judgment* that the position of national parliaments was weakened significantly through the reduction of unanimity within the decision-making process and the 'supra-nationalisation' of competences.[47] For the FCC, the principle of subsidiarity offers some degree of protection against centralisation through its application as both a political and a legal principle. Its enforcement is strengthened procedurally by national parliaments being recognised institutionally within the Treaty and through being granted specific procedural influence and control mechanisms, but question marks about the effectiveness of subsidiarity monitoring remain.

4. HOW EFFECTIVE IS SUBSIDIARITY MONITORING?

Until the Treaty of Lisbon and the inclusion of Protocol 2 subsidiarity control consisted primarily of a process of self-regulation by which the Commission provided the justification for a draft legislative proposal. However, the drawback with this process of self-regulation was that it encouraged the Commission to generalise subsidiarity justifications by references to the need for harmonised legislation on grounds of the 'efficient functioning of the Internal Market'.[48] Such justifications, which tended to be used as a matter of course, could not be considered as a reliable instrument by which to correctly justify the exercise of EU competence. Furthermore, at the level of the EU institutions the European Parliament could not be considered as a reliable partner to control subsidiarity, as European parliamentarians have little interest in identifying a breach and would not challenge Commission justifications. This is because their political power lies in their participation in the ordinary legislative procedure through which they share legislative powers with the Council. In the Council, the Member States tend to tolerate breaches of the subsidiarity principle or crossing the limits of legislative competence in circumstances when these may be aligned with, or where the

[47] Judgment of 20 June 2009 *Bundesverfassungsgerich*t, BVerfG, 2 BvE 2/08 at paragraph 251.

[48] See further the discussion in Chapters 2 and 5.

legislative proposal corresponds to, their own political interests.[49] To this extent, it is clear that subsidiarity monitoring must be considered as an *independent* political activity for national parliaments and which Protocol 2 generally achieves.

4.1 The Allocation of Votes to National Parliaments

The primary question raised by Protocol 2 is whether the instruments of subsidiarity monitoring and judicial review that are available to national parliaments can operate as an effective weapon by which to contain the exercise of powers by the EU, and thus can compensate for the progressive 'dispossession' of legislative competence. In short, is Protocol 2 merely a more effective form of substitute sovereignty, by comparison with the Amsterdam Protocol, which acts as a political and judicial counterbalance to the EU institutions and helps to secure improved legislative accountability? A problem with the early warning mechanism, at least in its current form, is that it constricts national parliaments rather than empowering them. This is because national parliaments, whether unicameral or bicameral, must comply with the eight week period in which to formulate their reasoned opinion, thereby reducing subsidiarity monitoring to a very procedural form. Moreover, the necessary quorum to initiate the early warning mechanism must be met in order to advance a complaint to the Commission, but this complaint has no mandatory force and only requires the Commission to review the legislative proposal.[50] This requires a suitably efficient internal organisation of the respective houses of parliament in order to reach the decision in time to raise a subsidiarity complaint.[51] This efficient co-operation *inter se* between parliamentary chambers must also be matched externally through horizontal political dialogue amongst parliaments of other Member States to reach the necessary quorum that the early warning mechanism requires. This horizontal co-ordination between national parliaments is very problematic to secure, not least because the eight weeks allocated for completion of scrutiny is a challenging period of time in which to

---

[49] For example, the United Kingdom government did not raise subsidiarity objections to the extent of the German government in the *Tobacco Advertising* case because it was itself pursuing a rigorous domestic regulatory agenda to prohibit tobacco advertising.

[50] Article 7 (2) Protocol 2. See further the discussion in Kiiver, P. (2012) *The Early Warning System for the Principle of Subsidiarity* at 110.

[51] Judgment of 20 June 2009 *Bundesverfassungsgerich*t, BVerfG, 2 BvE 2/08 at paragraph 305.

secure this level of agreement, and the evidence indicates that, to date, this has not been particularly successful.[52] Given that the early warning mechanism requires one-third of the total number of votes allocated to the national parliaments (there are a total of fifty-four out of the twenty-seven Member States pre accession of Croatia), then the quorum is only reached at eighteen votes. These figures illustrate that the bar to reach the quorum is set quite high, not to mention the 50 per cent of the total allocated votes which have to be reached under the provisions of Article 7 (3) of Protocol 2. One reason for not attaining the quorum is that the reasoned opinions submitted by national parliaments and chambers tend not to raise the same subsidiarity objections. The distribution of votes under the early warning mechanism is problematic in itself since every national parliament, whether unicameral or bicameral, is granted two votes, regardless of the population size of a Member State. At best it may be possible to conclude that such a configuration of votes is unbureaucratic and provides a non-controversial political solution to a problem which is more complex; to this extent unfavourable comparisons can be made between the distribution of votes in the early warning mechanism and QMV under the ordinary legislative procedure. For example, by comparison with the allocation of QMV votes under the ordinary legislative procedure, where population size has always been a significant factor, the solution in Protocol 2 fails to encompass the complexity of securing legislative legitimacy by reference to the population rather than by reference to an institution. The problem can be illustrated through the following comparison. The Maltese House of Representatives represents slightly more than 400,000 citizens, while the *Bundestag* and *Bundesrat* represent more than 80 million citizens. While the allocation of equivalent votes to the national parliaments may not be unobjectionably democratic, it does make the subsidiarity control system look flimsy. In the case of smaller Member States, with different economic and social challenges by comparison with larger, more industrialised countries, the response may be to adopt the stance of a 'bystander' parliament and not raise a complaint on grounds of subsidiarity because the legislative proposal has little or no material bearing upon the exercise of its legislative competences. Despite these criticisms of the early warning mechanism, national parliaments have, for the first time, an instrument in their own hands which, if used efficiently, *may*

[52] With the exception of the Draft Regulation on the Exercise of the Right to take Collective Action within the Context of the Freedom of Establishment and the Freedom to Provide Services. See further at note 68 below.

achieve a level of political influence within the Commission. Even if the necessary quorums are not met, a substantial number of parliamentary complaints cannot fail to have an effect, because the European institutions can hardly ignore such protest under public pressure. Moreover, improved legislative legitimacy identified within the Laeken Declaration demands that EU institutions pay attention to the views of national parliaments. This is particularly the case under the orange card procedure, where the quorum stands at 50 per cent of chambers. Any figure in excess of 40 per cent would already indicate the existence of a substantial minority of chambers which have expressed specific subsidiarity objections. It may be the case that the early warning mechanism is an instrument that will be used in the rarest of cases, because it is likely that strong and broadly expressed concerns are already being taken into account beforehand. The primary obstacle to the effective operation of Protocol 2 is that the Protocol does not guarantee political dialogue and there remains the practical problem of a horizontal co-ordination amongst national parliaments to raise the same subsidiarity objections directly to the Commission and in the correct form as reasoned opinions. Article 12 TEU and Protocol 2, irrespective of both provisions formally allocating the task of subsidiarity monitoring, fail to create a coherent horizontal bloc of parliaments which are all engaged in EU scrutiny to the same degree. In short, while the Treaty may have standardised the task of subsidiarity monitoring to be carried out by all parliaments, it does not standardise internal parliamentary procedures. These continue to be heterogeneous, and national parliaments previously categorised as weak actors in EU affairs are likely to remain so.

4.2 The Role of COSAC

To help make the early warning mechanism as effective as possible a co-ordinating role by COSAC is essential, and this is recognised by Article 8 of Protocol 1.[53] That said, inter-parliamentary co-operation is not a new development introduced by the Treaty of Lisbon and sharing information amongst national parliaments as part of the scrutiny process has been in existence since COSAC was first established in 1989. However, post-Lisbon the need for horizontal co-ordination to secure the necessary consensus is crucial because this can be considered as a prerequisite of the early warning mechanism and is strongly implied by the overall aims of Protocol 2. It is, however, questionable whether

[53] See Article 10 of Protocol 1.

national parliaments will be able, with sufficient regularity, to co-ordinate any more effectively than they have already achieved pre-Lisbon. Irrespective of developments such as IPEX,[54] which has existed since 2006 and acts as a repository for national parliaments to deposit their documentation arising from their scrutiny activities, neither Article 12 TEU nor Protocol 2 compels national parliaments. The Amsterdam Protocol formally recognised COSAC and its role in improving parliamentary scrutiny by enabling it to inter alia 'address to the EU Institutions any contribution it deems appropriate on the legislative activities of the Union'. Article 9 Protocol 1 goes further, with COSAC identified as a forum to debate policy and an information exchange,[55] which suggests that the respective activities are more than complementary. Through co-operation 'in accordance with the Protocol on the Role of National Parliaments',[56] this will inevitably require some consensus between the European Parliament and national parliaments on the application of the subsidiarity principle, but, as already discussed in this chapter, such co-ordination is not a given and largely presupposes that national parliaments broadly share the same subsidiarity concerns, which the evidence indicates will not necessarily be the case.[57] Despite the limitations with parliamentary co-ordination through COSAC and document repositories such as IPEX, the principle of national parliaments seeking to act with greater unity should not be dismissed. Improved inter-parliamentary communication and co-ordination through COSAC at the centre will only be for the benefit of improving subsidiarity monitoring. So far, COSAC has led a shadowy existence despite its good intentions and efforts. With the new position of national parliaments under the Treaty of Lisbon COSAC has a new opportunity to reposition itself and

---

[54] IPEX is the Interparliamentary EU Information Exchange and contains parliamentary documents and information from national parliaments concerning the EU. It also includes all Commission documents since 2006 and a parliamentary calendar. All information is available online at www.ipex.eu.

[55] The conference may communicate with the European Parliament; the Council and the Commission may not bind national parliaments or 'prejudge their positions'; 'shall' promote exchange of information and best practice; may organise inter-parliamentary conferences.

[56] Article 12 (f) TEU.

[57] In the course of this pilot project several subsidiarity objections were raised by a number of national parliaments, but these were on different provisions within the legislative proposals and suggested the absence of a single definition of subsidiarity and how it was to be applied. See further the discussion at 68 below and Kiiver, P. (2012) *The Early Warning System for the Principle of Subsidiarity* at 77–78.

play a more direct leadership role within the early warning mechanism. This is crucial, not least because of the very tight eight week deadline provided for within the Treaty. In the next section the practical experience of the early warning mechanism since the Treaty of Lisbon is considered and whether the objective of improved subsidiarity has been realised.

4.3 Subsidiarity Monitoring in Practice

Under the Council's Rules of Procedure, the Committee of the Permanent Representatives of each Member State (COREPER) ensures that the subsidiarity and proportionality principles are respected. In the European Parliament compliance is verified by the committees in charge of specific legislative dossiers, together with the Committee on Legal Affairs. The Council and the European Parliament each have their own procedures for implementing the subsidiarity control mechanism. The European Parliament's Rules of Procedure ensure that the reasoned opinions of national parliaments are taken into consideration within parliamentary discussions. The Council's Rules also stipulate that national parliaments are consulted on legislative initiatives originating from a group of Member States. A new development within the Treaty of Lisbon is that the CoR expresses its views when it is consulted or in its own initiative opinions. The Treaty of Lisbon has also empowered the CoR to challenge *ex post* the validity of legislation that could violate the subsidiarity principle, but only in the areas in which it is to be consulted. In 2010 the CoR amended its Rules of Procedure to the effect that all its opinions should contain an explicit reference to the subsidiarity and proportionality principles. By the end of 2012 the CoR's Subsidiarity Monitoring Network, launched in April 2007, included 113 regional partners. The specific contribution of the CoR and sub-national government to subsidiarity monitoring is considered in Chapter 7.

In 2005 COSAC organised a Subsidiarity Monitoring Pilot Project on the 3rd Railway Package[58] to test the subsidiarity early warning mechanism that was proposed by the Constitutional Treaty. The COSAC secretariat received reports on the pilot project from thirty one of the thirty-seven national parliamentary chambers that participated in the test. In total fourteen parliamentary chambers indicated that they found that one or more of the legislative proposals in the 3rd Railway Package

---

[58] COM (2004) 104, final, 3.3.2004 *Communication from the Commission 'Further Integration in the European Rail System: Third Railway Package'*.

breached the principle of subsidiarity and eleven of these chambers adopted a reasoned opinion. In addition, a further three national parliaments expressed doubts as to whether one or more of the four proposals conformed to the principle of subsidiarity. The national parliaments did not, however, identify problems with the same legislative proposals, indicating a wide variation in the definition and application of subsidiarity, and reinforcing the point that the absence of a normative definition of subsidiarity hinders the operation of the early warning mechanism. Subsequent projects carried out in 2009 – including a proposal for a Directive on Standards of Quality and Safety of Human Organs Intended for Transplantation[59] and a proposal for Council Framework Decision on the Right to Interpretation and Translation in Criminal Proceedings[60] – highlight that lack of consensus on both the definition and application of subsidiarity remained an obstacle to improved subsidiarity monitoring. In the case of the latter inquiry the objections raised by several national parliaments, including the Maltese and Irish parliaments, that the proposal went too far suggest an evaluation by these parliaments with the principle of proportionality rather than confining their inquiry to determining subsidiarity compliance and illustrate a common mistake made by national parliaments. In its 18th Report on Better Lawmaking the Commission noted[61] that since 2006 it had, within the framework of the political dialogue of the Barosso Initiative,[62] transmitted all new proposals to national parliaments, and replied to their opinions.[63]

As from 1 December 2009, this framework of the Barosso Initiative and the improved transmission of a greater variety of documents direct to national parliaments have been used in parallel with the subsidiarity control mechanism. In 2010, the Commission had sent out eighty-two draft legislative proposals falling within the scope of the Protocol and received 211 opinions. While most of the opinions concentrated on the content of the proposal, a total of thirty-four opinions did raise specific subsidiarity

---

59 Directive 2010/5/ EU of the European Parliament and Council of 7 July 2010.

60 COM (2009) 338 final *Proposal for a Council Framework Decision on the Right to Interpretation and to Translation in Criminal Proceedings*.

61 See COM (2011) 344 final *Report from the Commission on Subsidiarity and Proportionality* (18th Report on Better Law Making Covering the Year 2010) at 6–10.

62 Ibid. See also footnote 16 of COM (2006) 211 *Communication from the Commission to the European Council – A Citizens' Agenda: Delivering Results for Europe*.

63 See note 17 above.

concerns. In 2010, the Commission received, in the case of five legislative proposals, more than one reasoned opinion,[64] but in all of these cases the threshold for a yellow card was far from being reached. In 2011, the Commission received sixty-four reasoned opinions from national parliaments, an increase of almost 75 per cent by comparison with the 2010 statistics, the first year of functioning of the subsidiarity control mechanism following the conclusion of the ratification process for the Treaty of Lisbon. Despite this increase, these sixty-four reasoned opinions still represent slightly less than 10 per cent of the total number of 622 opinions received by the Commission in 2011 as part of its broader political dialogue with national parliaments.[65] This can be in large part put down to the fact that the focus of national parliaments' reasoned opinions remains quite disparate. Of the sixty-four reasoned opinions received in 2011, twenty-eight related to different Commission proposals. Moreover, most of the reasoned opinions focussed on legislative proposals in the fields of taxation, agriculture, the Internal Market and justice.

The proposals which elicited the highest number of reasoned opinions concerned the Common Consolidated Corporate Tax Base (nine opinions), the temporary reintroduction of border controls at internal borders in exceptional circumstances (six), the Common European Sales Law (five) and the Single CMO Regulation (five) for the organisation of a single agricultural market. The national parliaments most active in issuing reasoned opinions were the Swedish *Riksdag*, the Luxembourg *Chambre des Députés* (lower chamber) and the Polish *Sejm* and *Senat* (lower and upper chambers).[66] In none of the 2011 cases were the thresholds for triggering the yellow or orange cards met. In the case of the proposed Directive for a European Sales Law, which has been considered in Chapters 2 and 5, the overriding subsidiarity concerns of the United Kingdom Parliament that the measure failed to meet the necessity and value added tests required for EU legislation was not shared by many other parliaments, with only five reasoned opinions in total. Apart from the above mentioned legislative proposals, the vast majority of the twenty-eight legislative proposals on which national parliaments issued a reasoned opinion in 2011 elicited at most three reasoned opinions. This evidence points to the existence of a weak horizontal dialogue and no consensus on how to apply the principle of

---

64 See Maurer, A. (2001) 'National Parliaments in the European Union Architecture'. Further details are available on the IPEX website.

65 COM (2012) 373 final, *Report from the Commission on Subsidiarity and Proportionality*.

66 Ibid. at 4.

subsidiarity, leading to criticisms that political dialogue constitutes no more than a talking shop.[67] Until the end of 2011 the success of the early warning mechanism to secure co-ordinated agreement on the application of the subsidiarity principle can be described, at best, as largely ineffective. There is no doubt that different political priorities and the absence of a single definition of subsidiarity that is accepted by Member States continue to hamper the early warning mechanism. While it may be the case that indeed none of the legislative measures reviewed have raised any *real* subsidiarity questions, it cannot be ignored that even when national parliaments did raise an objection, this was often for different reasons by comparison with other parliaments and which usually related to political priorities within the Member State. However, on one occasion in 2012 a political consensus was reached with respect to the proposal for a Draft Regulation concerning the posting of workers and the right to take collective action.[68] On this occasion, national parliaments reached the threshold to show a yellow card. What makes this legislative proposal stand out from previous ones where only a few subsidiarity objections were raised and a yellow card did not result? Can this yellow card merely be dismissed as being only coincidental[69] and that inevitably there will always be a few instances where the subsidiarity interests of national parliaments are more broadly aligned? In the case of the proposal for a Regulation for the posting of workers and collective action this may be explained, in large part, by the politically and constitutionally controversial nature of the proposal. However, does this yellow card mark a change in approach within national parliaments which, after two years of political dialogue, are beginning to work more closely together, and which may have helped to determine a clearer understanding of the application of the subsidiarity principle?[70]

---

[67] See Bengston, C. (2007) 'Inter-Parliamentary Cooperation in Europe' at 61.

[68] COM (2012) 130 *Draft Regulation on the Exercise of the Right to take Collective Action within the Context of the Freedom of Establishment and the Freedom to Provide Services.*

[69] See Kiiver, P. (2006) *The National Parliaments in the European Union* at 162–164, who described any such consensus on the application of a yellow card as amounting to no more than a 'phantom collective' which would be achieved by coincidence rather than by design.

[70] When addressing the French National Assembly on 3 February 1994, the Foreign Minister Alain Juppé had expressed his hope that national parliaments would be empowered to challenge EU laws on the grounds that they violated the subsidiarity principle. While many of the proposals calling for a chamber of national MPs had argued that such a body should have a role in monitoring the

4.4 The First Yellow Card: A New Dawn for National Parliaments?

The circumstances surrounding this proposed Regulation can be traced back to the judgment of the European Court of Justice in *Viking*,[71] where the dispute concerned the decision of a Finnish company, Viking Lines, to reflag its vessel in Estonia. In response, the Finnish seaman's union called its members out on strike. The Court held that the trade union's proposed action amounted to a restriction on Viking's freedom of establishment. In its defence the trade union put forward the argument that strike action was justified on the ground of worker protection, an argument which the Court generally accepted.[72] However, in dismissing the action of the trade union the Court considered the proportionality of the trade union's action and concluded that industrial action should be a last resort and national courts would need to verify that all other avenues had first been exhausted. The primary effect of this judgment is that, in the context of the Internal Market and the removal of barriers to free movement, the Court had been asked to determine whether collective action may operate as a barrier to the freedom of establishment and concluded that it could. By doing so the Court, probably unwittingly, restricted a wide range of social rights and values. For example, it ignored that the right to collective action was protected by the Finnish Constitution, which itself raises a clear subsidiarity question in the context of this dispute, and that the right to take collective strike action was itself enshrined in Article 28 of the Charter of Fundamental Rights. The main reason for this proposed Regulation was an attempt by the Commission to reconcile that which the Court had not been able to; namely, the protection of the fundamental Treaty right of establishment with the right of workers to take protected action. As has already been mentioned, the Finnish Constitution, together with some other Constitutions such as those of Sweden and Denmark, protect the right to take collective strike action, indicating that EU legislation should not be necessary. Though this constitutional guarantee is not true of all Member States and, for example, in the United Kingdom industrial relations legislation is very much less employee friendly, there is a real question mark regarding whether harmonising legislation is the most appropriate

---

compliance of EU legislation with subsidiarity, the kind of mechanism that emerged during the Convention was by and large a novelty. See further Rittberger, B. (2005) *Building Europe's Parliament* at 191, 196.

[71] Case C-438/05 *International Transport Workers' Federation* v *Viking Line* [2007] ECR I-10779.

[72] Ibid., paragraph 77.

way to mitigate the harshness of the judgment in *Viking*. The Commission's explanatory memorandum states that:

> the present proposal aims to clarify the general principles and applicable rules at EU level with respect to the exercise of the fundamental right to take collective action within the context of the freedom to provide services and the freedom of establishment, including the need to reconcile them in practice in cross-border situations. Its scope covers not only the temporary posting of workers to another Member State for the cross-border provision of services but also any envisaged restructuring and/or relocation involving more than one Member State.[73]

Article 2 of the proposed Regulation addresses the relationship between fundamental rights and economic freedoms. The Commission describes the effect of this Article as follows:

> While reiterating that there is no inherent conflict between the exercise of the fundamental right to take collective action and the freedom of establishment and the freedom to provide services enshrined in and protected by the Treaty, with no primacy of one over the other, Article 2 recognizes that situations may arise where their exercise may have to be reconciled in cases of conflict, in accordance with the principle of proportionality in line with standard practice by courts and EU case law. The general equality of fundamental rights and the freedoms of establishment and to provide services in terms of status implies that such freedoms may have to be restricted in the interest of protection of fundamental rights. However, it equally implies that the exercise of such freedoms may justify a restriction on the effective exercise of fundamental rights.[74]

As ever the Commission produced an Impact Assessment[75] in which it sought to justify the legislative proposal with regard to Article 5 TEU. The Impact Assessment identified what the Commission considered to be the negative economic and social impacts and continuing legal uncertainty of the effect of the *Viking* judgment which could lead to a loss of support for the Internal Market by an important constituency of the stakeholders and create an unfriendly business environment including the possibility of protectionist behaviour. In essence, the justification is based

---

[73] COM (2012) 130 final *Proposal for a Regulation on the Exercise of the Right to take Collective Action within the Context of the Freedom of Establishment and the Freedom to Provide Services* at 10.

[74] Ibid. at 12.

[75] SWD (2012) 63 final, Commission Staff Working Document, *Impact Assessment Revision of the Legislative Framework on the Posting of Workers in the Context of Provision of Services*.

upon a very weak argument that without this legislation there could be a deterioration in employment relations which would be to the detriment of the Internal Market. In addition, this would create a negative impact on the protection of workers' rights and Article 28 of the Charter of Fundamental Rights. For the Commission, the positive impact of a legislative intervention in the form of a Regulation provides for more legal certainty than a soft law approach, but this suggests an 'over-regulation' by the Commission of a problem which has not explicitly manifested itself. In the view of the Commission a legislative intervention would express a more 'committed political approach'[76] by the Commission to respond to a problem that it concluded was viewed with great concern by the trade unions and parts of the European Parliament.[77] It is not unsurprising that the proposed legislative act led to a yellow card, with nineteen votes being cast from twelve Member States,[78] even though the figure of nineteen votes was only one more than the minimum quorum. In its reasoned opinion the House of Commons EU Scrutiny Committee stated that the draft Regulation fails to comply with the principle of subsidiarity because the Commission has failed to adduce clear evidence of the necessity for EU legislative action including how it will achieve its stated objectives.[79] Perhaps the most significant criticism that can be aimed at the Commission is that, in seeking to justify necessity, the Commission has in the case of this legislative proposal fallen well short of its own standards of providing quantitative and qualitative justifications for harmonising legislation. In short, the Commission's assertion that this Regulation amounts to a 'more political approach' is an attempt to replace independent evidence of the necessity to act with a weak political perception to demonstrate a justification that legislative action is necessary. Indeed it may be argued that the Commission's reliance upon the judgment of the Court in *Viking*, and its perceived negative socio-economic and political effects, is itself an incorrect justification. This is because, first, the judgment in *Viking* can be considered to be both clear and proportionate, and secondly the Commission's Impact Assessment offers no correlative evidence of an impairment of the right to establishment in the aftermath of this judgment. Moreover, there was no explicit evidence that the right to

[76] Ibid. at 66.

[77] Ibid. at 67.

[78] The following parliaments raised either one or more objections: Sweden, Finland, Denmark, Latvia, Portugal, Estonia, Poland, Malta, Belgium, France, United Kingdom and the Netherlands.

[79] Reasoned opinion of 22 May 2012 at paragraph 16.

collective action within the Member States had been impaired by comparison with the pre-*Viking* position or that industrial relations had deteriorated to the extent that this constituted a barrier to the functioning of the Internal Market.[80] In addition to the absence of clear evidence, which justifies an argument of necessity, the proposed Regulation fails to satisfy the primary test of Article 5 TEU that the legislative measure cannot be achieved by the Member States acting independently. Given the subject matter of the Regulation, it is beyond question that within the EU, national legislation is to be preferred because this will more accurately reflect the socio-economic and political dynamics of each Member State to an extent which the proposed Regulation cannot. This further raises the question of whether following the judgment in *ex parte British American Tobacco*, there is a *genuine* cross-border issue which requires harmonising legislation.[81] On this analysis, the test of Article 5 TEU is met; namely that Member States *can* achieve the objective acting independently and indeed already do through the operation of national constitutions and primary legislation. Though the extent of this protection may differ across the Member States, and some systems such as the United Kingdom may offer lower levels of employee protection, it cannot be argued that the Regulation would significantly improve collective bargaining and simultaneously improve the freedom of establishment by removing barriers for companies to establish business in other Member States. The proposed Regulation would also appear to fail to satisfy the criteria of an identifiable value added arising from EU legislative action. The final observation that arises from this proposed Regulation is that the yellow card confirms that subsidiarity monitoring is, first and foremost, a political rather than a judicial concept. The yellow card was the conclusion of a political debate that national parliaments had with the Commission, but one question is still unclear: was the yellow card merely a coincidence or did it arise from a horizontal political dialogue between national parliaments which shared similar concerns? There is no doubt that national parliaments shared similar concerns,[82] but on the question of whether the EU should legislate and not on the specific substance of the

---

[80] In the face of this opposition the Commission withdrew the proposal on 11 September 2012.

[81] Case C-49/01 *R* v *Secretary of State for Health ex parte British American Tobacco and Imperial Tobacco* [2002] ECR I-11453 in particular paragraphs 177 and 185.

[82] A review of the nineteen reasoned opinions available on the IPEX database indicates that the general consensus was that this was an issue that was sufficiently regulated by national law and did not require harmonising legislation.

Regulation or on the question of collective action. If the Member States which objected are considered, they include countries such as Sweden and Finland which have constitutional guarantees for collective action, and the United Kingdom and Poland, which have fewer and weaker labour laws, especially in the field of collective action. On this basis, the yellow card served its purpose and national parliaments, perhaps for primarily divers domestic reasons, objected to the legislative proposal. That said, the objection was only slightly above the bare minimum at nineteen, which indicates that some parliaments either failed to share the subsidiarity arguments, supported the regulation or had not engaged in any form of scrutiny. When all the circumstances of this Regulation and the yellow card are considered, this cannot be said to constitute the foundation of a regular horizontal co-ordination, if indeed this yellow card was the result of detailed and precise horizontal co-ordination. It should be remembered that national parliaments could, pre-Lisbon, communicate their concerns to the Commission about the compatibility of a legislative proposal with Article 5 TEU and inform their minister, who could vote against the legislative proposal in Council. In the case of this Regulation it is very likely that there would have been sufficient votes under QMV against the proposal in the Council to prevent the measure being passed.[83]

5. CONCLUDING REMARKS

This chapter has argued that while the allocated task of subsidiarity monitoring is a collective one, national procedures implemented to monitor subsidiarity remain largely individual. Though the dual requirements of ministerial accountability and subsidiarity monitoring will overlap and can be executed simultaneously, the primary focus of

The documentation is available at http://www.ipex.eu.IPEXL-WEB/dossier.document/COM20120130.do (accessed 26 November 2012).

[83] It is possible to argue that the whole subsidiarity control mechanism presents no major change as national parliaments have always been able to voice concerns about subsidiarity breaches as part of their normal scrutiny of EU documents. Also the Commission has justified its proposals in terms of subsidiarity, and according to an inter-institutional agreement also the Council and the European Parliament must examine whether the Commission's initiatives comply with the subsidiarity principle. See further Kiiver, P. (2006) *The National Parliaments in the European Union* 153 and Maurer, A. (2008) 'National Parliaments in the Architecture of Europe after the Constitutional Treaty' at 93.

national parliaments continues to be executive accountability and protecting national interests. Moreover, though the Treaty may have 'harmonised' the task of subsidiarity monitoring, which is now the responsibility of all national parliaments, the scrutiny procedures of national parliaments remain varied. This leaves scope for differentiated participation in subsidiarity monitoring, as the experience post-Lisbon demonstrates. While not perfect, the post-Lisbon Treaty position can be considered favourably even by comparison with the Constitutional Treaty. Practical innovations such as the IPEX database and the improved position of COSAC no doubt aid the horizontal political dialogue which is at the core of Protocol 2 but certainly do not guarantee it. From this perspective the 'package' of post-Lisbon developments does provide the foundations of a rudimentary framework within which horizontal parliamentary co-ordination on the question of subsidiarity may be achievable. Whether by design or otherwise a yellow card has been shown in the case of Regulation concerning the posting of workers and the right to take collective action, and so the early warning mechanism clearly can fulfil the function intended. In the light of the Commission's response to the yellow card, which has been to reconsider the proposed Regulation, this may act as a catalyst to empower national parliaments to be more proactive and strive to co-ordinate their scrutiny activities more closely, but only time will tell if this is to be a realistic proposition.

7. Accountability and legitimacy in a multi-level context

1. INTRODUCTION

Prior to the Treaty of Maastricht there was no formal recognition within the Treaties of a multi-level governance structure which had de facto existed through the presence of strong regional government in several Member States, most notably Germany. Under the Treaty of Rome 1957 and the Single European Act 1986 the overriding purpose of European integration was economic integration through the harmonisation of the laws of Member States, and this process generally bypassed regional governance. In particular, this focus on economic integration by *Member States* failed to take into account that, in several Member States, for example Belgium and Germany, regional governance was a key constitutional component which assumed significant legislative responsibility and was charged with the task of implementing significant parts of EU legislation. This is because the internal constitutional arrangements of Belgium and Germany allocated constitutional guaranteed legislative competences to federal States.

Since the Treaty of Maastricht an identifiable constitutional trend in many Member States has been to decentralise and create more formal structures of sub-national government[1] and Chapter 2 highlighted how this has also been identified as a component part of deparliamentarisation. Since the Treaty of Maastricht, Member States such as Spain, the United Kingdom and Italy have granted increased political and legislative

[1] In 2002 the Commission launched a consultation process, which built upon the COM (2001) 428 *European Governance – A White Paper*, 11 December 2002, to map out a strategy for greater participation by regional actors in EU affairs. See COM (2002) 709 *A Framework for Target-Based Tripartite Contracts and Agreements between the Community, the States and Regional and Local Authorities*, 11 December 2009.

autonomy to sub-national legislatures,[2] which has resulted in the transfer of significant legislative competence to sub-national institutions. This development has helped to shape what today is referred to as the EU's multi-level governance structure,[3] which formally recognises that EU integration has a distinct regional dimension.[4] The primary question that this raises is, with its enhanced constitutional standing, what role should sub-national government have within the overall structure of securing legislative accountability and legitimacy? The EU Treaties have been slow to reflect these internal constitutional developments, leading to criticism that the Treaty exhibited 'regional blindness'.[5] This criticism was all the more pertinent because the Committee of the Regions (CoR), which had been established by the Treaty of Maastricht, had failed to provide any form of effective representation for the interests of sub-national governance within the legislative process, having only an advisory function. The overriding justification for this criticism is that, notwithstanding increased decentralisation within the Member States, the Community method remained a State-centric and centralising legislative process,[6] and that the definition of subsidiarity, introduced by Article 5 EC of the Treaty of Maastricht 1993, only recognised that the EU shared competence with the Member States. Article 5 EC therefore failed to reflect the constitutional reality of regional autonomy under which the EU increasingly shared competence with regional rather than national institutions,[7] and thus failed to adequately protect regional competences. Working Group I of the Constitutional Convention acknowledged these

---

[2] See Ross, A. and Crespo, M. (2003) 'The Effect of Devolution on the Implementation of European Community Law in the United Kingdom and Spain' at 475.

[3] See generally on the development of multi-level governance in the EU, Marks G. (1996) 'An Actor Centred Approach to Multi-Level Governance' at 20; Jeffrey, C. (ed.), (1997) *The Regional Dimension of the European Union*; Pernice, I. (2009) 'The Treaty of Lisbon' at 349.

[4] See Keating, M. (2004) 'Regions and the Convention on the Future of Europe' at 192; Longo, M. (2003) 'European Integration' at 475.

[5] See Weatherill, S. (2005) 'The Challenge of the Regional Dimension in the European Union' at 3.

[6] See Wincott, D. (2002) 'The Governance White Paper, the Commission and the Search for Legitimacy' at 379.

[7] This was noted in Declaration 3 concerning Germany, Austria and Belgium on Subsidiarity of the Inter-Governmental Conference leading to the Treaty of Amsterdam. The Conference noted that in the case of the German, Austrian and Belgian governments, action taken by the European Community in accordance with the principle of subsidiarity not only concerns the Member

shortcomings and that the growth of regional autonomy necessitated improved recognition and protection of regional competences.[8] In response, the Treaty of Lisbon included, in Article 5 TEU, a revised version of the subsidiarity principle which encompasses 'regional and local' institutions and, under Protocol 2, allocates the task of subsidiarity monitoring to the CoR alongside national parliaments. Working Group I further concluded that competence monitoring by the CoR, including the right of the CoR to seek judicial review for violation of subsidiarity, may contribute to the overall improvement of accountability and legitimacy of the Community method.[9] This chapter explores how EU multi-level governance participates in subsidiarity monitoring and whether, and if so how, the improved recognition of regional governance under the Treaty of Lisbon may help to create what has been described as a 'Europe of the Regions'.[10] In particular what new opportunities for improved legislative accountability and legitimacy does the Treaty of Lisbon provide to sub-national actors and institutions and how can this assist national parliaments in their quest for improving accountability of the EU's legislative institutions?

2. MULTI-LEVEL GOVERNANCE IN THE EU

In 2001 in its White Paper on European Governance[11] the European Commission identified five principles underpinning good governance: openness, participation, responsibility, effectiveness and coherence. These principles were considered in Chapter 1 and are undoubtedly crucial components within the policy-making and legislative processes to secure effective accountability within the EU. They are also equally applicable in the context of examining what role regional governance should play within the EU when seeking to review the exercise of EU competences. This is important because in an EU of twenty-eight Member States with heterogeneous constitutional traditions and no consensus with regard to the allocation of regional competences, a

States but also their entities to the extent that they have their own law-making powers conferred upon them under national constitutional law.

[8] See CONV 286/02 Conclusions of Working Group I on the Principle of Subsidiarity.

[9] Ibid., at 8.

[10] See Thielemann, E. (1999) 'Institutional Limits of a "Europe with the Regions"' at 399.

[11] COM (2001) 428 final *European Governance – A White Paper*.

multi-level governance structure in which all levels of governance contribute to decision-making ensures that these principles are implemented, maintained and enhanced. Within the EU the implementation of multi-level governance depends on respect for the principle of subsidiarity to guard against excessive and unnecessary centralised decision-making and to prevent decision-making being restricted to a single tier of government. Because the post-Lisbon version of Article 5 TEU explicitly refers to the legislative capacity of regional governance to fulfil the policy objective, this means that formal consideration of regional competences, together with the legislative capacity of regional institutions, is part of the legislative process. This ranges from consideration of the regional impact of a legislative proposal within the Commission's Impact Assessments to the ability of regional institutions to seek judicial review of a legislative proposal for non-compliance with the principle of subsidiarity. Respect for the principle of subsidiarity and multi-level governance cannot be separated; the former indicates the responsibilities of the different tiers of government, while the latter emphasises their interaction within the legislative process. Multi-level governance should not simply be viewed as a question of translating European or national objectives into local or regional action, but must also be understood as a process for integrating the objectives of local and regional authorities within the strategies of the EU.[12] Moreover, multi-level governance should reinforce and shape the responsibilities of local and regional authorities at national level and encourage their participation in the co-ordination of European policy, in this way helping to design and implement EU policies. This strategy is very much at the heart of the EU's Agenda 2020 Programme, where there is a significant emphasis placed upon the delivery of EU policy objectives by sub-national governance through improved procedures of policy co-ordination. The conditions for good multi-level governance largely depend on the Member States themselves.

This is because there is no single model for sub-national government in the EU and its participation in EU affairs, and responsibility for the implementation of EU legislation is wholly dependent upon domestic constitutional provisions. Although there is a clear trend within the EU towards a process of decentralisation,[13] which though not uniform is nonetheless widespread, the conditions for this shared governance have

---

[12] See Carter, C. (2000) 'Democratic Governance Beyond the Nation State' at 429.

[13] See Scott, C. (2002) 'The Governance of the European Union' at 59.

not yet been met in full. The principles and mechanisms of consultation, co-ordination, co-operation and evaluation recommended at the EU level must first be applied within the Member States. Multi-level governance presupposes the existence of mutual loyalty and co-operation between all levels of governance to reach common goals within the integration process. This also includes applying the subsidiarity principle, as a fundamental principle of EU law, so that legislative responsibility is exercised appropriately. The institutional framework of multi-level governance and the formal allocation of competences that accompanies this are fundamental but, on their own, are not enough to guarantee good governance. On the contrary, co-operation between the institutions across multi-level governance with regard to the exercise of legislative powers is absolutely vital to enable each level of governance to fulfil its legitimate political and democratic roles. The CoR's White Paper on Multi-Level Governance[14] highlighted that European democracy would be reinforced by more inclusive and flexible inter-institutional co-operation and by more sustained political co-operation between the various levels of governance. Because of the political nature of the CoR and the European Parliament, it is logical that they should work closely together to strengthen the democratic legitimacy of the process of European integration, both in the context of the European political groups and also in the context of their various decision-making bodies.[15] However, for reasons discussed below such co-operation between the CoR and the European Parliament on the question of subsidiarity is likely to be to the detriment of national parliaments in the operation of Protocol 2. Inter-parliamentary co-operation is increasingly becoming a vital component of the process of seeking democratic legitimacy and of the process of drafting European legislation. Multi-level governance and its institutional arrangements are a way of also involving all local and regional authorities more explicitly in the process. In particular, under the early warning mechanism in Protocol 2, regional parliaments and regional legislative assemblies have a specific role of appraising the application of the subsidiarity principle. Whether this helps to safeguard the exercise of regional competences guaranteed under domestic constitutions, and more generally to ensure

---

[14] CdR 89/2009 final *The Committee of the Regions' White Paper on Multi-Level Governance* at 7.

[15] In its opinion on the European Parliament's new role and responsibilities implementing the Treaty of Lisbon, the Committee on Regional Development of the European Parliament stresses the importance of its relations with the Committee of the Regions (PE404.556v02-00 (30 May 2008)).

along with national parliaments that the subsidiarity principle is applied, remains questionable.

2.1 The EU's Third Level of Governance

Many Member States have established forms of devolved, regional or 'meso' government.[16] While this sub-State level is heterogeneous in economic, social, cultural and political terms, the fact remains that for nearly three decades the EU has witnessed a rise in what has been generically termed a 'third level' of government.[17] It is beyond question that the EU has played a significant role in creating and shaping this third level, and a 'Europe of the Regions' has been fashioned through, inter alia, the use of instruments such as structural funds and regional aid, which are designed to promote economic and social cohesion. The establishment of the CoR is itself recognition, albeit only rudimentary, that the EU legislative process must acknowledge regional interests and priorities. Multi-level governance rejects what can be described as a pyramidal form of governance and presupposes that *all* layers of governance are stakeholders in decision-making and share responsibility for policy delivery. Within the EU's paradigm of multi-level governance this consists of 'the existence of overlapping competences among levels of governance and the interaction of political actors across those levels'.[18] In circumstances when competences are concurrent it is the principle of subsidiarity in Article 5 TEU that regulates their exercise. However, it is apparent, both politically from the Commission's Better Regulation Agenda and from the judgments of the Court of Justice, that the presumption of legislative efficiency will necessitate that, notwithstanding Article 5 TEU and Protocol 2, competences will continue to be exercised, more often than not by the EU. Within the EU's multi-level polity the constitutional status of regions has been historically weak

---

[16] See Jones, B. and Keating, M. (eds) (1995) *The European Union and the Regions* and Börzel, T.A. (2002) *States and Regions in the European Union*. See also European Institute of Public Administration and European Centre for the Regions (2010) *The Role of Regional Parliaments in the Process of Subsidiarity Analysis within the Early Warning System of the Treaty of Lisbon*, available at http://portal.cor.eu/subsdiarity/Documents (accessed 16 May 2012). This Report illustrates that the heterogeneity of sub-national governance and the political prominence it has within domestic constitutions undoubtedly influence the extent to which it will be involved in subsidiarity monitoring.

[17] See Jeffrey, C. (ed.) (1997), *The Regional Dimension of the European Union*.

[18] See Marks, G. (1996) 'An Actor Centred Approach to Multi-Level Governance' at 360.

because, notwithstanding any improved Treaty recognition, there is an absence of a universal statement of *which* competences are, or should be, allocated to regions. The Treaty has not codified regional competences and their distribution continues to be determined solely through the public law of Member States. In the Treaty, Article 4 (2) TEU insipidly states that the EU will 'respect regional and local self-government' when legislating and the revised definition of subsidiarity in Article 5 TEU refers, in general, to the need to 'consider local and regional competences'.[19] Under Protocol 2 the Commission is obliged that, before proposing a legislative act, its consultations shall, where appropriate, take into consideration the regional and local dimensions of the envisaged act,[20] and every EU draft legislative act must include an assessment of its potential impact upon local and regional levels.[21] Article 5 of Protocol 2 provides that, in the case of draft directives, the Commission must explain the implications for Member States, including any regional legislation that will be required. These Treaty provisions undoubtedly target criticisms of regional blindness by mainstreaming regional considerations into the collective thoughts of the legislators, but they stop well short of creating a comprehensive system of checks and balances that adequately protects regional competences. However, regional competences, though real and important, should not be considered in isolation from Member States' competences. The protection of regional competences remains very much of relevance to central governments, which have a responsibility to ensure that domestic constitutional norms are upheld. Though the Treaty refers to 'regions', and thereby implies some form of collective homogeneity amongst regional actors, it would be incorrect to conclude that regions constitute a single entity within the EU whose exercise of competences is uniform. On the contrary, though regions form a constituent part of the multi-level polity, they do not, whether individually or within the CoR, share a common political or legislative agenda with regard to the boundaries of EU integration. Furthermore, the creation of a 'Europe of the Regions' has been undermined by the eastward expansion of the EU, and since 2004 the EU has admitted Member States which do not have developed regional structures. To this end a 'Europe of the Regions' is very much a western European phenomenon and this has undoubtedly weakened the position

---

[19] Article 5 (3) TEU.
[20] See Article 2 of Protocol 2.
[21] Ibid., Article 5.

of regional governments and made it more difficult to resolve the regional question within the EU.[22]

2.2 Sub-National Governance and the Allocation of Competences

Multi-level governance requires an a priori clear and rational vertical allocation of exclusive and concurrent competences, but the position of regions is weaker by comparison to the Member States, which remain the primary contracting parties under the Treaty. By contrast with the Member States, whose relationship with the EU is based upon the duty within Article 4 (3) TEU,[23] regional participation in EU affairs is determined by, inter alia, the individual public law arrangements within the Member States. In recognition of the multi-level polity and to address criticisms of competence creep the Treaty of Lisbon includes a clearer legal statement concerning the division of competences between the EU and its Member States. However, though Articles 4 and 5 TEU, together with Title I of the TFEU, describe and codify the division of competence more clearly, there is no specific reference to the exercise of 'regional competences' within the Treaty.[24] This omission can be criticised for not fully reflecting the constitutional reality within many Member States. The competence debate within the EU has embraced both normative and constitutional questions of competence distribution,[25] focussing upon the necessity for EU action and the extent to which legislative powers are transferred to the EU. Within the Constitutional Convention this debate embraced the need for improved accountability and legitimacy of the legislative process which post-Lisbon comes in the form of subsidiarity monitoring.[26] For regional governance, the competence debate is more complex and clouded by additional considerations of the operation of internal public law. For example, internal constitutional disputes between autonomous regions and central government may arise in circumstances

[22] See further Hopkins, W.J. (2010) 'A Tale of Two Europes' at 55.

[23] Article 4 (3) TEU blandly states, 'The Member States shall take any appropriate measure, general or particular, to ensure the fulfilment of the obligations arising out of the Treaties or resulting from the acts of the institutions of the Union.'

[24] Article 4 TEU states that the 'Union shall respect the equality before the Treaties of … regional and local self-government'.

[25] Ibid. See also Bogdany, A.V. and Bast, J. (2002) 'The European Union's Vertical Order of Competences' at 227 and de Witte, B. and de Burca, G. (2002) 'The Post-Nice Delimitation of Powers' at 201.

[26] See CONV 286/02 Conclusions of Working Group I on the Principle of Subsidiarity and Weatherill, S. (2009) 'Competence and Legitimacy' at 17.

when the Member State, as the primary contracting party to the Treaty, assumes overall responsibility for the implementation of EU law. Implementation of EU law by regional legislatures is addressed within most public law and circumstances of legislative override are rare. However, this question must be considered within the overall duty of Member States under Article 4 (3) TEU.[27] This duty, to ensure that obligations arising under the Treaty are fulfilled, suggests that, on efficiency grounds, centralised implementing legislation will be expedient. For some autonomous regions this means potentially fighting the competence battle on two fronts: first to protect their own internal constitutional privileges, and, secondly, to scrutinise the exercise of EU competences through subsidiarity monitoring. Article 5 TEU states that the limits of EU competence are governed by the principle of conferral under which the 'Union shall act only within the limits of the competences conferred upon it by the *Member States* in the Treaties to attain the objectives set out therein'.[28] Despite the reference to only the 'Member States' in Article 5 TEU the impact of Europeanisation upon national and sub-national government would appear to be similar – both will cede powers to the EU where it has exclusive competence and both will look to apply the subsidiarity principle when competences are shared. However, regional institutions are in a considerably weaker position by contrast to national parliaments, if for no other reason that the Council is predominantly composed of national ministers accountable, in the first instance, to a national parliament. Institutionally, the regions are also at a disadvantage, in comparison with national parliaments, because under the subsidiarity monitoring of the early warning mechanism in Protocol 2 *only* national parliaments have been allocated a pre-legislative intervention device through which they may challenge a legislative proposal for non-compliance with subsidiarity. The CoR, under Protocol 2 TEU, may have acquired the power to monitor subsidiarity, but this does not extend to direct participation in the early warning mechanism, raising the question of exactly *how* the CoR may discharge this task.

---

[27] This raises questions of State liability for failure to comply with EU law. In the context of Article 4 (3) TEU Member States remain liable at all times for any breach, even if committed by a sub-national legislature. In these circumstances regional liability is only indirect and will arise if national rules require the region at fault to reimburse central government.

[28] Emphasis added.

3. SUBSIDIARITY MONITORING BY THE COR

Multi-level governance brings together a distinctive configuration of multiple levels, institutions and non-State actors. The Treaty of Lisbon harnesses this political arrangement and, through competence monitoring by the CoR, identifies an additional opportunity by which legislative accountability may be pursued. Subsidiarity regulates the allocation of competences within multi-level governance[29] and it is appropriate that the CoR, as the institutional representative of the regions, participates in guarding the exercise of those competences. However, notwithstanding the increased prominence for the CoR within the Treaty, and its participation in subsidiarity monitoring, it is important to remember the practical limitations within which the CoR operates. Not only does the CoR suffer from a formal lack of legislative powers and have only a limited consultative function, but the regional representatives which constitute the CoR membership are appointed in a variety of ways. This varied composition further underscores the point that an absence of uniformity, in terms of both political power and representative function, weakens the position of the CoR as an institutional actor[30] which manifests itself in its subsidiarity monitoring activities.

3.1 Article 5 TEU in a Regional Context

As has been discussed in earlier chapters, Article 5 TEU defines the parameters of the efficiency argument which underpins the presumption of EU action in circumstances of concurrent competences. In its revised form post-Lisbon it states that EU action should only take place 'in so far as the objectives cannot be achieved by the Member States, either at central level *or at regional and local level*'.[31] This reference to regions, though a development from the Treaty of Amsterdam, constitutes only a rudimentary acknowledgement of the existence of sub-national governance and multi-levelism more generally. The major weakness that arises from the current Treaty is that, by failing to formally acknowledge that in

---

[29] See Popelier, P. and Vandenbruwaene, W. (2011) 'The Subsidiarity Mechanism as a Tool for Inter-Level Dialogue in Belgium' at 205–207. See also the Report by the European Institute of Public Administration and European Centre for the Regions (2010) *The Role of Regional Parliaments in the Process of Subsidiarity Analysis within the Early Warning System of the Treaty of Lisbon*, available at http://portal.cor.eu/subsdiarity/Documents (accessed 16 May 2012).

[30] See further Hopkins, W.J. (2010) 'A Tale of Two Europes'.

[31] Emphasis added.

the exercise of concurrent competences the EU does not share legislative power with the Member State, this ignores that sub-national legislature has been granted constitutionally guaranteed powers. To this extent, it may be questioned whether Article 5 TEU makes any significant improvement either to the protection of regional competences, or to improving the legitimacy and accountability of the legislative process more generally. The weakness exhibited by the post-Lisbon arrangements is even starker when contrasted with the constitutional status afforded to regional competences in Member States within federal constitutions such as Belgium and Germany. In Germany, for example, subsidiarity provides a constitutional safeguard, guaranteed by the Federal Constitutional Court, against the centralisation of legislative power. Within the German Constitution this arrangement provides an important political contribution to the overall system of constitutional checks and balances that exists within the Federal Republic.[32] However, neither Article 5 TEU nor Protocol 2 create the necessary sophisticated form of political accountability within the EU's supra-national Treaty framework which monitoring the application of the subsidiarity principle requires. It will be recalled from earlier discussions within this book that legislative justifications of necessity by the Commission have proved difficult to rebut. On this basis it is unlikely that the CoR will be any more successful than national parliaments in applying the principles within Article 5 TEU and securing the effective political accountability of the Commission and other legislative actors which the Treaty of Lisbon was supposed to deliver.

3.2 CoR and Impact Assessments

It will be recalled from Chapter 2 that Impact Assessments form the starting point for national parliaments against which they benchmark a legislative proposal for its compliance with the principle of subsidiarity. The same is true for the CoR if it is to fulfil the task of subsidiarity monitoring that it has been allocated under Protocol 2. The use of the Impact Assessment by the CoR presupposes that, at least in principle, national parliaments and the CoR are considering similar, if not the same, subsidiarity implications. This would be logical, especially since the exercise of competence at the EU level ought to be the same upon both regional and national competences. However, any synergy between the

[32] For a more detailed discussion of the *Bundesrat* in EU affairs see Cygan, A. (2001) *National Parliaments in an Integrated Europe* Chapter 9.

CoR and national parliaments with regard to the application of subsidiarity is likely to be sporadic for two reasons. First, as an EU institution, the CoR is likely to share with the European Parliament the integrationist objectives that come from EU legislative action. By contrast, national parliaments have been much more guarded about whether EU legislation is required and more rigorous in their application of subsidiarity.[33] Moreover, the CoR is a newcomer to this form of scrutiny and is unlikely to be able to draw upon the same level of experience that exists within national parliaments. Secondly, the membership of the CoR, which is drawn from regional governance from across the EU, has benefited significantly from the expansion of EU regional policy and related policies, for example EU Structural Funds. To the extent that such tangible economic or social benefits continue for EU regions, the CoR will remain a co-operative partner within the legislative process.[34] However, irrespective of whether the CoR may be a willing participant in deeper integration, it is questionable whether the CoR is indeed representative of regional governance and especially whether, as an institution, it offers an effective forum for the protection of regional competences. Article 13 (4) TEU defines the role of the CoR as 'assisting' the institutional actors within the Community method in an 'advisory capacity'. This includes a process of institutionalised dialogue with the Commission through which the CoR may contribute to Impact Assessments[35] undertaken as part of the Commission's Better Regulation Agenda. By contrast to the early warning mechanism, which is only activated once a legislative proposal is sent to the national parliaments,[36] an Impact Assessment is produced at the commencement of the decision-making process.

A practice of formal consultation in the formulation of an Impact Assessment regularises the CoR's participation in policy-making and

---

[33] See Weatherill, S. (2005) 'The Challenge of the Regional Dimension in the European Union' at 8.

[34] Ibid.

[35] See Document R/CdR 86/2007 *Agreement Governing Cooperation between the European Commission and the Committee of the Regions* at paragraph 3a. The value added by the CoR in formulating the Impact Assessment has been acknowledged as a priority when determining subsidiarity. See further Carroll, W.E. (2011) 'The Committee of the Regions' 353.

[36] Article 2 of Protocol 2 requires that the CoR is involved in formulating the Impact Assessment and this is intended to improve the regulatory environment through the value added of specific local and regional perspectives.

enables the CoR to raise competence questions *directly* with the Commission, and at a much earlier stage than would otherwise be available through the early warning mechanism. For regional institutions this is probably more efficient than undertaking their own scrutiny of a legislative proposal and feeding through their findings to the national parliament to incorporate into the reasoned opinion. Moreover, participation by the CoR in the Impact Assessment process enables it to move upstream within decision-making. This offers the prospect of contributing to the input legitimacy of the legislative proposal which national parliaments will not necessarily do in the same way, even under the improved provision of documentation under the Barosso Initiative. Thus the CoR looks to have more dynamic opportunities for participation in legislative formulation by contrast to national parliaments whose review of the draft proposal within the early warning mechanism only takes place during the latter stages of the legislative process with the purpose of securing output legitimacy.[37] Participation by the CoR in Impact Assessments *may* boost regional voices in the Community method, but the Impact Assessment does not offer a universal solution for improved legislative legitimacy, nor can this be considered as sufficient to protect regional competences. The experience post-Lisbon indicates that participation by regional institutions in Impact Assessments is likely to have only minor impact upon either the content or quality of legislation.[38] Improved consultation and dialogue may aid, more generally, in the creation of regional networks and alliances, but this form of co-operation is largely unstructured, and its conclusions are unlikely to rebut the presumptions, within Article 5 of Protocol 2, that EU action is required because it is efficient and necessary. The improved Treaty recognition for regions needs to be

---

[37] See Cygan, A. (2011) 'The Parliamentarisation of EU Decision-Making?' at 478.

[38] See R/CdR 57/2011 *Subsidiarity Annual Report 2010 of the CoR* at 22. This Report confirms the limited subsidiarity monitoring undertaken by the CoR through two pilot exercises which tested the operation of the Subsidiarity Monitoring Network amongst regional institutions. The first, in March 2009, was carried out in connection with a Commission Initiative on the Reduction of Health Inequalities. The second pilot, in October 2009, concerned a future Directive on Water Quality replacing Council Directive 93/83/EC. Both pilots brought together a network of regions which communicated regional perspectives on both proposals and raised awareness amongst EU officials of regional perspectives, but neither submission could be described as having a substantive impact upon policy due to the lack of participation by regional institutions and the absence of agreement concerning what actually constitutes a breach of subsidiarity.

cited within the overall Treaty objectives to draw together the strands of efficient policy delivery with the requirement of legitimate, democratic and more inclusive decision-making.[39] To this end, subsidiarity monitoring by the CoR undoubtedly resonates with the twin objectives of delivering tangible benefits to the citizen while simultaneously enhancing legislative legitimacy, but its ability to consistently improve legislative legitimacy, in a regional context, should not be overstated.[40] This is primarily because of the absence of Treaty provisions which allocate clearly defined regional competences and which subsidiarity monitoring by the CoR could consistently protect. Under current constitutional arrangements, where regional actors do not share a uniform political and legislative agenda, competence monitoring by the CoR will remain sporadic and inconsistent and subject to the political priorities of what may be defined as 'strong' regional institutions such as the *Länder*. The ongoing debate surrounding competence and accountability in the EU focusses upon subsidiarity as a means of securing improved protection for the exercise of competences within a multi-level framework. However, participation in EU affairs by regional actors is not confined to competence monitoring by the CoR; on the contrary, it must be remembered that the EU's regions, as individual entities, also occupy a significant constitutional position in the multi-level polity. This is because, in circumstances where regional institutions have acquired legislative autonomy, then, in the context of Article 4 TFEU, the EU shares competence with regional rather than national institutions. This raises specific political questions of subsidiarity for regional institutions and how these can be most effectively protected.

3.3 The CoR and the Early Warning Mechanism

Prior to the Treaty of Lisbon the CoR was a peripheral institutional actor within the legislative process and had very limited rights of participation. The primary prerogative of the CoR was that it would be consulted in the circumstances of a legislative proposal where competence was shared by the EU with the Member States. In doing so, and as a means of injecting a distinct regional dimension into the legislative process, the CoR

[39] See Kiiver, P. (2011) 'The Composite Case for National Parliaments in the European Union' at 236.

[40] See Popelier, P. and Vandenbruwaene, W. (2011) 'The Subsidiarity Mechanism as a Tool for Inter-Level Dialogue in Belgium' at 207.

established an institutional practice of subsidiarity monitoring.[41] However, due to the informal nature of this practice and the political inexperience of the CoR, the results of this subsidiarity monitoring were generally ineffective[42] and had only limited impact upon the legislative process. Article 5 of Protocol 2 TEU formally embraces the CoR in the task of subsidiarity monitoring, alongside national parliaments, which requires the CoR to engage in a political assessment of proposals' compatibility with Article 5 TEU.[43] This indirect Treaty recognition of regional governance and regional competences is intended to improve legislative legitimacy and offer guarantees that regional competences are not simply bypassed within the legislative process. However, as is the case with national and sub-national legislatures, the CoR is hampered by the absence of a normative definition of subsidiarity when seeking to review its application. By comparison with national parliaments, the CoR's contribution is considerably less effective, not least because of the construction of Protocol 2. The key feature of Protocol 2 is that it permits *only* national parliaments to issue reasoned opinions concerning alleging the non-compliance of a draft legislative proposal with Article 5 TEU. This leaves the outstanding question of what form of intervention CoR participation should take and whether this has any real relevance in the application of Protocol 2. While Protocol 2 engages both the CoR and national parliaments in subsidiarity monitoring, the early warning mechanism only provides an opportunity for political review to lead to the delivery of a reasoned opinion for national legislatures.

The significance of this goes back to the question of output legitimacy whereby national parliaments, through participation in subsidiarity monitoring, may be considered as fulfilling the function of providing legislative legitimacy in the manner referred to in the Laeken Declaration. By contrast, the CoR, which only provides a loose form of indirect representation for regional governance, cannot be considered as offering the same possibilities of providing legislative legitimacy through its political processes, which remain by and large informal. On this analysis the early warning mechanisms can be characterised as a State-centric process of

---

41 See Loughlin, J. (2005) 'The Regional Question, Subsidiarity and the Future of Europe'; Cygan, A. (2013) 'Regional Governance, Subsidiarity and Accountability within the EU's Multi-Level Governance' at 907.

42 See CONV 843/03 The Consultative Powers of the Committee of the Regions.

43 As a consequence the CoR revised its rules of procedure to reflect the new prerogatives offered under Protocol 2. See Committee of the Regions Rules of Procedure OJ L 6/14, 9.1.2010.

subsidiarity review whose objective is to improve the accountability of and inject democratic legitimacy into an equally State-centric legislative process. As will be recalled from the discussion in Chapter 6, the early warning mechanism presupposes a significant degree of horizontal co-ordination between national parliaments to attain the thresholds within Protocol 2 to show a yellow or orange card. However, the CoR cannot issue the equivalent of a yellow or orange card and regional institutions are not counted as 'parliaments or chambers' for this purpose and may be considered as broadly superfluous to the process of political dialogue under Protocol 2. This casts considerable doubt over exactly *what* influence the CoR may bring to bear under Protocol 2, though it remains open to regional chambers to co-ordinate their subsidiarity objections and include them in the CoR's response or for regional legislatures to have their subsidiarity assessments included in that of the national parliament. However, this will require a horizontal political dialogue between sub-national actors which is largely sporadic and in the light of the varied constitutional arrangements in the Member States may be considered as an unrealistic proposition.[44] For example, it is difficult to see how or even why the *Länder* would want to enter into discussions with relatively weak regional or local institutions. Perhaps the most effective way will be for regional legislatures to co-ordinate their responses with national parliaments. Under Article 6 of Protocol 2 this is anticipated as being the norm and 'it will be for each national parliament or each chamber of national parliament to consult, where appropriate, regional parliaments with legislative powers'. This encourages a vertical dialogue between domestic political institutions, but the onus rests upon the sub-national institutions to feed up their views to national parliaments. Though Article 6 provides an acknowledgement that EU decision-making is a multi-levelled process this does not guarantee that a distinct regional voice will be identified within the early warning mechanism because of the absence of a structured horizontal dialogue between regional institutions. Though the CoR has established the Subsidiarity Monitoring Network (SMN), which provides a forum for political dialogue, similar in nature to COSAC, it is questionable whether this can formulate a definitive regional position on the question of subsidiarity which will come through in the reasoned opinions of national parliaments. Furthermore, under the early warning mechanism the time limits for national parliaments are

---

[44] Under Rule 51 of the Rules of Procedure of the Committee of the Regions, 'all Committee opinions shall carry an explicit reference to the application of the subsidiarity and proportionality principles'.

very short, with a maximum of eight weeks to complete scrutiny prior to the Council confirming the common position. Under these circumstances regional institutions will have even less time to complete a review and with a lack of expertise and resources they will generally struggle to formulate meaningful contributions within the short deadlines.

3.4 The Subsidiarity Monitoring Network

The underlying premise of subsidiarity monitoring is that, to be effective, the process must achieve a substantial degree of agreement between the key stakeholders and actors who participate in it. In particular this necessitates the existence of a vibrant political dialogue amongst political institutions. Though national parliaments and the CoR are both allocated the task of subsidiarity monitoring it would be incorrect to assume that they share the same agenda with regard to subsidiarity monitoring. The CoR, as an EU institution, is likely, on many if not most occasions, to be closer to the European Parliament in terms of the exercise of EU competence. For example, with regard to the proposed Regulation on the right to take collective strike action which was discussed in Chapter 6,[45] and on which national parliaments had reached the threshold to show a yellow card, the CoR broadly shared the favourable view of the proposal held by the Commission and European Parliament. Though the CoR welcomed the withdrawal of the proposal, its reasons for doing so reflect a strongly articulated view that the proposal did not go far enough in the protection that it was offering, and that it failed to reform other legislation such as Directive 96/71/EC on the posting of workers in the framework of the provision of services.[46] However, irrespective of its political preferences the CoR will only be able to have its voice heard if, like national parliaments, there is some degree of collectivity to its subsidiarity monitoring activities, which appears to be evident, to some extent, in relation to the proposed Regulation for collective strike action. At the very least this would appear to indicate that there is scope for the existence of a distinct regional position with regard to legislative proposals arising from a horizontal political dialogue between regional actors, and which is distinct from that of national parliaments. However, whether

[45] COM (2012) 130 *Draft Regulation on the Exercise of the Right to take Collective Action within the Context of the Freedom of Establishment and the Freedom to Provide Services.*

[46] Directive 96/71/EC of the European Parliament and of the Council of 16 December 1996 concerning the posting of workers in the framework of the provision of services. OJ L 018, 21.01.1997, at 1–6.

the difference arises in relation to the application of the subsidiarity principle is a moot point. In the case of the Draft Regulation on collective strike action, the CoR's position appeared to be one of *more* EU intervention rather than questioning EU competence, which certainly was the case with the nineteen reasoned opinions received by the Commission from national parliaments. This raises real questions of how much assistance to national parliaments the CoR's intervention was. To help facilitate improved co-ordination on the application of the subsidiarity principle across a diverse range of sub-national institutions and actors the SMN was launched in April 2007. In recognition of the constitutional heterogeneity of sub-national governance across the Member States, the SMN's members include parliaments and governments of regions with legislative powers, local and regional authorities without legislative powers and local government associations in the EU. It is also open to CoR national delegations and chambers of national parliaments. The primary purpose for the establishment of the SMN was to facilitate the exchange of information between local and regional authorities in the EU and at the EU level regarding various documents and legislative and political proposals from the European Commission which, once adopted, will have a direct impact on these authorities and the policies for which they are responsible. However, the CoR has itself determined that fulfilling this task using this modus operandi does not guarantee that its influence will be brought to bear. This is because different constitutions have allocated different legislative and administrative competences to sub-national governments, leading to the existence of varied subsidiarity priorities across sub-national government. The SMN aims at enabling local and regional authorities to be active in monitoring the implementation of the subsidiarity and proportionality principles through four identifiable ways:

1. Raising awareness as regards the practical implementation of the subsidiarity and proportionality principles.
2. Keeping CoR rapporteurs and members informed about contributions regarding subsidiarity and proportionality from a representative network of local and regional stakeholders.
3. Identifying measures for better law-making, cutting red tape and increasing the acceptance of EU policies by EU citizens.
4. Acting as a laboratory for the identification and exchange of best practices and experience between local and regional authorities on the application of the subsidiarity principle and the decentralised implementation of EU policies at the local level.

In practice, the network operates through its website, indicating that its purpose is to gather and disseminate information from a diverse range of sub-national institutional actors rather than to formulate its own policy position in advance of a plenary debate. This is confirmed by the modus operandi of the SMN under which it operates as an access point enabling all of its partners to obtain information and express their views within the legislative process.[47] Network partners are free to submit their assessments of all political or legislative documents which are the subject of a CoR opinion. In addition, they can be invited by a CoR rapporteur drafting an opinion on an EU legislative initiative to give their views, whether on subsidiarity and proportionality aspects or on specific substantive matters. A summary report of the contributions is forwarded to rapporteurs and the relevant CoR commissions to serve as input for political debate within the commissions and during plenary sessions. After this the CoR may express a formal position on the application of subsidiarity. The overriding evaluation of this contribution to subsidiarity monitoring by the CoR is that it can be defined primarily as a 'soft' form of political involvement which can be categorised as being reactive and whose impact does not go much beyond raising regional issues with the legislative institutions.[48] On this analysis it is hard to see how much benefit this brings to national parliaments under Protocol 2.

---

[47] In 2009 the CoR launched its first Action Plan under which it aims to identify experiences and best practices in the application of the subsidiarity principle in the EU's regions and cities. The methodology of the Action Plan is that it is divided into 'pillars' corresponding to policy areas where the application of the subsidiarity principle is considered to be especially relevant and where evidence of best practice exists. The pillars cover the integration of migrants, fighting climate change, social policy and social rights, health policy and innovation. The key feature of these pillars is that they are primarily those policy areas where the EU has pursued Europeanisation through policy co-ordination rather than through legislative harmonisation, and as such soft law has been utilised.

[48] See R CdR 57/2011 *Subsidiarity Annual Report 2010 of the CoR* at 22. This Report confirms the limited subsidiarity monitoring undertaken by the CoR through two pilot exercises which tested the operation of the SMN amongst regional institutions. The first, in March 2009, was carried out in connection with a Commission Initiative on the Reduction of Health Inequalities. The second pilot, in October 2009, concerned a future Directive on Water Quality replacing Council Directive 93/83/EC. Both pilots brought together a network of regions which communicated regional perspectives on both proposals and raised awareness amongst EU officials of regional perspectives, but neither submission could be described as having a substantive impact upon policy due to the lack of

4. JUDICIAL REVIEW BY THE CoR

In Chapter 6 it was noted that the limited success of actions for judicial review before the Court on grounds of infringement of the subsidiarity principle arose from the significant margin of appreciation that the Court has granted, in particular, to the Commission when evaluating whether EU legislative action is 'necessary'. With regard to the CoR and its newly acquired powers to seek judicial review under Article 263 TFEU, it is not anticipated that it will be any more successful should it decide to pursue such a challenge. Yet it is the very existence of this opportunity, guaranteed by Protocol 2, which is noteworthy because it recognises that direct judicial review is a key component of accountable decision-making.[49] It should also not go unmentioned that judicial review for infringement of the subsidiarity principle has been allocated to what can be characterised as one of the more peripheral EU institutions which does not have any direct representative functions. Constitutionally, the value of the CoR to seeking judicial review under these circumstances must be considered as questionable.

4.1 Article 8 of Protocol 2

It is within this context that Article 8 of Protocol 2 provides two new opportunities for judicial intervention by the CoR to challenge decision-making under the Community method. First, under Article 263 TFEU the CoR has the power to protect its own institutional prerogatives to ensure that its right to consultation within the legislative process is fulfilled. This opportunity is limited to policy areas where the Treaty requires that the CoR should be consulted by the Council and/or European Parliament as part of the legislative process. This constitutes an important recognition that established rights of political participation cannot be circumscribed.[50] Secondly, the CoR may commence an action for an alleged

---

participation by regional institutions and the absence of agreement concerning what actually constitutes a breach of subsidiarity.

[49] See further CONV 548/03 Praesidium Conclusions of the Convention on the Future of Europe: Summary Report on the Plenary Session 6 and 7 February 2003.

[50] The right of consultation in the decision-making process is one that has been recognised by the Court in Case C-70/88 *Parliament* v *Council (Chernobyl)* [1990] ECR I- 2041, where the Court spoke at length of the need to protect the European Parliament's prerogatives within the legislative procedure. The primary reason for this was that, where the Treaty provided for it, consultation of the

infringement of the subsidiarity principle and request that the Court annuls the legislation following a vote by a simple majority of its members. Acquiring the status of a semi-privileged applicant under Article 263 TFEU provides an additional opportunity for institutional accountability of the Council and Parliament. If used strategically, this right could offer some challenge to the political authority of the Council and Parliament, not least because an action for judicial review by the CoR has the potential to apply a brake to the legislative process. While these opportunities to seek judicial review can be considered to only marginally improve accountability within the legislative process, they are still significant for several reasons. First, judicial review for breach of the subsidiarity principle is a right which the Treaty has not extended directly to national parliaments, which may similarly conclude that a legislative proposal infringes subsidiarity.

As discussed in Chapter 6, under Protocol 2 national parliaments continue to rely upon the proxy representation of their national governments to commence such an action, and in this sense these provisions offer nothing new for national parliaments by comparison with the pre-Lisbon position. Secondly, the right of the CoR to seek an annulment of a legislative proposal which infringes its prerogatives is arguably disproportionate to its position within the decision-making process. The CoR may commence an action against a legislative act adopted in the framework of a policy domain for which the Treaty foresees that the CoR should have been consulted. This is a very low threshold to satisfy because not only is the CoR an unelected institution, but also a failure to consult constitutes the removal of a participatory right, rather than amounting to the restriction of a direct representative function. Again, by contrast, national parliaments through their scrutiny of EU legislation are fulfilling a broader constitutional function of not only exerting accountability over the individual minister, but through the operation of the early warning mechanism are tasked with injecting accountability into the EU legislative process. This political accountability is all the more relevant because national parliaments may, unlike the CoR, exert enough political pressure to bring the legislative process to a halt, as occurred in the case of the proposed Regulation for collective redundancies. This adds further support to the proposition, made in Chapter 6, that it is more likely to be the political process rather than judicial review which will be the most

Parliament promoted democratic accountability and helped to maintain institutional balance, both of which can be attributed to, and arise from, the representative functions of the Parliament.

effective mechanism through which to enforce subsidiarity. Yet the opportunity in Article 8 of Protocol 2 for the CoR to bring judicial review proceedings has not been completely dismissed as ineffective. For example, Lenaerts has expressed a permissive interpretation of Article 263 (3) TFEU[51] and argues that the mere threat of judicial review, citing breach of subsidiarity as grounds for review, could improve the CoR's *ex ante* political control of the legislative actors who may consider the threat of legal action as sufficient incentive to review a legislative proposal.[52] Lenaerts further argues that, in addition to becoming a willing litigant, were the CoR to become a proactive participant in subsidiarity monitoring, the Court may be more inclined to protect its prerogatives through recognition that the CoR's input into the formulation of Impact Assessments constitutes a formal part of the decision-making process. If this assertion is correct – and it remains open to question – then it may be argued that the CoR and national parliaments engage in subsidiarity monitoring at two different points of the legislative cycle, and on this analysis their tasks are complementary. For these reasons Lenaerts argues that the CoR acquiring the status of a semi-privileged applicant under Article 263 TFEU should not be dismissed altogether because it offers the CoR an independent opportunity to directly protect its participatory rights and to ensure that legislative proposals comply with the subsidiarity.[53] This may contribute to a more comprehensive system of subsidiarity review but this analysis fails to grasp that the CoR, as an EU institution, maintains a vested interest in EU legislative action which national parliaments do not share. It is most likely that the commencement of any action by the CoR would be determined by the Commission's explanation and justification within the Impact Assessment and the preamble to the legislation. As Chapter 2 highlighted, the absence of substantive quantitative evidence by the Commission in support of the need for EU legislation remains a concern for national parliaments. In determining whether there is a cause of action on grounds of infringement of the subsidiarity principle the CoR should consider how the Impact Assessment has embraced its views and those of the reasoned opinions of national parliaments, and whether the Commission gives an adequate justification of how and why the proposal complies with subsidiarity. In the absence of this justification the CoR could commence judicial review proceedings, insisting that the Commission had failed to

51 See Lenaerts, K. (2010) 'Regions and the European Court' at 626–627.
52 *Chernobyl* judgment at paragraph 23.
53 See Lenaerts, K. (2010) 'Regions and the European Court' at 628–629.

discharge its duty, but significant procedural question marks remain over how the CoR exercises the rights within Article 263 (3) TFEU.

4.2 Procedural Challenges

Perhaps the biggest obstacle to the CoR commencing an action is a procedural one because prior to the commencement of any judicial review proceedings is a political decision which requires the approval of the Plenary Assembly of the CoR. Any decision to commence proceedings for judicial review requires a simple majority vote by the Plenary Assembly members.[54] Though not impossible, securing this majority will be a cumbersome political process, not least because obtaining a consensus amongst inexperienced regional politicians, who may not grasp the full purpose of subsidiarity monitoring, will be problematic. Any such consensus may be further undermined by the independent actions of strong regions, such as the German *Länder*, which may conclude that fulfilling the procedural requirements of Article 263 (3) TFEU is either unattainable or unhelpful. Rather than get embroiled within the CoR, where political consensus is not a given, the *Bundesrat* could use Article 52 (3) (a) of the Basic Law together with Rule 45 of the Rules of Procedure of the *Bundesrat*[55] to compel the Federal Government to bring an action before the Court if it believes that *Länder* competences are infringed. In addition, the Rules of Procedure also enable the *Bundesrat* to petition the Court of Justice directly, as the de facto German Member State, when EU legislation affects the exercise of exclusive *Länder* competences.[56] Either of these options is likely to prove a more efficient proposition for the *Bundesrat* by comparison with the pursuit of political consensus within the CoR. Not only does this question the efficacy of the CoR's judicial prerogatives, but it further underlines the constitutional limitations of the CoR's representative capacity[57] and raises substantive questions about the value of Article 8 of Protocol 2 as a means by which to secure accountability. A failure to consult the CoR undoubtedly constitutes a breach of Article 13 TEU which the Court may strike down. But a failure to be consulted can be considered of less political significance by comparison with the Commission ignoring the conclusions of a substantial number of national parliaments which, within the early warning mechanism, may conclude that a legislative proposal

54 This requires 176 out of 350 votes.

55 Rule 45 (c), paragraph 7 of the *Bundesrat*'s Rules of Procedure.

56 Ibid.

57 See Börzel, T.A. (2002) *States and Regions in the European Union.*

infringes subsidiarity. Though the example of the proposal for a Regulation on collective strike action indicates that the Commission is likely to withdraw the legislative proposal, there is no guarantee that this will always occur in every case of a yellow card being shown. This is why a major weakness with Protocol 2, and the political influence this has given national parliaments, is that the exercise of these political procedures is not reinforced by effective judicial review procedures for national parliaments and judicial review by the CoR is not an adequate substitute for direct actions by national parliaments. Clearly there are practical and procedural barriers for national parliaments to bring an action and such actions would probably be very rare. But the opportunity to do so would indicate that within multi-level governance, where accountability between the legislative levels is crucial, an opportunity for judicial review exists for *all* institutional actors. While judicial review may unlock new opportunities for the CoR to exert pressure within the Community method, and it is open for the CoR to become a proactive litigant, it is unlikely that this will be a regular occurrence. Politically, the CoR is caught between a rock and a hard place with regard to subsidiarity monitoring because it will not want to be perceived as obstructive to the integrationist objectives it generally shares with other institutions, and especially with the European Parliament. This must suggest the infrequent use of Article 263 (3) TFEU by the CoR, leaving significant questions concerning precisely the extent to which subsidiarity monitoring by the CoR can contribute to improved accountability and legitimacy of EU legislation.

5. CONCLUDING REMARKS

This chapter has considered the extent to which participation by sub-national government, especially through subsidiarity monitoring, offers additional opportunities for improved democratic legitimacy within the legislative process. The criticism that previous Treaties marginalised sub-national institutions from the legislative process and that the Treaty displayed regional blindness was undoubtedly correct, and while the Treaty of Lisbon can be said to have acknowledged this criticism, most notably through the allocation of subsidiarity monitoring to the CoR, the outcome can best be summed up as incoherent. The obligation of loyal co-operation within Article 4 (3) TEU continues to be placed solely upon the Member State. The Treaty of Lisbon may have recognised the constitutional relevance of sub-national governance, but these new provisions have not ended the debate on the future of multi-level governance within the EU. In particular, several unanswered questions remain, including the capacity of regional governance to ensure that its voice is consistently heard within decision-making. Subsidiarity monitoring by the CoR opens up new opportunities for political dialogue within the legislative process, but there is a real risk that because of the different constitutional and political priorities, national parliaments and the CoR will not necessarily co-ordinate their activities. The EU remains an organisation made up of States and not regions and while the Treaty fails to specifically recognise regional competences it is inevitable that regional governance will remain on the margins of the decision-making process.

8. National parliaments after Lisbon: A new dawn of accountability or remaining on the periphery?

1. INTRODUCTION

Parliaments remain central institutions in European systems of government. Notwithstanding the process of integration and Europeanisation, national parliaments retain their constitutional position within Member States and the need for their consent to approve each new Treaty reiterates that national parliaments retain a constitutional relevance. National parliaments also remain the embodiment of the nation State. The inclusion of Article 50 TEU within the Treaty of Lisbon to some extent underlines this point, by providing a withdrawal clause for Member States. This implies that withdrawal from the EU by a Member State is an issue which a national parliament can unilaterally determine without the need for prior consent from the EU.[1] While this suggests that the nation State remains a central concept within the EU, not too much should be read into the inclusion of Article 50 TEU within the Treaty. First, it offers no new powers for national parliaments; withdrawal from the EU could have been achieved prior to the Treaty of Lisbon and the main development of Article 50 TEU is that this exit clause offers the prospect of an orderly procedure for withdrawal. Secondly, confirming the relevance of national parliaments in the EU by reference to a Treaty provision that provides for the withdrawal of a Member State cannot be said to improve either legislative accountability or EU democracy. Therefore, while Article 50 TEU confirms that the EU remains a supra-national organisation made up of nation States, it is questionable whether this provision will encourage national parliaments to conclude that their democratic parliamentary credentials are any more relevant to EU integration than before the Treaty of Lisbon.

[1] See further Łazowski, A. (2012) 'Withdrawal from the European Union and Alternatives to Membership' at 523.

In reality the post-Lisbon debate surrounding the role of national parliaments remains one of securing improved accountability within the ordinary legislative process. After Lisbon, accountability can be pursued either through parliamentary scrutiny of the minister or through the subsidiarity monitoring under Protocol 2. In either case, however, the impact of national parliaments is limited and in the case of Protocol 2 national parliaments struggle to consistently apply the principle of subsidiarity in a uniform way, which undoubtedly restricts the impact of Protocol 2. While the first yellow card concerning the proposed Regulation on collective strike action may be hailed as a success of Protocol 2, the decision to show it may be an isolated one, or at least one which is infrequently repeated. As the discussion in Chapter 6 illustrates, the yellow card may be explained because of the controversial nature of the legislative proposal, rather than the result of some co-ordinated action on the parts of national parliaments. Though many national parliaments have raised subsidiarity objections with regard to a variety of different legislative proposals, it is questionable whether this can be said to result in the creation of some alternative or additional function that national parliaments may assume and which is not explicitly included in Protocol 2. Yes, national parliaments can demonstrate their influence in a variety of ways and may have attributed to them some subsidiary classification such as a *Conseil d'Etat*, but this 'role' should not be viewed as an adequate substitute to the execution of subsidiarity monitoring under the terms of Protocol 2.[2] There is no doubt that Protocol 2 is a step forward and offers new opportunities for national parliaments to become involved in EU affairs. The full extent to which this is possible is highly debatable[3] given the heterogeneous nature of EU scrutiny procedures across the Member States, but one thing is clear: in the post-Lisbon era national parliaments must become more 'EU focussed' if they are to exert any significant control over their own executives or the EU institutions. However, Europeanisation is not uniform and the ordinary legislative procedure, to which Protocol 2 applies, is only one method by which centralised regulation can be achieved. Legislative harmonisation may no longer be appropriate in all circumstances, but this does not mean that the EU will return competences to the Member States. On the contrary,

---

[2] See Kiiver, P. (2012) *The Early Warning System for the Principle of Subsidiarity* at Chapter 6.

[3] For an overview of the debate on the operation of Protocol 2 see Barrett, G. (2008) '"The King is Dead, Long Live the King"' at 66; Cygan, A. (2011) 'The Parliamentarisation of EU Decision-Making?' at 478 and Kiiver, P. (2012) *The Early Warning System for the Principle of Subsidiarity* at Chapter 3.

arguably the biggest challenge facing Member States in the post-Lisbon era is how to control the exercise of complementary competences under Articles 5 and 6 TFEU and inter-governmental processes such as the open method of co-ordination (OMC). Though the OMC promotes policy co-ordination processes through the use of soft law these remain formally outside the scope of Protocol 2. It is open to national parliaments to review policy co-ordination but this must be considered unrealistic within the terms of their overall responsibilities.

While there may be no legislative impact upon Member States in the form of a regulation or directive, the OMC still raises clear questions of subsidiarity and accountability which must be addressed. Yet it is not all bad news for national parliaments. In a domestic constitutional context they continue to be the primary political institutions with which citizens have the most affinity and tend to be the beneficiaries of sceptical attitudes towards 'Brussels'. Moreover, national parliaments continue to control the government, approve legislation and, as the bodies responsible for amending the Constitution, hold the ultimate power within society. However, this privileged constitutional position remains under challenge and, as was noted in Chapter 2, the EU is not solely responsible for the loss of legislative competence experienced by national parliaments. For example, the constitutional reform that has taken place within many Member States since the Treaty of Maastricht has seen a growth of regional legislatures whose exercise of legislative powers creates a new internal dynamic which includes the Member States' relationship with the EU.[4] In addition, there has been a more recent and arguably stronger challenge to the relationship of Member States with the EU in meeting the challenge of other external constraints such as globalisation and the financial crisis. The effect of both of these on the EU and its Member States has seen a lively debate post-Lisbon where the need for 'more Europe' to enable the EU to face these new challenges is a very prominent agenda. 'More Europe' means fewer legislative and regulatory powers for national parliaments and this would suggest that the Fiscal Treaty, agreed in 2012, is unlikely to be the last regulatory measure introduced by the EU.

---

[4] See Cygan, A. (2013) 'Regional Governance, Subsidiarity and Accountability within the EU's Multi-Level Governance Framework' at 907.

2. FACING AN UNCERTAIN FUTURE: NATIONAL PARLIAMENTS AND THE CHALLENGE OF SECURING ACCOUNTABILITY

The political crisis surrounding the EU since 2008 is not a new occurrence. The post-2008 crisis is an exaggerated form of the political crisis that has engulfed the EU since the Treaty of Maastricht. Moreover, the political crisis surrounding the ratification of the Treaty of Maastricht signalled the end of what has been described as 'the permissive consensus' of the public in favour of deeper European integration.[5] The Maastricht 'no' vote in Denmark and subsequent further popular opposition to new Treaties, together with the more general scepticism across the Member States, illustrate that EU citizens are not prepared to tolerate a highly technocratic form of integration driven by an isolated political élite. The Single European Act may have delivered the Internal Market, which provided enhanced free movement rights to be enjoyed by EU citizens, but this had created a highly centralised and distant governance structure and legislative process. It is perhaps this centralisation above all else which has hindered the EU's desire to pursue political integration. Following the Danish 'no', the governing élite realised that the passive approval of the EU citizens for deeper European integration could no longer be taken for granted.[6] The Danish 'no' had the effect of crystallising the concerns across the EU, which remain to this day, of a crisis of legitimacy.[7] European public opinion has on a number of occasions voiced its discontent with regard to the state of European integration and concluded that not only did EU citizens retain serious reservations concerning the direction of integration, but also the scepticism demonstrated by citizens across many Member States suggested that serious fault lines existed in the EU's plans for moving forward with deeper political integration.[8] In Germany, the Federal Constitutional Court (FCC) has consistently highlighted that EU integration takes place only through popular consent which, in its view, requires the consent of national parliaments. The perception which prevailed in the immediate

---

[5] See Føllesdal, A. (2004) 'Legitimacy Theories of the European Union' at 3–4.

[6] See Norris, P. (2007) 'Representation and the Democratic Deficit' at 276.

[7] See Dehousse, R. (1995) 'Constitutional Reform in the European Community' at 118. See also Andreev, S. (2007) 'The EU "Crisis of Legitimacy" Revisited' at 1.

[8] This expression draws from Hix, S. (2008) *What's Wrong with the European Union and How to Fix It.*

aftermath post-Maastricht and which still dominates today is that the EU has failed to adequately address the democratic deficit and especially how it may secure legislative legitimacy. To this extent the new provisions within the Treaty of Lisbon can be considered in the same context of failing to deliver sufficient accountability of decision-makers because subsidiarity monitoring cannot be said to provide the necessary output legitimacy which sufficiently bridges the gap between the EU and the citizen. This is in part because, despite the best efforts of democratisation, the European Parliament is not perceived as injecting input legitimacy into the legislative process.[9] Output legitimacy without sufficient input legitimacy is an empty vessel. Moreover, despite the debate in the Constitutional Convention and irrespective of the conclusion that subsidiarity monitoring could help to bridge the democracy gap,[10] there is no tangible evidence that national parliaments want to assume this role, maintaining an accountability and democracy vacuum within the EU which the Treaty of Lisbon was intended to address.

2.1 Deparliamentarisation: A Continued Democratic Deficit

The accepted view of the democratic deficit is that it has arisen from 'the absence or underdevelopment of the institutions and processes of *parliamentary* democracy at the European level'.[11] The intensive political and academic debate surrounding the democratic deficit has been dominated by reference to the 'parliamentary model' of government. In particular this conforms to the strict doctrine of the separation of powers and holds the principle that the executive should emanate from and be directly responsible to an elected parliament.[12] Yet, as has been highlighted at several points within this book, the EU does not have a parliamentary system out of which an executive is drawn, and to adopt this interpretation would wrongly suggest that the core of the EU's democratic deficit arises solely from the process of Europeanisation and the accompanying transfer of competences to the EU from national parliaments. Arguably,

---

[9] Judgment of 20 June 2009 *Bundesverfassungsgericht*, BVerfG, 2 BvE 2/08 at paragraph 259.

[10] See CONV 67/1/02 The Role of National Parliaments in the European Architecture at 8–10.

[11] See Majone, G. (2006) 'The Common Sense of European Integration' at 608–609, emphasis added.

[12] See Smismans, S. (2004) *Law, Legitimacy, and European Governance* at 3. See also Dehousse, R. (1995) 'Constitutional Reform in the European Community' at 118; Weiler, J.H.H. (1998) *The Constitution of Europe* at 77.

the more significant factor for the continued democratic deficit arises from the incomplete and piecemeal democratisation of the EU which has focussed upon institutional reform.

In particular this has granted greater legislative powers to the European Parliament. The justification for this development may be to secure improved input legitimacy in the legislative process, but the increased use of Trilogues and technocratic nature of decision-making confirm the continued existence of an opaque and broadly unaccountable decision-making process. The features of the decision-making process suggest that, irrespective of these institutional reforms, the EU remains broadly irrelevant to the daily lives of many citizens. The relationship between national parliaments and the EU has tended to be categorised in a negative manner. National parliaments have been described as 'victims' of Europeanisation[13] because the technocratic characteristics of EU decision-making have strengthened executives and the Council at the expense of national parliamentary practices.[14] This has created a definitive accountability gap, and arguably created a variant of the democratic deficit, which traditionally was considered as existing only at the EU level. One impact of the democratic deficit, which the Treaty of Lisbon does not sufficiently address, is that the Treaty has not offered processes by which to improve the accountability of ministers to their national parliaments in a way which alleviates the impact of qualified majority voting (QMV). The increased use of QMV has loosened the accountability of ministers to national parliaments, and while QMV is efficient it does not sit comfortably with the parliamentary system of government within the Member States where political accountability of the executive remains a central concept.

This deficit that arises with the increased use of QMV and majoritarian decision-making has not been bridged by granting increased legislative powers to the European Parliament. Though having the political and moral authority of being a directly elected institution which supposedly represents EU citizens within the political process, the European Parliament has not been strong enough to regain control over the Commission and to balance the power of national ministers acting collectively in the Council.[15] Moreover, the European Parliament, at least in terms of the legislative process, from the perspective of national parliaments, forms

[13] See Maurer, A. (2001) 'National Parliaments in the European Union Architecture' at 432.

[14] See Moravcsik, A. (1998) 'Introduction: The Choice for Europe' at 9.

[15] See Haltern, U.R., Mayer, F.C. and Weiler, J.H.H. (1995) 'European Democracy and its Critique' at 4.

part of the problem. Europeanisation has seen the European Parliament benefit from increased legislative competences being granted to the EU which have come at the expense of national parliaments. Notwithstanding the political disputes arising from the inter-institutional dynamic, the European Parliament remains an enthusiastic participant within the integration process. In such a scenario, the sort of inter-parliamentary co-operation that exists between the European Parliament and national parliaments through, for example, COSAC does not amount to a framework for multi-level parliamentary co-operation. This absence of any real parliamentary government, as discussed in Chapter 2, encapsulates the concept of 'deparliamentarisation' within the EU.[16] One ambitious but unrealistic solution put forward to remedy this was the creation of a 'parliamentary system of governance in the EU which would see the EU being transformed into a majoritarian democracy modelled upon those of its Member States would solve the democratic deficit of the EU'.[17] In an EU of twenty-eight Member States this is not constitutionally or institutionally feasible. Post-Lisbon the accountability debate and how the democratic deficit can be further addressed remain focussed on the role of the citizen and, in particular, how the EU can become more relevant in the lives of EU citizens.

This legitimacy deficit, in which EU citizens are also considered as marginalised from the governance process, remains a major constituent part of the wider democratic deficit within the EU. But while the Treaty has made a number of institutional reforms these have not, per se, placed citizens at the heart of the legislative process. Both the Laeken Declaration and the Convention on the Future of Europe articulated the concern that EU citizens felt isolated from the process of EU integration and that the EU must, as part of its objective of securing improved legitimacy, seek to connect more directly with citizens. The Convention highlighted that the EU must 'rethink its role, improve its operation and go down new avenues of progress and democracy'.[18] The Treaty of Lisbon acknowledged these criticisms and has sought to engage more directly with citizens through, for example, the Citizen's Initiative, but it is questionable whether this offers a comprehensive response to what remains a significant problem of citizen disconnection and alienation. Furthermore, even when considered together with Article 12 TEU and

---

[16] See Cygan,A. (2011) 'The Parliamentarisation of EU Decision-Making?' at 479–481.

[17] See Magnette, P. (2006) 'Democracy in the European Union' at 37.

[18] See CONV 67/1/02, The Role of National Parliaments in the European Architecture at 8.

Protocols 1 and 2, which seek to engage national parliaments, these developments fail to collectively bridge the democracy gap to citizens who remain largely ignorant of the EU legislative process. Despite the emphasis that has been placed by the EU upon 'the citizen', the objective of improved accountability has remained introspective. As already noted, the EU has remained focussed on democratisation and inter-institutional accountability rather than pursuing parliamentarisation. Though the Treaty of Lisbon has added Article 12 TEU and Protocols 1 and 2, the search for improved accountability, despite the citizen-focussed rhetoric, continues to position the European Parliament at the core through recognition of its democratic credentials. While the European Parliament is the only elected institution which directly represents EU citizens, there is a disjuncture between this constitutional position and its real relationship with EU citizens. Many of the functions which the European Parliament fulfils in the name of the EU citizen are technical and remote from the daily lives of citizens. This can be seen through its participation in the ordinary legislative procedure, in which the European Parliament 'co-decides' with the Council, and its joint decision-making in the adoption of the EU budget.[19] The European Parliament now also elects the President of the Commission and the Commission is also, as an entire body, subject to a vote of consent by the European Parliament. The Commission is responsible to the European Parliament and may, as a body, be dismissed by it following the adoption of a motion on censure.[20] These developments indicate an accountability chain within the EU polity because of the exercise of this political control by the European Parliament over the Council and Commission. This should not be underestimated and constitutes an improvement even on the post-Maastricht arrangements, but it is questionable if this complex and arguably remote form of accountability resonates with EU citizens, especially in circumstances where they have had no direct input into the appointment of senior political figures such as the President of the Council. Crucially, this political accountability does not encompass national parliaments, which have no direct say with regard to how the EU's institutions function.

---

19 Article 314 TFEU.
20 Article 17 (7) and (8) TEU; Article 234 TFEU.

2.2 The Future of EU Democracy: Citizens Rather than Parliaments?

Post-Lisbon the importance of the citizen to EU integration has undoubtedly received a new impetus and can be said to have become central to the EU's strategy through which it legitimises its actions. Though this emphasis upon the citizen must be treated with some caution, and in many respects offers nothing new to the sentiments being expressed about the citizen and the EU post-Maastricht, there does appear to be a greater sense of realisation that EU integration can only continue if citizens are *genuinely* engaged in its process and recipients of its benefits. Thus identifying tangible benefits to the citizen from legislative action, the Agenda 2020 Programme, the Citizen's Initiative and designating 2013 as the 'Year of the Citizen' all indicate that the EU is seeking legitimacy through delivery of policy benefits and being relevant in the lives of citizens. Yes, national parliaments are still considered to form part of this quest for legitimacy, but the EU appears to speak directly to citizens and in a manner which would seem to marginalise the democratic and representative characteristics of national institutions.

Treaty development, which seeks to address criticisms of the democratic deficit by changes to institutional architecture, though both necessary and logical, fails to engage the citizen, who continues to demonstrate little interest in EU affairs. The 'no' votes on the Constitutional Treaty and the Treaty of Lisbon illustrate not just a scepticism with deeper integration, but a fundamental lack of understanding of how EU integration benefits EU citizens. Though it is a directly elected institution the European Parliament's representative function is severely undermined by virtue of the poor turnout for European Parliament elections. As discussed in Chapter 3, the FCC considers that this limited form of Treaty recognition does not compensate for the continuing legitimation deficit arising from the representation provided by the European Parliament. The FCC in the *Lisbon Treaty judgment* identified the existence of a legitimation deficit with the European Parliament[21] as being central to its inability to supplant national parliaments within the EU polity. Bogdanor[22] identifies that it is this absence of the election of a government or leader which remains a weakness of these arrangements. Moreover, as already highlighted, the European Parliament has tended to focus on the relationship between itself and the Commission/Council and

---

[21] See Judgment of 20 June 2009 *Bundesverfassungsgerich*t, BVerfG, 2 BvE 2/08 at paragraph 253.

[22] See Bogdanor, V. (1997) *Power and the People* at 158.

has paid less attention to strengthening the relationship between the European Parliament and EU citizens.

The Constitutional Convention itself conceded that citizens will not necessarily feel connected with the EU if they themselves feel detached from the legislative process, even if the European Parliament can do a good job in scrutinising and influencing the Commission and Council. One notable institutional development in the Treaty of Lisbon which has sought to address the disconnection of citizens is the appointment of political 'figureheads' such as the President of the European Council. While this *may* raise the profile of the Council it remains unclear precisely how the President of the European Council, who is appointed by the Member States, can contribute to improved democracy and accountability, especially if citizens feel no affinity with the post-holder. Similar criticisms can be made of the wholly appointed Commission, which remains distant from the citizen and whose selection is not subject to any form of direct popular control. Though the European Parliament formally approves the Commission and will be prepared to flex its muscle where it believes a candidate is unsuitable for the role, this does not create a perception that it is the 'people who run Europe'.[23] This process does not resemble the election of a government being chosen from and accountable to a parliament, and only serves to reinforce an omni-present technocratic interpretation of EU integration. Such arrangements erode the legitimacy of the EU, leading to the conclusion that continued public apathy to the EU undermines the objective of the institutional reforms. Moreover, the appointment of such figureheads without reference to any popular electoral support merely serves to reinforce the argument that the democratic deficit is alive and well in the post-Lisbon EU and has morphed into a deficit which is the direct consequence of a process of incoherent institutional democratisation and insufficient citizen participation. From a democratic standpoint, the limits of the parliamentary approach in EU integration have been highlighted by Scharpf and discussed in Chapter 1.

It will be recalled that Scharpf argued that 'by constructing blueprints for a majoritarian European constitution, the enthusiasts of European democracy tend to ignore the preconditions of legitimate *majority rule*'.[24] Indeed, European elections are still considered 'second-order national elections' where EU issues are not adequately debated (other than the 'in'

---

[23] Ibid. at 164.

[24] Scharpf, F.W. (2006) 'Problem Solving Effectiveness and Democratic Accountability in the EU' at 18.

or 'out' debate that is prominent in many Member States). More importantly, a major social prerequisite for legitimate majority rule is lacking; that is to say that the EU does not possess the collective identity, or demos, which is the overriding characteristic of nation States and national democracies. According to Scharpf, 'the confusion and frustration of present debates can only be overcome if the distinction between input- and output-oriented democratic legitimacy is accepted'[25] and if it is realised that it is only by delivering outputs that citizens demand that the EU, as a problem-solving polity, can hope to reinforce its legitimacy in the absence of a European demos. But, and as has already been suggested earlier in this chapter, output legitimacy which is justified by reference to the results delivered cannot be considered as a sufficient substitute for a legislative process which derives its legitimacy from a process of rigorous accountability. For example, it is difficult to envisage that national parliaments would view it as compatible with their obligations under Article 12 TEU and Protocol 2 to accept legislation which breaches the principle of subsidiarity, but which the Commission's Impact Assessments conclude are in the best interests of EU citizens. Institutional mechanisms which secure direct political legitimacy are also required, indicating that some form of parliamentary governance or parliamentarisation in the EU remains an important criterion if improved democratic legitimacy is to be secured. The inevitable question this raises is whether an increased role for national parliaments, which remain the embodiment of national political and socio-economic aspirations, can help to fill this legitimacy void and provide a mechanism through which the EU can connect with citizens. This was certainly a feature of the debate in the Constitutional Convention, and though review of subsidiarity by national parliaments may provide some output legitimacy to EU legislation, it is extremely doubtful that national parliaments view themselves as a central component of the solution to bridge the gap with the citizen. Notwithstanding the Treaty reforms and the view of Herman van Rompuy,[26] national parliaments are *not* part of the EU institutional architecture and remain on the periphery of the decision-making process. Subsidiarity monitoring is an important political task which Protocol 2 of the Treaty has assigned to national parliaments as those institutions which have an interest in ensuring its application. Yet despite these new provisions and the more direct engagement of national parliaments in EU

---

[25] Ibid.

[26] See EUObserver.com, 28 February 2012, 'Van Rompuy: National Parliaments are EU Institutions' available at http://euobserver.com/institutional/115395 (accessed 1 March 2012).

decision-making, criticisms that Europeanisation continues to challenge national sovereignty remain. For example, in the case of subsidiarity monitoring the execution of this task by national parliaments has no direct influence on 'upstream' policy formulation, which is arguably the point at which the biggest political influence can be brought to bear. Subsidiarity monitoring, though an important exercise which seeks to ensure that EU competences are exercised appropriately, could be considered as the fulfilment of a limited procedural function of competence monitoring at the 'fag end' of the decision-making process which is unlikely to have significant bearing upon a legislative proposal. Though proponents of Protocol 2 may highlight the yellow card shown in May 2012, there is no doubt that this occurrence must be considered within its political and constitutional setting and does not indicate that this will be a regular occurrence. There have been other equally controversial proposals where the subsidiarity principle has been applied and where no yellow card has been shown.[27] Though subsidiarity monitoring by national parliaments may inject some form of output legitimacy into EU decision-making, this does not build a bridge between citizens and the EU. Even in those circumstances where national parliaments have confirmed that competence is appropriately exercised at the EU level, questions can remain whether the legislation is disproportionate or even necessary. For citizens, the issue of their disconnection from the EU arises not just from their lack of participation in selecting the members of the Commission or the President of the Council, but from a more widespread perception that EU legislation is over-intrusive in their daily lives and that it lacks relevance. Without addressing these substantive questions about the content and scope of EU legislation, it was acknowledged within the Convention that the EU would continue to lack legitimacy amongst citizens. In particular, it was accepted by the Convention that technical procedures for subsidiarity monitoring would not, independently, be sufficient to provide either increased legislative accountability or sufficient guarantees against over-intrusive legislation.[28] If benchmarked against these criteria then the Treaty of Lisbon has failed to deliver the more legitimate, accountable and transparent decision-making that was being sought.

---

[27] See further the discussion in Kiiver, P. (2012) *The Early Warning System for the Principle of Subsidiarity* at 76–91.

[28] See CONV 74/02 Mandate of the Working Group on National Parliaments at 3.

3. NATIONAL PARLIAMENTS AFTER LISBON: AN INFLUENTIAL COLLECTIVE BLOC OR A PLETHORA OF INDIVIDUAL ACTORS?

The concept of 'national parliaments in the EU' gives an impression that, notwithstanding different constitutional norms and traditions, there is some degree of homogeneity in terms of both procedure and purpose amongst national parliaments in the context of EU affairs, and especially with regard to the scrutiny activities of national parliaments. As already noted, the Treaty does not define national parliaments and at no point does it recognise that the fulfilment of their scrutiny functions elevates them to some form of 'collective' institutional status. While it would be incorrect to conclude that national parliaments do not exhibit some similar values and practices in relation to EU affairs, it may be wrong to conclude that they engage in EU scrutiny and EU affairs to the same extent, or that the Treaty of Lisbon has created a cogent horizontal bloc of parliamentary institutions which will be monitoring subsidiarity in precisely the same way. While the task of subsidiarity monitoring may be uniform and to be undertaken by all Member States, the procedures used to achieve this vary immensely.[29]

3.1 Identifying 'National Parliaments' in the Treaty

The new powers which have been conferred by the Treaty of Lisbon upon national parliaments have led to some national parliaments amending their rules of procedure to adapt to the requirements of subsidiarity monitoring.[30] From research conducted by COSAC[31] it is evident that there is no normative or single model by which national parliaments have implemented the requirement of Article 12 TEU and Protocols 1 and 2. Notwithstanding the internal parliamentary reforms to procedure and practice post-Lisbon, significant disparity continues to exist between the internal modus operandi of national parliaments which enables the criticism to continue that national parliaments are classified as either

---

[29] See Wyrzykowski, M. et al. (2011) 'General Report' at 50.

[30] Parliamentary procedures were amended in the Belgian *Chambre des Deputes*, the Czech *Poslanecka*, the Finnish *Eduskunta*, the French *Assemble nationale*, the Dutch *Ereste Kamer* and *Tweede Kamer*, the Swedish *Riksdag* and the House of Lords.

[31] See COSAC Secretariat (2010) *Thirteenth Bi-annual Report: Developments in European Union. Procedures and Practices Relevant to Parliamentary Scrutiny*, Madrid.

'strong' or 'weak' actors in respect of their EU oversight activities. Indeed, it may be argued that it will only be those parliaments which are considered strong parliaments that will amend their internal procedures in an attempt to ensure that their scrutiny activities remain relevant. The Treaty of Lisbon sought to address the criticism of strong and weak actors through assigning to national parliaments the task of subsidiarity monitoring[32] and introduces a harmonised minimum standard for their EU scrutiny activities. This presumes that effective subsidiarity monitoring necessitates a political dialogue within an organised horizontal collective of parliaments. Moreover, subsidiarity monitoring undertaken by a 'collective' bloc of national parliaments implies that citizens are more likely to accept legislation if their national parliaments have uniformly confirmed its compliance with the exercise of EU competences. To secure this level of consent Protocol 2 includes a process of political dialogue which has been singled out as an opportunity through which national parliaments may reposition themselves within the EU polity. For example, Passos has argued that national parliaments have become a 'new actor in the European Union legislative process to be added to the existing European Parliament–Council–Commission triangle'.[33] However, whether national parliaments are elevated to an institutional or even quasi-institutional status can be challenged on several grounds, not least because simply executing the task of subsidiarity monitoring, which the evidence post-Lisbon indicates is itself sporadic, does not create an institutional role for national parliaments. There is a broad consensus about the impact of European integration on national parliaments and any recognition of them as a collective entity has tended to be for the wrong reasons. In the context of the negative effects of EU integration, most of the literature on the role of national parliaments in the EU polity has considered them as victims of European integration.[34] Constitutionally, this is probably correct and relatively straightforward to explain. Powers which previously were under the jurisdiction of national legislatures have been shifted upwards to the European level. In the Council of Ministers the increased use of QMV has made it increasingly difficult for national

---

32 For a comprehensive comparison of the provisions in the Constitutional Treaty and Treaty of Lisbon see Barrett, G. (2008) '"The King is Dead, Long Live the King"'.

33 See Passos, R. (2008) 'Recent Developments Concerning the Role of National Parliaments in the European Union' at 35; Kiiver, P. (2011) 'The Early Warning System for the Principle of Subsidiarity' at 98.

34 See Maurer, A. (2001) 'National Parliaments in the European Union Architecture'.

parliaments to force governments to make *ex ante* commitments before taking decisions at the European level, thereby impeding parliamentary scrutiny. Moreover, the extensive involvement of national ministers and civil servants in drafting and implementing EU legislation insulates or marginalises national parliaments, regardless of the Council's decision. The resulting information deficit has reduced the ability of MPs to control their governments in European matters. In fact, through the centrality of technical expertise in the EU policy process, the true winners of European integration have arguably been bureaucrats and organised private interests at all levels of government and not directly elected representatives who are considered as the traditional holders of legitimacy in European systems of parliamentary government.[35] While such pessimistic conclusions might actually underestimate the influence of national parliaments, the continuing challenges facing them deserve to be taken seriously. Active scrutiny by individual domestic legislatures of their governments is important to ensure some democratic control over the EU policy process, as the principal actors in the EU are still national governments that take decisions in the European Council and the Council. The main problem facing legislatures is how to reduce informational asymmetry in order to facilitate effective parliamentary accountability, and on this question the Treaty is silent.

3.2 From Individual to Collective Scrutiny: The Creation of a New Scrutiny Paradigm?

Notwithstanding Protocol 2 the scrutiny activities of national parliaments, as well as their constitutional arrangements for reviewing EU affairs, remain diverse. For national parliaments the primary role has been, and arguably continues to be, to scrutinise the activities of the minister in the Council and secure effective accountability to the national parliament in accordance with their constitutional traditions. In substance the Treaty of Lisbon does not change this. With the allocation of subsidiarity monitoring to national parliaments it may be argued that, over time, national parliaments could evolve from individual actors who pursue a monist objective of ministerial accountability to developing into some form of 'collective' horizontal bloc which through a process of political dialogue arrives at a single opinion on the question of subsidiarity compliance. This 'polycentric' methodology has been identified as a potential shift

[35] See Bergman, T. and Damgaard, E. (eds) (2000) *Delegation and Accountability in European Integration*; and Wessels, W., Maurer, A. and Mittag, J. (eds) (2003) *Fifteen into One?*

towards the creation of a single EU scrutiny paradigm through which parliaments cease to function as isolated individual actors and evolve into a proactive horizontal bloc.[36] Subsidiarity monitoring provides some opportunity for this mainly because this task is expected to be carried out by all national parliaments and based upon the same documentation. This would indicate the need for some degree of uniformity to the scrutiny activities of national parliaments, but this is far from the case given the heterogeneous procedures that continue to exist within national parliaments. The evolution of some new collective of national parliaments may be offered as one possible interpretation of the circumstances which led to national parliaments meeting the one-third threshold to show the yellow card in relation to the proposed Regulation for collective strike action. But, as the discussion in Chapter 6 illustrated, the 'consensus' achieved in this instance may have been one that arose by virtue of the circumstances and coincidence rather than necessarily being the conclusion of a co-ordinated political dialogue.

This analysis is perhaps a more appropriate inference, especially if the controversial nature of the proposal and the domestic constitutional and political circumstances in which national rules on collective strike action exist are considered. The diversity of legislative acts which regulate collective strike action across the Member States reflects the different socio-economic traditions that continue to exist within the Member States. The desire, on the part of national parliaments, to preserve what they considered to be important socio-economic values was undoubtedly a significant, if not the overriding, reason which led to these Member States raising subsidiarity objections. Though application of the subsidiarity principle was an important consideration in this case, it was arguably not the only concern for national parliaments, who felt that this was a matter of competence creep and the need to protect the exercise of a competence which should remain exclusively with Member States. On this analysis, the issue would not necessarily be a question of subsidiarity, but would illustrate a similar issue which arose in the *Tobacco Advertising Directive case*; namely that the EU had acted beyond its powers and legislated on a policy over which it had no competence. The use of reasoned opinions, as part of the process of subsidiarity monitoring, was perhaps the most effective and direct method for national parliaments through which to voice these concerns to the Commission, though it is very likely that this legislative proposal would not have

[36] See Besselink, L.M. (2006) 'National Parliaments in the EU's Composite Constitution' at 119.

secured the necessary votes within the Council primarily for the reason that there was no EU competence to legislate. The Treaty of Lisbon has formally allocated subsidiarity monitoring to national parliaments and provides a new procedural device, but the task of evaluating legislative proposals for their compliance with the principle of subsidiarity is not a new one. Furthermore, though distinct from ministerial accountability, subsidiarity monitoring should not necessarily be considered as inconsistent with the broader aims of national parliamentary scrutiny. This form of scrutiny by national parliaments, which took place without any horizontal co-ordination between national parliaments, illustrates clearly the argument, discussed in Chapter 2, that parliamentary scrutiny has traditionally constituted a form of substitute sovereignty. In the post-Lisbon era, where subsidiarity monitoring may be viewed as an end in itself, securing executive accountability by national parliaments remains an important objective. This is because it remains the only means by which national parliaments may exert any influence over the executive throughout the entire decision-making procedure. The Treaty of Lisbon reforms raise the question: is there scope for some new form of collective of national parliaments to emerge which is more fully engaged within the EU polity? In short, the answer is probably 'no', but the value and impact of more co-ordinated action by national parliaments should not be dismissed altogether, especially in the context of the political relationship with the EU institutions. This leaves the door slightly ajar for Kiiver's proposal that national parliaments could act as some form of *Conseil d'Etat* for the EU and circumstances such as the proposed Regulation for collective strike action illustrate how this may develop.[37] But this role is not included within Protocol 2 and even this form of action requires a significant degree of collectivity, raising real questions concerning how often this will occur.

4. CONCLUDING REMARKS

The key development in the Treaty of Lisbon is that, for the first time in the Treaties, national parliaments have been recognised as relevant actors within the EU polity through subsidiarity monitoring. New opportunities such as the Barosso Initiative further provide for improved political participation and dialogue with the Commission. Through the process of subsidiarity monitoring it is expected that national parliaments may

---

[37] See Kiiver, P. (2011) 'The Early Warning System for the Principle of Subsidiarity'.

contribute to the improvement of output legitimacy as part of the overall package of changes designed to address the persisting democratic deficit. In order to fulfil this function national parliaments now receive information directly from the EU institutions and monitor that the EU institutions respect the principle of subsidiarity.[38] Not only does this seek to bind national parliaments together and encourage them to act coherently, it has also sought to create a new democratic alliance between the European Parliament and national parliaments, which Article 10 TEU identifies as being a significant part of delivering representative democracy in the EU. However, this framework for improved co-operation between the European Parliament and national parliaments stops short of a parliamentary system of government or parliamentarisation of the EU, not least because in the context of subsidiarity monitoring, national parliaments will be reviewing the exercise of competence in a legislative process of which the European Parliament is a co-legislator. Perhaps it is more important for national parliaments to focus on what the Treaty of Lisbon *does* offer them. There is no question that the position of national parliaments has improved, even by contrast with the post-Amsterdam position. Scrutiny of EU affairs has evolved from being a sporadic activity, carried out inconsistently by national parliaments, to one which is a key component of the legislative process. Working Group IV concluded that 'national parliaments have a distinct role to play within the EU polity'. It concluded that their enhanced involvement would help to 'strengthen the democratic legitimacy of the Union and bring it closer to its citizens',[39] but this remains very much a work in progress. In particular, the Treaty of Lisbon does not offer an overall comprehensive package of reforms that address, with sufficient coherence, the democratic deficit. Indeed, as this book has argued, with the process of democratisation the democratic deficit has merely been shifted around the EU polity and for each improvement within the Treaty, for example subsidiarity monitoring, there is a new challenge created such as the increased use of complementary competences and soft law where traditional scrutiny methods and established practices and procedures may not be appropriate. In such circumstances it is difficult to see how national parliaments will be any form of collective in EU decision-making – except perhaps a collective of parliaments on the margins of

---

[38] See Piris, J.C. (2010) *The Lisbon Treaty* at 122–133. See Cygan, A. (2011) 'The Parliamentarisation of EU Decision-Making?' at 479–481.

[39] See CONV 353/02 Working Group IV The Role of National Parliaments, Final Report of Working Group IV on the Role of National Parliaments at paragraph 4.

that process. Though many national parliaments have been rather slow in adapting themselves to the challenges of EU integration there is no doubt that they are able to exercise much improved scrutiny over their national governments than they were even a decade ago. A key feature of the impact of EU integration upon national parliaments is that this has proved to be an organic process under which national parliaments must react to, amongst other things, changes in EU competences and changes in the legislative process. Subsidiarity monitoring has not re-centred national parliaments within the EU polity. Improved co-operation within COSAC and the Barosso Initiative *may* promote political dialogue, but these developments do not guarantee collectivity and influence; nor do they constitute parliamentarisation. Similarly, subsidiarity monitoring does not alter institutional balance and the fulfilment of this task does not presuppose the beginnings of a new EU organ. The Treaty of Lisbon continues the trend established since the Single European Act that, in parallel, the Treaties pursue Europeanisation and democratisation. These two objectives have not, formally or informally, sited national parliaments at the centre – except to ratify each new Treaty. The input of national parliaments in EU affairs and speaking out against competence creep *may* uphold subsidiarity and help inject some improved legitimacy into the legislative process, but national politicians must first see the value in the Treaty provisions and be willing to engage more directly and more often in EU affairs.

Bibliography

Andreev, S. (2007) 'The EU "Crisis of Legitimacy" Revisited: Concepts, Causes, and Possible Consequences for the European Politics and Citizens', *Political Perspectives* **1**, 1

Armstrong, K. (2011) 'The Character of EU Law and Governance: From Community Method to New Forms of Governance', *Current Legal Problems* **65**, 179

Armstrong, K. (2006) 'How Open is the United Kingdom to the OMC Process of Social Inclusion?', in J. Zeitlin and P. Pochet with L. Magnusson (eds), *The Open Method of Co-ordination in Action: The European Employment and Social Inclusion Strategies* (Brussels: Peter Lang) 287

Auel, K. (2007) 'Democratic Accountability and National Parliaments: Redefining the Impact of Parliamentary Scrutiny in EU Affairs', *European Law Journal* **13**, 487

Auel, K. and Benz, A. (2005) 'The Politics of Adaptation: The Europeanisation of National Parliamentary Systems', *Journal of Law and Society* **11**, 372

Baldwin, R. (2005) 'Is Better Regulation Smarter Regulation?', *Public Law* **46**, 485

Barber, B. (1984) *Strong Democracy: Participatory Politics for a New Age* (London: University of California Press)

Barnard, C. (ed.) (2007) *The Fundamentals of EU Law Revisited: Assessing the Impact of the Constitutional Debate* (Oxford: Oxford University Press)

Barnard, C. and Oduhu, O. (eds) (2009) *The Outer Limits of European Union Law* (Oxford: Hart Publishing)

Barnard, C. and Scott, J. (eds) (2002) *The Law of the Single Market: Unpacking the Premises* (Oxford: Hart Publishing)

Barrett, G. (2008) '"The King is Dead, Long Live the King": The Recasting by the Treaty of Lisbon of the Provisions of the Constitutional Treaty Concerning National Parliaments', *European Law Review* **33**, 66

Barrett, G. (ed.) (2007) *National Parliaments and the European Union: The Constitutional Challenge for the Oireachtas and Other Member State Legislatures* (Dublin: Clarus Press in association with the Institute of European Affairs)

Bengston, C. (2007) 'Inter-Parliamentary Cooperation in Europe', in J. O'Brennan and T. Raunio (eds), *National Parliaments within the Enlarged European Union: From Victims of Integration to Competitive Actors* (London: Routledge) 46

Bengtson, C. (2003) 'National Parliaments in European Decision-Making: A Real Prospect or Wishful Thinking?', *The Federal Trust Online Paper* 29/03, London, September

Bergman, T. and Damgaard, E. (eds) (2000) *Delegation and Accountability in European Integration: The Nordic Parliamentary Democracies and the European Union* (London: Frank Cass)

Besselink, L.M. (2006) 'National Parliaments in the EU's Composite Constitution: A Plea for a Shift in Paradigm', in P. Kiiver (ed.), *National and Regional Parliaments in the European Constitutional Order* (Groningen: Europa Law Publishing) 117–30

Best, E. and Settembri, P. (2008) 'Legislative Output after Enlargement: Similar Number Shifting Nature', in E. Best, T. Christiansen and P. Settembri (eds), *The Institutions of the Enlarged European Union: Continuity and Change* (Cheltenham, UK and Northampton, MA, USA: Edward Elgar) 183

Best, E., Christiansen, T. and Settembri, P. (eds) (2008) *The Institutions of the Enlarged European Union: Continuity and Change* (Cheltenham, UK and Northampton, MA, USA: Edward Elgar)

Beyers, J., Eising, R. and Maloney, W. (eds) (2010), *Interest Group Politics in Europe: Lessons from EU Studies and Comparative Politics* (London: Routledge)

Bogdanor, V. (1997) *Power and the People: Guide to Constitutional Reform* (London: Weidenfeld and Nicolson) 158

Bogdany, A.V. and Bast J. (2002) 'The European Union's Vertical Order of Competences: The Current Law and Proposals for its Reform', *Common Market Law Review* **39**, 227

Bogusz, B. (2004) 'Modes of Governance for an EU Immigration Policy – What Role for the Open Method of Coordination?', in B. Bogusz, R. Cholewinski, A. Cygan and E. Szyszczak (eds), *Irregular Migration and Human Rights: Theoretical, European and International Perspectives* (The Hague: Kluwer Law International)

Bogusz, B., Cygan, A. and Szyszczak, E. (eds) (2008) *The Regulation of Sport in the EU* (Cheltenham, UK and Northampton, MA, USA: Edward Elgar)

Bogusz, B., Cholewinski, R., Cygan, A. and Szyszczak, E. (eds) (2004) *Irregular Migration and Human Rights: Theoretical, European and International Perspectives* (The Hague: Kluwer Law International)

Börzel, T.A. (2002) *States and Regions in the European Union* (Cambridge: Cambridge University Press, 2002)

Bulmer, S. and Lequesne, C. (eds) (2005) *The Member States of the European Union* (Oxford: Oxford University Press)

Cabinet Office (2009) *Parliamentary Scrutiny of EU Documents: Guidance for Department*, Cabinet Office, 20 April

Carroll, W.E. (2011) 'The Committee of the Regions: A Functional Analysis of the CoR's Institutional Capacity', *Regional and Federal Studies* **21**, 341

Carter, C. (2000) 'Democratic Governance Beyond the Nation State: Third Level Assemblies and Scrutiny of EU Legislation', *European Public Law* **6**, 429

CdR 89/2009 final *The Committee of the Regions' White Paper on Multi-Level Governance*

COM (2012) 130 *Draft Regulation on the Exercise of the Right to take Collective Action within the Context of the Freedom of Establishment and the Freedom to Provide Services* (Brussels: European Commission)

COM (2012) 130 final *Proposal for a Regulation on the Exercise of the Right to take Collective Action within the Context of the Freedom of Establishment and the Freedom to Provide Services* (Brussels: European Commission)

COM (2012) 373 final *Report from the Commission on Subsidiarity and Proportionality: 19th Report on Better Law Making Covering the Year 2011* (Brussels: European Commission)

COM (2012) 375 final 10.7.2012 *Annual Report 2011 on Relations Between the European Commission and National Parliaments* (Brussels: European Commission)

See COM (2011) 344 final *Report from the Commission on Subsidiarity and Proportionality* (18th Report on Better Law Making Covering the Year 2010) (Brussels: European Commission)

COM (2011) 344 final 10.7.2012 *Annual Report 2010 on Relations Between the European Commission and National Parliaments* (Brussels: European Commission)

COM (2011) 635 final *Proposal for a Regulation of the European Parliament and of the Council on a Common European Sales Law* (Brussels: European Commission)

COM (2010) 368 (recast) *On Deposit Guarantee Schemes* (Brussels: European Commission)

COM (2010) 379 final *Proposal for a Directive on the Conditions of Entry and Residence of Third Country Nationals for the Purposes of Seasonal Employment* (Brussels: European Commission)

COM (2010) 543 final *Smart Regulation in the European Union* (Brussels: European Commission)

COM (2009) 15 final *Third Strategic Review of Better Regulation in the European Union* (Brussels: European Commission)
COM (2009) 338 final *Proposal for a Council Framework Decision on the Right to Interpretation and to Translation in Criminal Proceedings* (Brussels: European Commission)
COM (2009) 343 final 7.7.2009 *Annual Report 2008 on Relations Between the European Commission and National Parliaments* (Brussels: European Commission)
COM (2009) 490 final *Action Plan on Urban Mobility* (Brussels: European Commission)
COM (2008) 237 6.5.2008 *Final Commission Annual Report 2007 on Relations Between the European Commission and National Parliaments* (Brussels: European Commission)
COM (2008) 586 final *The Report of the European Commission on Subsidiarity and Proportionality 2007* (Brussels: European Commission)
COM (2006) 211 *Communication from the Commission to the European Council – A Citizen's Agenda: Delivering Results for Europe* (Brussels: European Commission)
COM (2005) 97 final *Communication from the Commission to the Council and European Parliament – Better Regulation for Growth and Jobs in the European Union* (Brussels: European Commission)
COM (2005) 494 final, *The Commission's Contribution to the Period of Reflection and Beyond: Plan-D for Democracy, Dialogue and Debate* (Brussels: European Commission)
COM (2004) 104, final, 3.3.2004 *Communication from the Commission 'Further Integration in the European Rail System: Third Railway Package'* (Brussels: European Commission)
COM (2002) 709 *A Framework for Target-Based Tripartite Contracts and Agreements between the Community, the States and Regional and Local Authorities* (Brussels: European Commission)
COM (2001) 428 *European Governance – A White Paper* (Brussels: European Commission)
COM (1989) 568 final *Communication from the Commission concerning its Action Programme relating to the Implementation of the Community Charter of Basic Social Rights for Workers* (Brussels: European Commission)
Commission of the European Communities (1996) 'Opinion to the Intergovernmental Conference 1996: Reinforcing the Political Union and Preparing for Enlargement', *EU Bulletin* 1/2-1996
Commission of the European Communities (1993) *Growth, Competitiveness, Employment: The Challenges and Ways into the 21st Century* (Luxembourg: EC)

CONV 548/03 Praesidium Conclusions of the Convention on the Future of Europe: Summary Report on the Plenary Session 6 and 7 February 2003. The European Convention, The Secretariat, Brussels

CONV 843/03 *The Consultative Powers of the Committee of the Regions.* The European Convention, The Secretariat, Brussels

CONV 67/1/02 The Role of National Parliaments in the European Architecture. The European Convention, The Secretariat, Brussels

CONV 71/02 Mandate of the Working Group on the Principle of Subsidiarity. The European Convention, The Secretariat, Brussels

CONV 74/02 Mandate of the Working Group on National Parliaments. The European Convention, The Secretariat, Brussels

CONV 81/02 Contribution from Mr Caspar Einem, Member of the Convention: National Parliaments. The European Convention, The Secretariat, Brussels

CONV 82/02 Contribution from Members of the Convention Representing the Finnish Parliament on the role of National Parliaments in the European Union Structure. The European Convention, The Secretariat, Brussels

CONV 84/02 Contribution from Ms Anne Van Lancker, Member of the Convention: Socio-economic Governance in the Constitutional Treaty. The European Convention, The Secretariat, Brussels

CONV 188/02 Summary of the meeting on 10 July 2002. The European Convention, The Secretariat, Brussels

CONV 204/02 Is there a Role for National Parliaments in Subsidiarity Monitoring? The European Convention, The Secretariat, Brussels

CONV 286/02 Conclusions of Working Group I on the Principle of Subsidiarity. The European Convention, The Secretariat, Brussels

CONV 353/02 Working Group IV The Role of National Parliaments, Final Report of Working Group IV on the Role of National Parliaments. The European Convention, The Secretariat, Brussels

Cooper, I. (2006) 'The Watchdogs of Subsidiarity: National Parliaments and the Logic of Arguing in the EU', *Journal of Common Market Studies* **44**, 281

COSAC Secretariat (2010) *Thirteenth Bi-annual Report: Developments in European Union. Procedures and Practices Relevant to Parliamentary Scrutiny*, Madrid

Couve de Murville, M. (1971) *Une Politique Etrangère 1958–1969* (Paris: Plon)

Craig, P. (2012) 'Subsidiarity: A Political or Legal Analysis', *Journal of Common Market Studies* **50**, 72

Craig, P. and de Búrca, G. (2011) *EU Law: Text, Cases and Materials* (5th edition) (Oxford: Oxford University Press)

Cullen, P. (1995) 'Competing Legitimacy at European and National Levels: The Ruling of the Constitutional Court and Parliamentary Scrutiny of European Union Affairs in Germany', in F. Laursen and S.A. Pappas (eds), *The Changing Role of Parliaments in the European Union* (Maastricht: European Institute of Public Administration) 61

Curtin, D. (2009) 'The Council of Ministers: The Missing Link?', in L. Vehey, P. Kiiver and S. Loeffen (eds), *Political Accountability and European Integration* (Groningen: Europa Law Publishing) 125

Curtin, D. and Egeberg, M. (2008) 'Tradition and Innovation: Europe's Accumulated Executive Order', *West European Politics* **31**, 639

Cygan, A., (2013) 'Regional Governance, Subsidiarity and Accountability within the EU's Multi-Level Governance Framework', *European Public Law* **19**, 907

Cygan, A. (2011) 'The Parliamentarisation of EU Decision-Making? The Impact of the Treaty of Lisbon on National Parliaments', *European Law Review* **36**, 478

Cygan, A. (2007) 'EU Affairs before the United Kingdom Parliament: A Case of Scrutiny as Substitute Sovereignty?', in O. Tans, C. Zoethout and J. Peters (eds) *National Parliaments and European Democracy* (Groningen: European Law Publishing) 75

Cygan, A. (2006) 'The EU Constitutional Treaty from the Perspective of the Parliament from the United Kingdom: An Improved Framework for Parliamentary Scrutiny?', in P. Kiiver (ed.), *National and Regional Parliaments in the European Constitutional Order* (Groningen: Europa Law Publishing) 15–27

Cygan, A. (2001) *National Parliaments in an Integrated Europe – An Anglo-German Perspective* (The Hague: Kluwer Law International)

Cygan, A. (1998) *The United Kingdom Parliament and European Union Legislation* (The Hague: Kluwer Law International)

Davies, G. (2006) 'Subsidiarity: The Wrong Idea, in the Wrong Place, at the Wrong Time', *Common Market Law Review* **43**, 63

De Schuter, O. and Deakin, S. (eds) (2005) *Social Rights and Market Forces: Is the Open Method of Co-ordination of Employment and Social Policies the Future of Social Europe?* (Brussels: Bruylant)

De Witte, B. and de Burca, G. (2002) 'The Post-Nice Delimitation of Powers', in A. Arnull and D. Wincott (eds), *Legitimacy and Accountability in the European Union after Nice* (Oxford: Oxford University Press) 201

Dehousse, R. (1995) 'Constitutional Reform in the European Community: Are there Alternatives to the Majoritarian Avenue?', *West European Politics* **18**, 118

Dimitrakopoulos, D.G. (2001) 'Incrementalism and Path Dependence: European Integration and Institutional Change in National Parliaments', *Journal of Common Market Studies* **39**, 405

Dobner, P. and Loughlin, M. (eds) (2010) *The Twilight of Constitutionalism* (Oxford: Oxford University Press)

Dougan, M. (2008) 'The Treaty of Lisbon 2007: Winning Minds Not Hearts', *Common Market Law Review* **45**, 617

Doukas, D. (2009) 'The Verdict of the German Federal Constitutional Court on the Lisbon Treaty: Not Guilty, but Don't Do It Again', *European Law Review* **34**, 866

Duina, F. and Oliver, M. (2006) 'To the Rescue of National Parliaments: A Reply to Raunio', *European Law Journal* **12**, 132

Duina, F. and Raunio, T. (2007) 'The Open Method of Coordination and National Parliaments: Further Marginalisation or New Opportunities?', *Journal of European Public Policy* **14**, 489

Economic and Social Committee (2010) *Opinion on the Implementation of the Lisbon Treaty: Participatory Democracy and the Citizen's Initiative* (OJ 2010 C 354/59)

Egan, M. (2001) *Constructing a European Market* (Oxford: Oxford University Press)

Estella, A. (2002) *The EU Principle of Subsidiarity and its Critique* (Oxford: Oxford University Press)

EUObserver.com (2012), 'Van Rompuy: National Parliaments are EU Institutions', 28 February, available at http://euobserver.com/institutional/115395 (accessed 1 March 2012)

European Institute of Public Administration and European Centre for the Regions (2010) *The Role of Regional Parliaments in the Process of Subsidiarity Analysis within the Early Warning System of the Treaty of Lisbon* (Maastricht: European Institute of Public Administration), available at http://portal.cor.eu/subsdiarity/Documents (accessed 16 May 2012)

Evans, A. (2003) 'UK Devolution and EU Law', *European Law Review* **28**, 475

Farrel, H. and Héritier, A. (2004) 'Interorganizational Negotiation and Interorganizational Power in Shared Decision-Making: Early Agreements under Codecision and their Impact upon the European Parliament', *Comparative European Political Studies* **37**, 1184

Føllesdal, A. (2004) 'Legitimacy Theories of the European Union', *ARENA Working Paper* No. 15/2004

Goetz, K. and Meyer-Sahling, H. (2008) 'The Europeanisation of National Political Systems', *Living Review of European Government*, available at http://www.livingreviews.org/lreg-2008-2 (accessed 12 April 2010)

Gonzalez, J.P. (1995) 'The Principle of Subsidiarity', *European Law Review* **20**, 355

Häge, F. and Kaeding, M. (2007) 'Reconsidering the European Parliament's Legislative Influence: Formal vs. Informal Procedures', *Journal of European Integration* **29**, 341

Halberstam, D. and Möllers, C. (2009) 'The German Constitutional Court Says "Ja Zu Deutschland!"', *German Law Journal* **12**, 1241

Haltern, U.R., Mayer, F.C. and Weiler, J.H.H. (1995) 'European Democracy and its Critique', *West European Politics* **18**, 4

Harding, C. (2000) 'Exploring the Intersection of European Law and National Criminal Law', *European Law Review* **25**, 374

Harlow, C. (2002) 'A Plethora of Parliaments', in C. Harlow (ed.), *Accountability in the European Union* (Oxford: Oxford University Press) 78

Harlow, C. (ed.) (2002) *Accountability in the European Union* (Oxford: Oxford University Press) 78

HC 563 (Session 2007–8) *Subsidiarity, National Parliaments and the Lisbon Treaty*

HC 34-xviii (2005–6) *Progress of European Scrutiny*

HC 152 xxxiii-I (2001–2) *Democracy and Accountability in the EU and the Role of National Parliaments*

Hix, S. (2008) *What's Wrong with the European Union and How to Fix It* (Cambridge: Polity)

Hix, S., Noury, A. and Roland, G. (2005) 'Power to Parties: Cohesion and Competition in the European Parliament', *British Journal of Political Studies* **35**, 209

HL 125 (Session 2008–9) *Codecision and National Parliamentary Scrutiny*

HL 62-I (Session 2007–8) *The Treaty of Lisbon: An Impact Assessment, Report*

HL 62-II (Session 2007–8) *The Treaty of Lisbon: An Impact Assessment, Minutes and Evidence*

HL 137 (2005–6) *A European Strategy for Jobs and Growth*

HL 101 (Session 2004–5) *Strengthening National Parliamentary Scrutiny of the EU – The Constitution's Early Warning Mechanism*

HL 48 (Session 2001–2) *A Second Parliamentary Chamber for the EU: An Unreal Solution to some Real Problems*

HL 80 (Session 1990–91) *Political Union*

Hodson, D. and Maher, I. (2001) 'The Open Method as a New Mode of Governance: The Case of Economic Policy Coordination', *Journal of Common Market Studies* **39**, 719

Hopkins, W.J. (2010) 'A Tale of Two Europes: European Regions from Berlin to Lisbon', *Australian and New Zealand Journal of European Studies* **3**, 55

Horsley, T. (2011) 'Subsidiarity and the European Court of Justice: Missing Pieces in the Subsidiarity Jigsaw?', *Journal of Common Market Studies* **49**, 1

House of Commons Research Paper 01/57 *The Irish Referendum on the Treaty of Nice*

Hrbek, R. (2003) 'The Role of the Regions in the EU and the Principle of Subsidiarity', *International Spectator* **38**, 59

Iglesias, G.C.R. and Blanco, L.O. (eds) (2011) *The Role of National Parliaments in the European Union: Proceedings of the FIDE XXIV Congress, Madrid 2010*, Vol. 1 (Madrid: FIDE)

Jancic, D. (2013) 'The French Parliament: A European Scrutineer or National Actor?', *European Public Law* **19**, 875

Jancic, D. (2012) 'The Barosso Initiative: Window Dressing or Democratic Boost?', *Utrecht Law Review* **8**, 78

Jancic, D. (2008) 'A New Organ of the European Union: "National Parliaments Jointly"', *Federal Trust Policy Commentary* February, available at http://www.fedtrust.co.uk/uploads/Parliaments_Jointly.pdf (accessed 10 January 2010)

Jeffrey, C. (ed.) (1997) *The Regional Dimension of the European Union: Towards a Third Level in Europe?* (London: Frank Cass)

Jones, B. and Keating, M. (eds) (1995) *The European Union and the Regions* (Oxford: Oxford University Press)

Jyränki, A. (ed.) (1999) *National Constitutions in the Era of Integration* (The Hague: Kluwer Law International)

Kardasheva, R. (2012) *Trilogues in the EU Legislature*, SSRN Working Paper Series, available at http://ssrn.com/sol3/papers.cfm?abstract_id=2119912 (accessed 14 August 2012)

Kassim, H. (2005) 'The Europeanisation of Member State Institutions', in S. Bulmer and C. Lesquene (eds), *The Member States of the European Union* (Oxford: Oxford University Press) 295

Kassim, H., Peters, B. and Wright, V. (2000) (eds), *The National Coordination of EU Policy: The Domestic Level* (Oxford: Oxford University Press)

Keating, M. (2004) 'Regions and the Convention on the Future of Europe', *South European Society and Politics* **9**, 192

Kendall, J. and Anheier, H.K. (1996) 'The Third Sector and the European Union Policy Process: An Initial Evaluation', *Journal of European Public Policy* **6**, 283

Kerse, C. (2007) 'Parliamentary Scrutiny in the United Kingdom Parliament and the Changing Role of National Parliaments in European

Union Affairs', in G. Barrett (ed.), *National Parliaments and the European Union: The Constitutional Challenge for the Oireachtas and Other Member State Legislatures* (Dublin: Clarus Press in association with the Institute of European Affairs) 349

Kiiver, P. (2012) *The Early Warning System for the Principle of Subsidiarity: Constitutional Theory and Empirical Reality* (London: Routledge)

Kiiver, P. (2011) 'The Composite Case for National Parliaments in the European Union: Who Profits from Enhanced Involvement?', *European Constitutional Law Review* **2**, 227

Kiiver, P. (2011) 'The Early Warning System for the Principle of Subsidiarity – The National Parliament as a *Conseil d'Etat* for Europe', *European Law Review* **36**, 98

Kiiver, P. (2006) *The National Parliaments in the European Union: A Critical View on EU Constitution Building* (The Hague: Kluwer Law International)

Kiiver, P. (ed.) (2006) *National and Regional Parliaments in the European Constitutional Order* (Groningen: Europa Law Publishing)

Kokott, J. (1999) 'Federal States in Federal Europe: German *Länder* and the Problems of European Integration', in A. Jyränki (ed.), *National Constitutions in the Era of Integration* (The Hague: Kluwer Law International) 175

König, T. and Mäder, L. (2009) 'The Myth of 80% and the Impact of Europeanisation on German Legislation', *MZES Working Paper* No. 1188

Lasok, D. and Bridge, J.W. (1994) *Law and Institutions of the European Union* (London: LexisNexis Mathew Bender)

Laursen, F. and Pappas, S.A. (eds) (1995) *The Changing Role of Parliaments in the European Union* (Maastricht: European Institute of Public Administration)

Łazowski, A. (2012) 'Withdrawal from the European Union and Alternatives to Membership', *European Law Review* **37**, 523

Lenaerts, K. (2010) 'Regions and the European Court: Giving Shape to the Regional Dimension of the Member States', *European Law Review* **35**, 609

Longo, M. (2003) 'European Integration: Between Micro-Regionalism and Globalism', *Journal of Common Market Studies* **41**, 475

Loughlin, J. (2005) 'The Regional Question, Subsidiarity and the Future of Europe', in S. Weatherill and U. Bernitz (eds), *The Role of the Regions and Sub-National Actors in Europe* (Oxford: Hart Publishing) 157

Louis, J.-V. (2008) 'The Lisbon Treaty: The Irish "No": National Parliaments and the Principle of Subsidiarity – Legal Options and Practical Limits', *European Constitutional Law Review* **4**, 429

Magnette, P. (2007) 'European Democracy between Two Ages', in C. Barnard (ed.), *The Fundamentals of EU Law Revisited: Assessing the Impact of the Constitutional Debate* (Oxford: Oxford University Press)

Magnette, P. (2006) 'Democracy in the European Union: Why and How to Combine Representation and Participation', in S. Smismans (ed.), *Civil Society and Legitimate European Governance* (Cheltenham, UK and Northampton, MA, USA: Edward Elgar Publishing) 37

Majone, G. (2006) 'The Common Sense of European Integration', *Journal of European Public Policy* **13**, 607

Majone, G. (1996) *Regulating Europe* (London: Routledge)

Marks, G. (1996) 'An Actor Centred Approach to Multi-Level Governance', *Regional and Federal Studies* **6**, 20

Marx, R. and Wulsdorf, H. (2002) *Translation of Quadrogesimo Anno, Papst Pius XI. (1931)*

Matilla, M. and Lane, J. (2001) 'Why Unanimity in the Council? A Roll-Call Analysis of Council Voting', *European Union Politics* **2**, 31

Maurer, A. (2008) 'National Parliaments in the Architecture of Europe after the Constitutional Treaty', in Gavin Barrett (ed.), *National Parliaments and the European Union: The Constitutional Challenge for the Oireachtas and Other Member State Legislatures* (Dublin: Clarus Press) 47

Maurer, A. (2005) 'The Convention and the National Parliamentary Dimension', *Arena Working Papers*, available at http://www.arena.uio.no/publications/papers/wp05_01.pdf (accessed 16 November 2009)

Maurer, A. (2001) 'National Parliaments in the European Union Architecture: From Latecomers' Adaptation Towards Permanent Institutional Change', in A. Maurer and W. Wessels (eds), *National Parliaments on their Ways to Europe: Losers or Latecomers?* (Baden-Baden: Nomos) 27

Maurer, A. and Wessels, W. (eds) (2001) *National Parliaments on their Ways to Europe: Losers or Latecomers?* (Baden-Baden: Nomos)

Menon, A. and Weatherill, S. (2002) 'Legitimacy, Accountability and Delegation in the European Union', in A. Arnull and D. Wincott (eds), *Accountability and Legitimacy in the European Union* (Oxford: Oxford University Press) 113

Møller Sousa M. (2008), 'Learning in Denmark? The Case of Danish Parliamentary Control over European Union Policy', *Scandinavian Political Studies* **31**, 441

Moravcsik, A. (1998) 'Introduction: The Choice for Europe', in A. Moravcsik (ed.), *The Choice for Europe: Social Purposes and State Power from Messina to Maastricht* (Ithaca, NY: Cornell University Press)

Norris, P. (2007) 'Representation and the Democratic Deficit', *European Journal of Political Research* **32**, 273

Norton, P. (1996) 'Introduction: The Institution of Parliaments', in P. Norton (ed.), *Parliaments and Governments in Western Europe* (London: Frank Cass) 1

Obholzer, L. and Reh, C. (2012) 'How to Negotiate Trilogues in the EU: Reforming Trilogues and First Reading Agreements', *CEPS Policy Brief* No. 270, May

O'Brennan, J. and Raunio, T. (2007) 'Deparliamentarisation and European Integration', in J. O'Brennan and T. Raunio (eds), *National Parliaments within the Enlarged European Union: From Victims of Integration to Competitive Actors* (London: Routledge) 1

O'Keefe, D. and Twomey, P. (eds) (1994) *Legal Issues of the Maastricht Treaty* (London: Wiley Chancery)

Passos, R. (2008) 'Recent Developments Concerning the Role of National Parliaments in the European Union', *ERA Forum* **9**, 25

Peers, S. (2005) 'Transforming Decision-Making on EC Immigration and Asylum Law', *European Law Review* **30**, 285

Pernice, I. (2009) 'The Treaty of Lisbon: Multilevel Constitutionalism in Action', *Columbia Journal of European Law* **15**, 349

Peters, J. (2009) 'The Role of National Parliaments: Checks and Balances between the EU and the Member States', in L. Vehey, P. Kiiver and S. Loeffen (eds), *Political Accountability and European Integration* (Groningen: Europa Law Publishing) 33

Peters, J. (2004) 'European Democracy after the 2003 Convention', *Common Market Law Review* **41**, 37

Piris, J.C. (2010) *The Lisbon Treaty: A Legal and Political Analysis* (Cambridge: Cambridge University Press)

Poiares Maduro, M. (1998) *We the Court* (Oxford: Hart Publishing)

Pollack, M. (1994) 'Creeping Competence: The Expanding Agenda of the EC', *Journal of European Public Policy* **14**, 95

Popelier, P. and Vandenbruwaene, W. (2011) 'The Subsidiarity Mechanism as a Tool for Inter-Level Dialogue in Belgium: On "Regional Blindness" and Co-operative Flaws', *European Constitutional Law Review* **7**, 204

Puntscher Riekman, S. (2010) 'Constitutionalism and Representation: European Parliamentarism in the Treaty of Lisbon', in P. Dobner and

M. Loughlin (eds), *The Twilight of Constitutionalism?* (Oxford: Oxford University Press) 120

Radaelli, C. (2007) 'Whither Better Regulation for the Lisbon Agenda?', *Journal of European Public Policy* **14**, 190

Raunio, T. (2010) 'Destined for Irrelevance? Subsidiarity Control by National Parliaments', *Real Instituto Elcano Working Paper* 36/2010, Madrid

Raunio, T. (2007) 'National Parliaments and OMC: Destined to Remain Apart?', Paper delivered at '50 Years of Interparliamentary Cooperation: Progressing Towards Effective Cross-Level Parliamentarism', Bundesrat, Berlin, 13 June, available at http://swp-berlin.org/en/get_document.php?asset_id+4124 (accessed 12 February 2010)

Raunio, T. (2006) 'Does the OMC Really Benefit National Parliaments?', *European Law Journal* **12**, 130

Raunio, T. and Hix, S. (2003) 'Backbenchers Learn to Fight Back: European Integration and Parliamentary Government', *Western European Politics* **23**, 142

Raunio, T. and Wiberg, M. (2009) 'How to Measure the Europeanisation of a National Legislature?', *Scandinavian Political Studies* **15**, 74

R/CdR 57/2011 *Subsidiarity Annual Report 2010 of the CoR*

R/CdR 86/2007 *Agreement Governing Cooperation between the European Commission and the Committee of the Regions*

Report on Relations between the European Parliament and the National Parliaments in European Integration, January 2002, A5-0023/2002

Rittberger, B. (2005) *Building Europe's Parliament: Democratic Representation Beyond the Nation State* (Oxford: Oxford University Press) 191

Ross, A. and Crespo, M. (2003) 'The Effect of Devolution on the Implementation of European Community Law in the United Kingdom and Spain', *European Law Review* **28**, 210

Saurugger, S. (2010) 'Interest Groups and Democracy in the European Union', in J. Beyers, R. Eising and W. Maloney (eds), *Interest Group Politics in Europe: Lessons from EU Studies and Comparative Politics* (London: Routledge) 164

Scharpf, F.W. (2010) 'Legitimacy in the Multi-Level European Polity', in P. Dobner and M. Loughlin (eds), *The Twilight of Constitutionalism* (Oxford: Oxford University Press) 89

Scharpf, F.W. (2006) 'Problem Solving Effectiveness and Democratic Accountability in the EU', *Political Science Series No. 107*, Institute for Advanced Studies, Vienna, 18

Scharpf, F.W. (1999) *Governing in Europe: Effective and Democratic?* (London: Routledge)

Scott, C. (2002) 'The Governance of the European Union: The Potential for Multi-Level Control', *European Law Journal* **8**, 59

SEC (2011) 1093 final. *28th Annual Monitoring of the Application of EU Law* (Brussels: European Commission)

SEC (2009) 1211, *Commission Staff Working Document on Urban Mobility* (Brussels: European Commission)

Shackleton, M. (2000) 'The Politics of Co-decision', *Journal of Common Market Studies* **38**, 325

Shackelton, M. and Raunio, T. (2003) 'Codecision since Amsterdam: A Laboratory for Institutional Innovation and Change', *Journal of European Public Policy* **10**, 171

Smismans, S. (2005) 'Reflexive Law in Support of Directly Deliberative Polyarchy: Reflexive Deliberative Polyarchy as a Normative Frame for the OMC', in O. De Schuter and S. Deakin (eds), *Social Rights and Market Forces: Is the Open Method of Co-ordination of Employment and Social Policies the Future of Social Europe?* (Brussels: Bruylant) 99

Smismans, S. (2004) *Law, Legitimacy, and European Governance: Functional Participation in Social Regulation* (Oxford: Oxford University Press)

Smismans, S. (2003) 'European Civil Society: Shaped by Discourses and Institutional Interests', *European Law Journal* **9**, 482

Special 320 Eurobaromoter Post Electoral Survey 2009

Steinbach, A. (2010) 'The Lisbon Judgment of the German Federal Constitutional Court: New Guidance on the Limits of European Integration?', *German Law Journal* **11**, 367

Steiner, J. (1994) 'Subsidiarity under the Maastricht Treaty', in D. O'Keefe and P. Twomey (eds), *Legal Issues of the Maastricht Treaty* (London: Wiley Chancery) 49

SWD (2012) 63 final, Commission Staff Working Document, *Impact Assessment Revision of the Legislative Framework on the Posting of Workers in the Context of Provision of Services*

Szyszczak, E. (2001) 'The New Paradigm for Social Policy: A Virtuous Circle?', *Common Market Law Review* **38**, 1125

Tans, O. (2007) 'Conclusion: National Parliaments and the European Union; Coping with the Limits of Democracy', in O. Tans, C. Zoethout and J. Peters (eds), *National Parliaments and European Democracy: A Bottom-Up Approach to European Constitutionalism* (Groningen: Europa Law Publishing) 229

Tans, O., Zoethout, C. and Peters, J. (eds) (2007) *National Parliaments and European Democracy* (Groningen: European Law Publishing)

Teasdale, A.L. (1993) 'The Life and Death of the Luxembourg Compromise', *Journal of Common Market Studies* **31**, 567

Thielemann, E. (1999) 'Institutional Limits of a "Europe with the Regions"', *Journal of European Public Policy* **6**, 399

Töller, A.E. (2006) 'How European Integration Impacts on National Legislatures: The Europeanisation of the German Bundestag', *Centre for European Studies, Programme for Study of Germany and Europe, Working Paper Series*, available at http://aei.pitt.edu/9283/1/toller.pdf (accessed 24 November 2011)

Toth, A.G. (1994) 'A Legal Analysis of Subsidiarity', in D. O'Keefe and P. Twomey (eds), *Legal Issues of the Maastricht Treaty* (London: Wiley Chancery) 37

Tridimas, T. and Nebbia, P. (eds) (2006) *Challenges for EU Law in the 21st Century: Volume 1* (Oxford: Hart Publishing)

Van Dijk, J. (2009) 'National Parliaments and Political Accountability in Europe', in L. Vehey, P. Kiiver and S. Loeffen (eds), *Political Accountability and European Integration* (Groningen: Europa Law Publishing) 85

Vasey, M. (1988) 'Decision-Making in the Agriculture Council and the Luxembourg Compromise', *Common Market Law Review* **25**, 725

Vehey, L., Kiiver, P. and Loeffen, S. (eds) (2009) *Political Accountability and European Integration* (Groningen: Europa Law Publishing)

Verhoeven, G. (1998) 'How Democratic Need European Union Members Be? Some thoughts after Amsterdam', *European Law Review* **23**, 217

Weatherill, S. (2011) 'The Limits of Legislative Harmonisation Ten Years after *Tobacco Advertising*: How the Court's Case Law has become a Drafting Guide', *German Law Journal* **12**, 827

Weatherill, S. (2009) 'Competence and Legitimacy', in C. Barnard and O. Oduhu (eds), *The Outer Limits of European Union Law* (Oxford: Hart Publishing) 17

Weatherill, S. (2008) 'On Overlapping Legal Orders: What is the Purely Sporting Rule?', in B. Bogusz, A. Cygan and E. Szyszczak (eds), *The Regulation of Sport in the EU* (Cheltenham, UK and Northampton, MA, USA: Edward Elgar) 48

Weatherill, S. (2006) 'Why Harmonise?', in T. Tridimas and P. Nebbia (eds), *Challenges for EU Law in the 21st Century: Volume 1* (Oxford: Hart Publishing) 22

Weatherill, S. (2005) 'The Challenge of the Regional Dimension in the European Union', in S. Weatherill and U. Bernitz (eds), *The Role of the Regions and Sub-National Actors in Europe* (Oxford: Hart Publishing) 1

Weatherill, S. (2005) 'Better Competence Monitoring', *European Law Review* **30**, 23

Weatherill, S. (2002) 'Pre-emption, Harmonisation and the Distribution of Competence to Regulate the Internal Market', in C. Barnard and J.

Scott (eds), *The Law of the Single Market: Unpacking the Premises* (Oxford: Hart Publishing) 58

Weatherill, S. (1996) 'After *Keck*: Some Thoughts on How to Clarify the Clarification', *Common Market Law Review*, **33**, 885

Weatherill, S. and Bernitz, U. (eds) (2005) *The Role of the Regions and Sub-National Actors in Europe* (Oxford: Hart Publishing)

Weiler, J.H.H. (1998) *The Constitution of Europe: 'Do the New Clothes Have an Emperor?' and Other Essays on European Integration* (Cambridge: Cambridge University Press)

Wessels, W. and Romestch, D. (1996) 'Conclusion', in W. Wessels and D. Romestch (eds), *The European Union and Member States: Towards Institutional Fusion* (Manchester: Manchester University Press)

Wessels, W. and Romestch, D. (eds) (1996) *The European Union and Member States: Towards Institutional Fusion* (Manchester: Manchester University Press)

Wessels, W., Maurer, A. and Mittag, J. (eds) (2003) *Fifteen into One? The European Union and its Member States* (Manchester: Manchester University Press)

Wincott, D. (2002) 'The Governance White Paper, the Commission and the Search for Legitimacy', in A. Arnull and D. Wincott (eds), *Accountability and Legitimacy in the European Union* (Oxford: Oxford University Press) 379

Wouters, P., Verhey, L. and Kiiver, P. (eds) (2009) *European Constitutionalism beyond Lisbon* (Antwerp, Portland and Oxford: Intersentia)

Wyatt, D. (2006) 'Could a Yellow Card for National Parliaments Strengthen Judicial as well as Political Policing of Subsidiarity?', *Croatian Yearbook of European Law and Policy* **2**, 1

Wyrzykowski, M. et al. (2011) 'General Report: The Role of National Parliaments in the European Union', in G.C.R. Iglesias and L.O. Blanco (eds), *The Role of National Parliaments in the European Union: Proceedings of the FIDE XXIV Congress, Madrid 2010*, Vol. 1 (Madrid: FIDE)

Zeitlin, J. (2005) 'The Open Method of Co-ordination in Question', in J. Zeitlin and P. Pochet (eds), *The Open Method of Co-ordination in Action: The European Employment and Social Inclusion Strategies* (Brussels: P.IE., Peter Lang) 19

Zeitlin, J. and Pochet, P. (eds) (2005) *The Open Method of Co-ordination in Action: The European Employment and Social Inclusion Strategies* (Brussels: P.IE., Peter Lang)

Zeitlin, J. and Pochet, P., with Magnusson, L. (eds) (2006) *The Open Method of Co-ordination in Action: The European Employment and Social Inclusion Strategies* (Brussels: Peter Lang)

Index